DRIVE-BY JOURNALISM

The Assault on Your Need to Know

Arthur E. Rowse

Common Courage Press

Monroe, ME

Library of Congress Cataloging-in-Publication Data

Rowse, Arthur E. (Arthur Edward)
    Drive-by journalism : the assault on your need to know / Arthur
Rowse.
        p. cm.
    Includes index.
    ISBN 1-56751-192-9 (paper) -- ISBN 1-56751-193-7 (cloth)
        1. Television broadcasting of news--United States. 2. United
States--Politics and government--1993- 3. Television advertising--
United States. I. Title.

PN4784.T4 R69 2000
070.1'95--dc21

                                                            00-025333

Common Courage Press
Box 702
Monroe, ME 04951

(207) 525-0900; fax: (207) 525-3068
orders-info@commoncouragepress.com

www.commoncouragepress.com

First Printing

To all the journalists still fighting
to free the news business from itself.

Contents

A Personal Note

My love affair with journalism began in Lexington, Mass., the town that bills itself as "the birthplace of American liberty" and holds a parade of its citizens each April 19 to honor the patriots of 1775. My career as a journalist began there at the age of 10 when my father brought me to his office one Saturday where I started playing with an old Remington typewriter. Soon I was publishing the weekly *Naborhood News*, so spelled because the correct letters from the stencils I had would not fit on the page.

My first bout with censorship came when my father objected to publication of his snide remark about a neighbor's baby. I rebelled by only slightly crayoning over the offending words. But I soon was censoring myself without realizing it. I also did not understand until many years later why so many neighbors were buying the paper. It was not so much for the news but to laugh at my juvenile *faux pas*.

My first encounter with advertising pressure came at *The Boston Globe* where we copy editors routinely waved at "JFR Musts" on their way to the typesetters. These were publicity releases from downtown business firms ordered into the paper by John F. Reid, the ad manager. In those days, the Boston papers would even distort the weather news to please local merchants. On a Good Friday after a blizzard blocked the city's shopping area, and with another storm predicted, the *Globe's* page-one banner declared: "GO BUY YOUR EASTER BONNET; FAIR AND WARMER EASTER." Boston papers have improved since then. So has the weather.

My first taste of predatory corporate practices came as a Newspaper Guild member at *The Boston Herald/Traveler* when I was summarily fired for refusing to take a temporary double promotion without getting the two pay differentials. Fortunately for my family of nine, *The Washington Post* came to my rescue ten weeks later with a "superscale" position on its city desk.

My first view of major political bias came in the 1952 election campaign when most major newspapers tailored the news about the Richard Nixon and Adlai Stevenson slush funds to fit their own prejudices. Later, I described these practices in a book, *Slanted News,* that Erwin D. Canham, editor of *The Christian Science Monitor,* said in the foreword was "written in just the right way." He meant it was by a practicing journalist without a big name or fancy subsidy.

This book is written in the same way. It is based on a lifelong labor of love as a reporter, editor, columnist and publisher of newsletters, pamphlets and books. Its topics are essentially the same destructive forces—self-censorship, predatory practices, commercial pressures and political bias—that plagued the press in my younger days. Only this time, the detrimental forces are stronger and the consequences more serious.

Political leaders continue to issue dire warnings about our potential destruction at the hands of enemies, this time the marginal military powers of Iraq, Iran, North Korea and China. But the main threats to freedom and democracy today don't come from abroad. They come from within our borders, from as close as the next apartment or the next block. They are the new American rebels, ones who don't trust their own government or the press that brings bad news. They proudly call themselves American citizens but most of them don't care enough about the nation's affairs to follow the news seriously or exercise the right to vote for their own political representatives. They want the United States to remain the strongest power in the world, but they don't know what's happening outside their own little circle. And they don't trust international organizations or treaties designed to keep peace and save the earth from manmade disaster.

They say they love liberty, but like Rush Limbaugh, they don't even believe in the Fairness Doctrine that once required broadcasters to offer opposing viewpoints a fair chance to be heard. These self-proclaimed patriots apparently believe that self-government is the root of all evil. And some talk heatedly about revolting against it, as Limbaugh did just weeks before the Oklahoma City bombing when he said: "The second American revolution is just about—I got my fingers about a quarter-of-an-inch apart—is just that far away. Because these people are sick and tired of a bunch of bureaucrats in Washington driving into town and telling them what they can and can't do with their land."

That was obviously much the way Timothy McVeigh felt before he bombed the Alfred P. Murrah building in Oklahoma City on Patriot's Day 1995, creating the worst example of domestic terrorism in the nation's history. Such attitudes still stir countless others who wouldn't bomb a building but who unknowingly foster equally destructive forces.

Yet the one institution that can counteract these forces—the news establishment—encourages them instead. Rather than using its freedom to foster the informed citizenry necessary for a vital democracy, the press has been merging competing voices into a homogenized newsamuse cartel. It exploits the First Amendment for commercial gain, diminishes important news in order to maximize profits, belittles self-government and narrows political debate for commercial gain, shaping politics to its own needs, allowing advertisers and publicity agents to color the news and destroying public servants with cheap, shallow "gotcha" journalism, the bastard child of informed investigative reporting.

Today's media complex is drunk with economic and political power, and still it seeks more. Yet it already comes close to controlling who runs for national office, who gets elected and what it all means. Making money seems to come before making sense of the world to the American people. To be sure, the news business is not responsible for all the country's problems, but it has the biggest role to play in resolving them because it controls the news and commentary that form the lifeblood of a free society.

In many respects, the American news media have never been better. They lead the world in speed, quantity and variety of choice for those who are interested. There are many conscientious people in key media roles, but they are finding it more and more difficult to focus on the public interest. Many of the best journalists have resigned or been forced out. Many others still at work would like to reverse the tide, but are trapped by the need to make a living. Even the working atmosphere has changed. What used to be an enjoyable occupation is often painful drudgery in an uptight corporate world.

The basic fault lines go back two centuries. The revered leaders who wrote the First Amendment made a major miscalculation. They assumed that a privately owned press with protection from government interference would naturally fulfill its obligation to keep the public informed sufficiently to maintain a vibrant democracy. They didn't foresee how a privately run press could turn into a mammoth oligopoly more intent on enhancing its power and profits than protecting freedom and democracy.

What brought such a change and when did it happen? The turning point was 1985 when all three commercial TV networks were taken over by larger firms. It proved to be the first wave of large media mergers that subordinated news operations to tiny corners of huge industrial conglomerates. Even before that, many family-owned newspapers and broadcasting outlets faced prohibitive inheritance taxes and the need to increase profits. So they went public or sold to a chain, actions that further elevated profits over public service. With investors demanding higher returns every three months, media managers have had to cut the heart out of journalism again and again. To attain maximum audiences, they have opted for personal scandal and disaster rather than news more relevant to citizens of a democracy. Drive-by journalism is one way to describe the syndrome.

This book is a call for help from those who run the news business. It's a call for its leaders to stop auctioning freedom and democracy and get down to the business they claim to do: reporting the news fully and offering a full forum for political debate. It's time to tell the American people why they are being represented so poorly in the nation's capital. And it's time to tell them about the press's own role in all this before it gets too late to discuss it freely.

Let Lexington's Old Belfry ring out the alarm again. Let it be a warning for the Fourth Estate to honor its obligation to educate and inform the American people so they—and it—can keep their freedoms from being overtaken by powers they no longer can control. And let the nation know of the need for urgent action.

In the words of Robert Maynard Hutchins, the former chancellor of the University of Chicago, "The death of democracy is not likely to be an assassination from ambush. It will be a slow extinction from apathy, indifference and undernourishment."

Arthur E. Rowse

CHAPTER I

Corrupting the News with Business Mergers

The major part of the nation's press is large-scale enterprise, close-ly interlocked with the system of finance and industry.

The Hutchins Commission

On the second day of the 21st century, eight days before announcing the momentous merger with America Online Inc., Time Warner Inc.'s chief executive Gerald Levin took part in a televised panel discussion on CNN about the global media. Although he knew of the startling deal, he couldn't let on. But he did have revealing thoughts about the future shape of society.

"The global media," he said, "is fast becoming the predominant business of the 21st century, and we're in a new economic age, and what may happen, assuming that's true, is it's more important than government. It's more important than educational institutions and nonprofits." Then he added:

"We're going to need to have these corporations redefined as instru-ments of public service because they have the resources, they have the reach, they have the skill base, and…that may be a more efficient way to deal with society's problems than bureaucratic governments."

There you have it. Many have long suspected that big media want-ed to take over government and society. But never had such a power-ful executive spelled out the idea with such candor and in public. According to Levin, media firms have become not only more impor-tant than government, schools and charitable institutions, but they will eventually replace them. All we need to do is to certify these profit-hungry giants as public services. They will solve the problems that government and society have been unable to solve. No need for messy elections or tedious political campaigns. Let AOL Time Warner and the free market system end homelessness and poverty, racial divisions, wipe out the national debt. With the combination of the world's largest Internet service provider and the largest entertainment complex, this new monstrosity would have approximately 25 million subscribers and the nation's second largest cable system (13 million homes). They could take over all the rest if those pesky competitors and nasty government regulators would simply get out of the way.

Rarely had any American business magnate voiced such grandiose plans. Or were they just dreams? Whatever they were, they were powerful headline material. But despite the presence of *Time* magazine's editor and journalists from CNN, Levin's musings faded into the ozone without notice.

It wasn't until the big merger hit the headlines that his words began to resonate in a few places. But the merger itself caused the news media to focus on what Levin and his counterpart, Steve Case of AOL, preferred to emphasize: all the wonderful new choices and services that would be available to consumers from this union of giant predators. Despite the sweeping scope of the deal, government approval was said to be assured since there was little direct overlap between AOL's dominant Internet business and Time Warner, the nation's largest media company. Yet in one stroke of a pen, they took a giant step toward destroying competition in this vast arena of communication and entertainment.

This chapter describes the frantic race for power and profit that is shrinking control of these huge industries into a small circle of corporate monsters. And it tells how such consolidation is corrupting the process that decides the news you get and how it affects your life and future.

In a few years, Levin's sweeping words may not seem so farfetched. Along with other large media empires, AOL Time Warner would have the power to influence much of what happens to ordinary people in this country and around the world, including:

- **Your choice of TV channels on cable systems.** Millions of television viewers have learned what it is like to lose favorite programs because of turf disputes between media companies. In 1996, Time Warner sought to block News Corporation's Fox News, a competitor of its CNN network, from Time Warner's dominant New York City cable systems. In response, Mayor Rudolph Giuliani, a beneficiary of strong political support from Fox TV and News Corporation's *New York Post*, promptly added Fox to a city-owned TV channel. But a court ruled that such action violated Time Warner's press freedom not to carry Fox, which eventually got its way. Four years later, nearly half a million cable subscribers in Virginia, Texas and Ohio temporarily lost popular programs because of a similar dispute between Fox and Cox Communications. Then in May 2000, approximately 7 million people lost nearly two days of ABC programs because of a blackout instituted by Time Warner in a running dispute over how much it should pay Disney to add ABC programs to its cable systems, the second largest in the nation.

- **Your choice of Internet service provider via cable.** Before its merger with Time Warner, AOL was lobbying governments around the country to require cable companies to share their high-speed links to the Internet with rival firms. AOL was worried that some big cable operators would not give their subscribers a free choice. After the merger, AOL changed its mind. Although its officials repeated their pledge of open access, they said they would prefer that the market decide the matter rather than the government. Other competing firms also expressed concern that they might lose favored places in AOL's home page and its online distribution vehicles.

- **Your choice of services on the Internet.** With more subscribers than the total of its 20 nearest competitors, AOL Time Warner can make or break Web sites on the Internet by the way it designs and words its homepage. Its sheer volume of traffic guarantees a big advantage to any service it prefers, such as airline ticket selling, banking, shopping and its alliances with such other organizations as General Motors, HomeGrocer, Sears and PBS, plus its ability to pump up sales of Time Warner magazines, books and other items. The firm's huge customer base allows it to offer bigger sales discounts than any competitor can. With such unchallenged power, it can also discourage innovative ideas so vital to the computer world.

- **Your choice of news and commentary.** AOL's choice of "top stories" is a highly selective editing process. Whether a particular item is included or excluded can have a huge effect on the nation and the world simply because of its impact on the thinking of so many people. Although subscribers are free to go elsewhere for news and commentary, they can't go far from the influence of these firms. The big blackout in May 2000 showed how even news and discussion programs are subject to the whim of these media behemoths.

MORE POWERFUL THAN GOVERNMENT

As such forces gain power over people's lives, people lose power to govern themselves. The making of Media Central means the unmaking of democracy, because it transforms the press from its role as a protector of the people from runaway government to the ultimate conglomerate seeking to exploit the gullible public and steal favors from government. In the past few decades, the news business has become more powerful than government in determining whether 45 million Americans finally get health insurance, whether millions of elderly get federal help in paying for prescription drugs and whether politicians continue to be purchased by wealthy interests that defeat the wishes of the general public. The fate of such proposals as gun control, tax rates, corporate subsidies, environmental protection and the right to sue for damages from defective products is influenced more by the news media than any other force.

With their ability to decide what news is reported and how it is told, the media determine who runs for public office, who gets elected and what it all means. But such a situation is not what the Founding Fathers had in mind for American democracy. They knew that an independent press was vital for democracy and that it must function as a private business. So they protected it from government interference with the famous words of the First Amendment prohibiting Congress from abridging press freedom. They assumed that in exchange for that freedom, the press would recognize its responsibility to supply enough information to keep democracy functioning properly. They never dreamed that the press—now including print, broadcast, cable, satellite and the Internet—would use its freedom so extensively to make money and so little to communicate the nation's needs. They could not have envisaged a press so tied into the commercial world and with so little interest in serving the public.

They would be especially upset to see what has happened to democracy itself: the failure of most Americans to vote or follow the news in a serious way and the consequent widespread ignorance of political affairs. They would be equally disturbed to see the extent to which private interests have taken over the election process and lawmaking in the nation's capital. And they would be shocked to see how poorly the general public is represented in government, how extensively government itself has become a subject of contempt, and how much the public distrusts the information system that is so essential to a functioning democracy.

The news business is not the only factor responsible for the disintegration of American democracy. But none has a larger role to play or more at stake. Press freedom is usually the first one to be killed by autocratic rulers. So one might expect that those who run the news media would do whatever is necessary to maintain that freedom if only for their own salvation.

PROFIT OVER PUBLIC SERVICE

But instead, they are steadily abdicating their responsibility in order to maximize profits. Responsibility to the commonweal clearly did not enter the minds of Rupert Murdoch and John C. Malone when those two influential media moguls began maneuvering to buy General Motors in March 2000. Nor did it play a role in the Tribune Company's decision in the same month to buy Times Mirror and merge these two conglomerates into the third largest newspaper company.

The urge to merge is not new in the news business. From its beginning, independent voices have been under constant assault by economic aggressors. The first scourge was the newspaper chain, with names like Hearst and Scripps. The next was the media conglomerate, such as Time Warner, with holdings confined mostly to journalism. Then the industrial conglomerate, such as General Electric and

Microsoft, where journalism is relegated to a tiny corner. Next came the transmission firm, such as AT&T, with cable and telephone networks covering their entry into the news business. The merger of AOL and Time Warner will greatly expand the media reach to the vast Internet. Journalism's responsibility to the public welfare took a step backward with each of these mergers, especially since the mid-1980s when the biggest firms jumped into the pool.

That was when all three major networks were gobbled up by industrial conglomerates. Capital Cities, led by billionaire investor Warren Buffet, purchased ABC; Loews Corp., led by Lawrence Tisch, bought CBS; and General Electric, led by Jack Welch, took over RCA, which included NBC. In the same year, Rupert Murdoch and his News Corporation acquired six large Metromedia television stations, which became the nucleus of his Fox network. A year earlier, he had taken control of Twentieth Century Fox, a major film studio in Hollywood. The next big year for mergers was 1995, when Disney bought Capital Cities/ABC, Westinghouse purchased CBS, and Time Warner took over Turner Communications along with its cable channels CNN, TBS and TNT.

Many of the earlier mergers were born when family-owned media firms, especially newspapers, discovered that estate taxes raised serious impediments to passing along their greatly enriched properties to future generations. The solution was either a sale or a public offering of stock. In either case, ownership usually shifted from local control to the stock market. Among today's major media companies, Hearst and Newhouse (Advance Publications) are rare exceptions as privately owned chains. It is estimated that three-quarters of all daily newspapers are now publicly owned, and four-fifths of them are chain-owned.

The transfer of media control to Wall Street has led to relentless demands for constantly higher profits far exceeding even those of the most avaricious families of the past. The difference between ownership on Main Street and on Wall Street is usually between a profit motive tempered by public responsibility and a profit motive with little or no public responsibility. A purchaser of stock in a media company on the public exchange is concerned only with dividends and increased valuation.

Such pressures weigh heavily on executives of publicly held news organizations. They have had to constantly cut costs while trying to raise the impact of each news report to the fullest in order to maximize profits. This helps explain why so much of the news in recent years has been devoted to trivia and emotional pitches, the angles deemed most likely to attract large audiences. It also helps explain why news relating to people as citizens is downplayed. And it may indicate why so many people are losing faith in the news business as it has become more consolidated.

Media mergers not only alter the character of news and weaken public trust in the press, they also alter the dynamics of politics and democracy. Lost in all the talk about media mergers has been any serious consideration of the media's role in turning people away from the ballot box and away from following public affairs seriously.

Democracy—as well as journalism—is diminished when First Amendment freedoms and obligations are packaged and sold along with baseball teams, theme parks and nuclear reactors under the same corporate umbrella. Responsibility to the public gets lost under the bundle of assets to be auctioned and then turned into "corporate synergy" and "brand names" by multi-billionaires with little or no journalism background or interest in it. As this is written, the ultimate media conglomerate is rapidly taking shape as the number of corporate players diminishes.

FROM 50 TO 5 FIRMS IN TWO DECADES

In the good old days 18 years ago, author and media critic Ben Bagdikian was alarmed to find only 50 firms in control of the entire news and entertainment industry, including television, radio, cable, movies, magazines and books.[1] In 1996, he said the number had dropped to only 10 with virtually the same degree of control. By the year 2000, the select group was in the process of being cut to five: AOL Time Warner, General Electric, Viacom/CBS, News Corporation and Walt Disney. If the AOL/Time Warner deal is eventually cleared, these five firms will essentially control what is available.

•**AOL** will bring to the Time Warner merger not only its dominant Internet service, with branches in about a dozen other countries, but also numerous consumer services ranging from news to airline and theater ticket-selling, plus numerous "chat rooms" with free-ranging discussions. It also owns Netscape, Spinner Networks, Compuserve and holds partnerships with Wal-Mart and Bell Atlantic, minority shares in Gateway, Hughes Electronics and SBC Communications, the largest regional telephone service. Time Warner adds not only the nation's second largest cable network but also CNN, the Turner Network movie studios, theme parks, sports teams, retail stores, record companies, Warner Music and a large array of publishing entities from the Book-of-the-Month Club to magazines, such as *Time*, *Fortune* and *People*.

- **Disney** has ABC with its 10 owned-and-operated TV stations, 44 radio stations and 219 affiliated TV stations. Other holdings include the Disney Channel, Toon Disney, six daily papers, six magazine subsidiaries, Disney theme parks, book publishers, recording companies, theatrical productions, a cruise line, professional sports teams, Disney stores and several movie studios including Touchtone Pictures and Miramax Films.

- **General Electric** owns NBC, with its 13 owned-and-operated television stations and 212 affiliated stations, as well as cable holdings such as CNBC (shared with Dow Jones), MSNBC (shared with Microsoft), the History Channel (with Hearst), Rainbow Media Holdings (with Cablevision), Sports Channel (with News Corporation). In addition, GE owns numerous financial services, insurance companies and facilities to manufacture everything from aircraft engines, appliances, light bulbs, plastics, X-ray, MRI to nuclear equipment.

- **News Corporation** has 22 owned-and-operated television stations in this country, the Fox network with its 159 affiliated stations, plus *The New York Post* and *The Weekly Standard*, Twentieth Century Fox movie studios, Madison Square Garden, numerous pro sports teams plus cable holdings, magazines, satellite systems, book publishers, sheep ranches and more than 130 newspapers outside the United States.

- **Viacom**, and its CBS division, own and operate 35 TV stations with 200 affiliated stations, 160 radio stations, 6,000 Blockbuster film rental stores, plus Paramount film studios, Spelling Entertainment Group, Simon & Schuster and other book publishers. Viacom also owned the UPN broadcast network, which specializes in wrestling shows. Viacom planned to sell CBS's share in Home Team Sports. Cable properties include the Nashville Network, Country Music Television and King World. The combined company reaches more than 35 percent of the national TV audience, the limit allowed by the FCC.

In sum, these five firms own and operate all four major commercial television networks and their programming affiliations reaching nearly every major station in the country. Along with AT&T, they also control close to half of the nation's cable hookups. And they dominate cable programming, movie-making, music-making, book and periodical publishing. In addition, they have large chunks of the radio business, professional sports and amusement parks. Even the Internet, once envisioned as a glorious free-for-all of independent voices, is rapidly coming under the control of these large firms not only because of AOL's lion's share of paid subscribers but because of the dominance of major firms in providing the information that attracts large audiences and massive advertising on the World Wide Web.

And they're going global. American media giants are racing foreign conglomerates—such as Canada-based Seagrams and Germany's Bertelsman—to expand their power around the globe. Although Rupert Murdoch's News Corporation is based in Australia, it has satellite systems and TV stations covering large parts of Europe, South America and Asia but does much of its business in the United States. In some ways, the men who run these growing empires are like the explorers who sailed the unknown five centuries ago. Murdoch was once described by Sumner Redstone, head of Viacom, as one who "basically wants to conquer the world." But the phrase also describes Redstone, whose firm took over CBS in 1999, as well as Gerald Levin and Steve Case of AOL Time Warner and Murdoch himself. They want government to get out of the way.

ROUNDING OUT THE CARTEL

On a different level, another ten firms round out the media cartel, especially with their dominance in daily newspapers. All have contributed to the concentration of media power and remain likely participants in future mergers. They include:

- **Advance Publications,** the fourth largest newspaper chain, known as Newhouse newspapers in 22 cities and many magazines, including *The New Yorker, Vanity Fair, House & Garden, Vogue* and *Parade*.

- **AT&T/TCI,** a combination of the largest long-distance telephone network and the largest cable hookup in the country, TeleCommunications Inc., known as TCI. Also included is Liberty Media, with major interests in programming, including the Discovery Channel and MacNeil/Lehrer Productions. AT&T also owns a share in Excite@Home, an Internet service provider, and through a stake in Media One, would share ownership of TW Entertainment with Time Warner. AT&T also has moved in on Internet telephony with a one-third stake in Net2Phone and plans to take over majority control with partners British Telecommunications and Liberty Media.

- **Clear Channel Communications,** owner of 19 TV stations, over 800 radio stations and about 200,000 billboards as well as SFX Entertainment, which controls 120 concert, theater and sports venues, all of which allows the firm to dominate out-of-the-home entertainment as well as a large portion of the nation's news channels.

- **Dow Jones,** owner of the Dow Jones Industrial Average, *The Wall Street Journal*, the nation's largest circulation newspaper, *Barron's* and 34 newspapers around the globe, plus a share in CNBC Europe and CNBC Asia.

- **Gannett Company,** the second largest newspaper chain with over 90 daily papers including the country's second largest, *USA Today*, plus 19 television stations, a national news service, a printing company, a retail advertising firm, multimedia cable TV, a direct marketing and a telemarketing company, a computer systems installation service and Gannett New Business and Product Development Co.

- **Knight Ridder,** the nation's largest newspaper chain, with 31 papers, two newsprint manufacturing firms, plus Internet access provider InfiNet, an advertising agency and a joint classified advertising venture with Tribune, Gannett, Times Mirror and the Washington Post Co., among others.

- **Microsoft,** the world's largest software manufacturer before its pending breakup, has growing stakes in media operations, including ownership of the MSN portal and CarPoint, *Slate* magazine, an equal share with GE in MSNBC cable and a share in Comcast, a cable system serving 4.5 million people.

- **New York Times Co.,** the fifth largest newspaper chain and owner of *The New York Times, The Boston Globe,* the New York Times News Service, eight television stations, 23 other newspapers and half of *The International Herald-Tribune.*

- **Tribune Co.,** whose purchase of Times Mirror in March 2000 made it the third largest newspaper chain, anchored by *The Chicago Tribune, Los Angeles Times* and 11 other newspapers, plus 22 TV stations, four radio stations, the Chicago Cubs, numerous magazines, stakes in America Online and the WB Network, and an equal share in the Los Angeles Times-Washington Post News Service.

- **Washington Post,** owner of *The Washington Post* and *Newsweek,* plus 36 newspapers, six television stations, a cable system, a newsprint producer, Kaplan Educational Centers, half of the Los Angeles Times-Washington Post News Service and an equal share with The New York Times Co. in *The International Herald Tribune.*

THE NEWS PACE-SETTERS

Two of the above firms deserve special mention because of their dominance over the basic news process. They are *The New York Times* and *The Washington Post.* A news story can emerge from many places, but its destiny depends more on those two organizations than any others. This is especially frustrating for journalists with other companies. According to Larry Lipman, Washington bureau chief for *The Palm Beach Post,* "Issues don't rise to the national conscience unless they've been in those two papers."[2] Both papers also have more than 600 customers for their own news services, which spread their influence around the world. With their choices of which news to feature and which to ignore, these two papers set the national pattern of news and discussion each day.

The Associated Press brings to the cartel its near monopoly on supplying news dispatches from around the world. Funded by media members and non-media subscribers, this sprawling cooperative has 3,500 employees at some 240 bureaus feeding words, sounds and pictures to nearly every news outlet in the nation. Its nearest competitor in distributing general news is British-based Reuters, with relatively few subscribers in the United States.

Other organizations with major roles in determining the news are *The Wall Street Journal*, the four major networks, the *Los Angeles Times* and Knight Ridder. But the two East Coast papers essentially dictate the day's news emphasis. The *Times* is in a class by itself because of its completeness and seriousness. Many news organizations take their cues for the following day from its page-one layout that is sent to many other news organizations the night before publication. Its front-page stories form the basis for many of the next day's radio and TV network reports as well as for major papers, magazines and Web sites.

Competition for audiences and profits is still vigorous among the 17 media firms cited here. But the tendency to cooperate on various fronts is beginning to overcome business rivalries. And as the level of joint ventures and shared services grows, so does the convergence of forces heading toward the creation of a media super-conglomerate.

Shared services include press facilities in public places, pooling operations that cover such common news sources as the White House and Congress, advertising solicitation cooperatives, the Associated Press, trade associations, journalistic societies and play pens such as the Gridiron Club, plus joint operations of opinion and tracking polls. The sharing often includes the same law firms and lobbyists.

Beyond this power circle in Washington, owners and managers of the top media conglomerates belong to an informal media clique of their own that holds an annual picnic of sorts at the summer camp of investment banker Herb Allen in Sun Valley, Idaho. This select gathering, which is chronicled nearly every year by Ken Auletta in *The New Yorker,* gives out awards and hears a few informal talks, but its main business is camaraderie and big deals. Among the stars at the 1999 affair, according to Auletta, were Microsoft co-founders Bill

Gates and Paul G. Allen, AT&T president A. Michael Armstrong, USA Networks chief Barry Diller, CBS chief Mel Karmazin, Liberty Media's John C. Malone, Viacom's Sumner M. Redstone, NBC chief Robert Wright, Washington Post Company's Katherine Graham and News Corporation's Lachlan Murdoch, substituting for his father, Rupert.[3]

SHARING DILUTES COMPETITION

Joint ventures range from common ownership of cable channels and Web sites to joint ownership of news organizations. The latest example involves the massive conversion to digital television, with its promise of extra-sharp images and separate channels for sending data. By March 2000, long before many of the new services would be ready for business, hundreds of TV stations were banding together with data-casting services. Numerous big wheels, such as the New York Times Company, Post-Newsweek Stations, Cox Broadcasting and Tribune Broadcasting, formed something called iBlast, including more than 140 stations. Smaller firms with a total of some 250 stations created Digital Broadcasters Cooperative.

Media firms also are linked to each other as well as to non-journalistic businesses through interlocking memberships on their boards of directors. One might expect organizations sporting world-class news operations to limit potential conflicts of interest by appointing educators, historians, philanthropists and the like to their boards. Indeed, a rare few do hold such seats, but most outside directors of media firms represent other big businesses, thus adding still more potential embarrassments to their journalistic functions.

Among the outside connections represented by directors of ABC's parent Walt Disney in 1999, for example, were Cisco Systems, Northwest Airlines, Phillip Morris Co. and the law/lobby shop of Verner Liipfert, Bernhard *et al.* CBS's board before its merger with Viacom included directors serving in the same capacity at Amazon.com, Atlantic Richfield, Prudential Insurance, Rockwell International, Chase Manhattan Bank, Warner-Lambert, Union Pacific, U.S. Airways, UAL Mart Stores, Banc One, Gillette, New York Life, Smithkline Beecham and American Express. Viacom's board before the CBS alliance had directors also representing Bell Atlantic, American Home Products, CVS Corp., Allied Signal,

GEAOLDISNEYFOXATTMICROVIACOM INC.

Let's see now, the big five news-entertainment conglomerates—AOL Time Warner, General Electric, Walt Disney, News Corporation and Viacom/CBS—compete with each other and with AT&T and Microsoft as well as big newspapers.

But through joint ownership of cable channel MSNBC, Microsoft and General Electric are partners. And so are Microsoft, AT&T and AOL Time Warner through Microsoft's ownership stake in AT&T, which will own part of Time Warner through cable system MediaOne, which AT&T is buying. AT&T also has a share in Excite At Home, a high-speed Internet access competitor of Road Runner, which is jointly owned by Time Warner, Microsoft and MediaOne. AOL Time Warner also shares ownership of AOL Europe with the large German media conglomerate, Bertelsmann, which is buying a share of Time Warner's Book-of-the-Month Club.

By sharing ownership of MSNBC with Microsoft, GE/NBC also is an indirect partner with AT&T and AOL/TW, which is allied with Viacom/CBS through their joint ownership of Comedy Central cable channel and with ABC/Disney and Hearst through their joint ownership of Arts & Entertainment (A&E) and The History cable channels. GE/NBC also shares fortunes with Rupert Murdoch's News Corporation and its Fox News Network through joint ownership of the National Geographic cable channel.

Through its Liberty Media subsidiary, the engorged telephone company is in the news business through its ownership of *The Salt Lake Tribune*, its majority stake in MacNeil/Lehrer Productions and minority interest in News Corporation. And it can influence how *TV Guide* operates through its stake in that magazine.

So these seven conglomerates that appear to be journalistic competitors are all partners where it counts most: through profit-making agreements.

Hartford Finance, Avnet, Bear Stearns and Credit Suisse First Boston, among others. The boards of other media conglomerates contain similar ties to corporate America. (See Appendix E for more details.) Some even share the same directors. They include:

- **Steve Case**, chair of AOL Time Warner, who serves also on the board of MCI Worldcom, owner of UUNet, the next largest Internet service provider.

- **Stephen F. Bollenbach**, president of Hilton Hotels Corp. and former executive vice president of Walt Disney Co., who sits on the board of Time Warner;

- **James Ireland Cash Jr.**, a board member of General Electric and Knight Ridder;

- **Robert F. Erburu**, retired chairman of Times Mirror and director of Cox Communications;

- **Sherry Lansing**, chair and CEO of Paramount Pictures, a subsidiary of Viacom, who is a director of Times Mirror;

- **David D. Williams**, president and CEO of Tribune Media Services, part of Tribune Co., who is a director of Knight Ridder; and

- **Vernon Jordan**, close friend of President Clinton, who holds many directorships, including one at Dow Jones. Until December 1999, he also was a partner in the law/lobby firm of Akin, Gump, Strauss, Hauer and Feld, whose clients included AT&T, Time Warner, and CBS's former parent, Westinghouse.

Such alliances, of course, can be a positive force. Cross fertilization of business enterprises has helped inspire amazing technological advances in communicating news and information. But thay also create potential conflicts of interest for journalists. For those who want news details, they are readily available from numerous sources. The two C-SPANs and various Web sites offer as much background as any person could use.

For those who can't or won't watch the regular evening TV news shows, there are 24-hour cable networks. For those who want world news or want to tune into U.S. news while abroad, there is CNN. And for those who want a lot of news outlets, the number grows by the day.

Sharing with competitors now includes journalists themselves. More and more are being traded like professional athletes. In 1999, MSNBC, a cable channel shared by GE and Microsoft, contracted to have *New York Times* reporters give the news and be interviewed. They were soon replaced by journalists from *The Washington Post* and its *Newsweek* magazine, while the *Times* journalists found a new home on PBS's *NewsHour* and at ABC News.

Post media writer Howard Kurtz immediately raised questions about the NBC deal with his paper. "Both sides," he wrote, "will maintain editorial independence, but the thicket of joint ventures and cross promotion raises questions about potential conflicts of interest. It means, for example, that the Post Co. is in business with a network that is owned by General Electric and partners with Microsoft, both major companies covered by the *Post* and *Newsweek*."[4] Meanwhile, *Wall Street Journal* reporters were assigned also to present news and analysis on CNN, and Dow Jones business journalists were told to provide news for GE's financial channel, CNBC, whose overseas operations are jointly owned by the same two firms. The in-word for this phenomenon is co-peting, a cross between competing and cooperating.

CONGLOMERATES FOSTER CONFLICTS

Such alliances, of course, are designed to put a gloss on news packages. They also can reduce expenses while they make the news business look increasingly like one large corporate family. More serious are the growing conflicts between business and journalistic interests. Every merger of a business conglomerate and a news operation increases tensions for journalists: pressures for greater corporate efficiency through budget cuts, the need to attract new audiences and keep older ones from leaving plus the urge to downsize serious news and replace it with trivia and scandal.

In its venture into the news business, the Walt Disney Company has learned about some of these problems. Soon after it took over ABC, the giant entertainment firm thought it might be nice to create a new brand name for the well-known network and offer special deals to entice journalists to visit the Magic Kingdom. Disney officials were not prepared for the negative response that killed both initiatives. But nothing could stop Disney from constructing a new storefront studio in New York City to showcase its morning news show. It decked out the place with so many Disney logos that it resembled another theme park, which was essentially the aim.

Things got even sillier one day in February 2000. GMA hosts Charles Gibson and Diane Sawyer broke into giggles when their chief guest turned out to be a comical sock puppet used to help sell dog food on Pets.com. It looked like innocent fun to many in the nationwide audience except for information that was not revealed: Disney had recently purchased a stake in Pets.com and was boldly publicizing its trademark gimmick. Gibson and Sawyer claimed not to know, and so did top officials. Such gimmickry is growing more common on news shows.

Similar conflicts also dog other networks. NBC frequently faces a dilemma on how to handle unfavorable news about some branch of its giant industrial guardian General Electric, a firm with a long record of incurring regulatory complaints and criminal prosecutions. Time Warner has a continuing problem of using its periodicals to promote its movies. *Time* has gained fame for the frequency with which it has given Time Warner films cover-story treatment and the frequency of promoting films and other corporate entertainment in general.

Budding retail ventures are also adding potential conflicts. One involves ABC's plan to build an Internet superstore for selling compact disks, videos, books, T-shirts and the like, which were already sold in the nationwide network of Disney stores. NBC has some three dozen Internet facilities plus its "NBC Experience Store" which features a studio tour "and so much more." In March 1999, the network decided to invest in Value Vision International, a home-shopping channel, in order to peddle online jewelry and clothing inspired by its soap opera "Passions." CBS also has a growing online presence, including some two-dozen enterprises.

WHEN TO STOP THE PRESSES

The number and variety of these attempts at corporate reach and synergy show not only how gregarious large media firms are becoming but how little they care about the impact of such ventures on their journalistic functions. The problem is occasionally illustrated when a book publishing deal is canceled because it becomes too embarrassing to the company. One example erupted in 1998 in connection with a book highly critical of the Walt Disney Company by Peter and Rochelle Schweizer. Its title: *The Mouse Betrayed*. Its message: The news media don't report that pedophiles prey on underage visitors to Disney World and employee accident rates there are more than double the industry average. Prior to publication, the authors and their publisher, Regnery Publishing, got ABC's *20/20* interested in doing a major segment. Its investigative unit checked the authors' sources and found additional cases of pedophilia not in the book.

But a month later, ABC decided to can the project. The Schweizers immediately suggested that ABC had buckled to demands from Disney, and some media observers pointed to the immortal words of Michael Eisner one month earlier: "ABC News knows that I would prefer them not to cover [Disney]." ABC officials refused to talk to reporters about it, and Brian Ross, the correspondent on the story, told *Brill's Content* that higher officials gave him no reason for the rejection.[5] The absence of a journalistic reason left the appearance of top-level censorship even if no orders were given.

When Rupert Murdoch discovered in 1998 that his book publisher, HarperCollins, had released a book critical of China without his knowledge, he ordered the firm's top editor, Stuart Proffit, suspended. When the incident hit the headlines, Murdoch blamed staffers for the foul-up. Earlier, he had published a book by the daughter of Chinese Premier Deng Xiaoping praising her father highly. Murdoch wanted to do business in China at the time.

After the tidal wave of large media mergers in 1985, it didn't take long for a new degree of corporate embarrassments to follow. Lawrence K. Grossman, who was president of NBC at the time, later disclosed a phone call from GE chief Jack Welch, a hard-nosed foe of organized labor and government regulators. Grossman said Welch was fuming about NBC news reports about the calamitous dive of the stock market the day before, Oct. 19, 1987. He reportedly insisted that reporters stop using such phrases as "Black Monday" and "precipitous drop" because they were depressing the price of General Electric shares.

Grossman said he ignored the high-level request but soon got an "even more revealing" indication of corporate values the next month in the form of a memo from Welch's lieutenant in charge of NBC, Robert C. Wright, suggesting strongly that news employees contribute to the company's new political action committee. The memo warned:

"Employees who elect not to participate in a giving program of this type should question their own dedication to the company and their expectations." Grossman said the whole news division decided to exclude itself, declaring in Grossman's words, "it was entirely inappropriate for newsmen and women to grind a political ax even for their own company."[6]

GE's deep involvement in the business of electric power, Pentagon contracts and nuclear energy has continually created ethical challenges for NBC journalists as well as the thousands of others around the country who benefit indirectly from GE advertising. The company's numerous manufacturing plants have dumped so many pollutants into public waterways that they account for more than 70 sites slated for cleanup under the Superfund law. They include several miles of the Housatonic River in Massachusetts and at least 40 miles of the Hudson River in New York state. For nearly half a century, the firm sent cancer-causing pollutants into the nation's waterways without notice or penalty. It wasn't until September 1998 that the company finally agreed to clean up two miles of the Housatonic, and it won't be until December 2000 that it will even announce its plans to restore some 40 miles of the Hudson, which it says should clean itself. Not much of this continuing story has gotten onto NBC's *Nightly News*.

BLOWING SMOKE AT THE NETWORKS

A classic case of journalistic conflict of interest due to conglomerate activities arrived almost simultaneously in duplicate for two networks. For ABC News, it was a severe case of corporate letdown at a crucial time. Reporter John Martin and producer Walt Bogdanich worked for months to nail down a 1994 story providing strong evidence that the tobacco industry manipulated the nicotine content of cigarettes. Phillip Morris Co. responded with a $10 billion lawsuit that landed just as ABC was in negotiations with the Walt Disney Company to buy the network. According to Steve Weinberg, who investigated the matter for the *Columbia Journalism Review*, in-house ABC lawyers took over the case from outside ones more experienced at handling libel. Next came an announcement that ABC would settle and agree to apologize.[7] The decision angered ABC news employees, including Martin and Bogdanovich, who were confident that the report was unassailable. The settlement left a question as to whether top network executives who were due to reap millions with a sale to Disney were swayed by that fact or by their feeling that defending the story in court would be too costly.

CBS was hit by a similar downer the following year. It happened as *60 Minutes* prepared to air an interview with a whistleblower named Jeffrey Wigand who had incriminating things to say about his employer, Brown & Williamson. Three days before the Wigand interview was to be aired, CBS lawyers ordered it killed. When news of the decision got out to the press, some CBS journalists were enraged. Network lawyers explained that a Wigand interview could have exposed the corporation to a rare type of suit called tortious interference, although no suit was ever filed. The network happened to be negotiating at the same time with Westinghouse, which had offered to buy CBS.[8] A *Washington Post* story quoted anonymous CBS employees as saying that several top officials of the network did not want the story to interfere with a takeover that could bring them more than $1 million each in stock gains. *60 Minutes* later broadcast a watered-down version of the story after *The Wall Street Journal* published the details.

In addition to coping with conflicts caused by mergers, journalists and their superiors have been struggling against increasing efforts to corporatize news operations. The problem started years ago as media firms hired business managers and accountants to make their operations more efficient. As James Fallows, author of *Breaking the News*, observed, "The problem with the media structure…is not the identity of the ultimate owners: Westinghouse, Disney, GE and so on. The more basic concern is the conversion of the news business to just another corporate operation, where whoever is in charge must be as driven by the demands of the financial market as their counterparts in the banking and steel-making and fast food industries."[9]

CEREAL KILLER ON THE LOOSE

Even the best news organizations have been caught in the rush to corporatize news operations. One was the Times Mirror Co., the conglomerate that owned the *Los Angeles Times* and other papers before it was purchased in 2000 by Tribune Co. Long on everyone's list of the nation's best newspapers, the *Times* had changed substantially from the days when Otis Chandler and earlier Chandlers played an active role in running the paper. In 1995, the Chandler family hired Mark H.

Willes from General Mills to jack up profits. He soon became known as the "cereal killer" as he slashed almost 2,000 jobs in the newspaper division and folded the New York edition of *Newsday* because it wasn't making enough money. He also began requiring editors to meet regularly with heads of other departments, a breach of the traditional wall between them.

A month after Willes named himself publisher of the *Los Angeles Times* in 1997, editor Shelby Coffey III bowed out, concluding there was no room for him in such a business-oriented approach to the news. Despite widespread criticism of Willes by journalists around the country, however, management remained happy with the hefty rise in stock prices. To help promote the profit motive, Willes installed stock tickers around the plant tracking Times Mirror fortunes up to the second. At many media companies, news managers have been softened up with stock and stock options, powerful incentives for them to drop any resistance to profit pressures.

By 1998, at least 192 daily and weekly newspapers had "marketing committees" including newsroom representatives, according to a *Presstime* poll. It meant that the old buffers insulating reporters and editors from commercial operations were fast eroding. Edward W. Jones, managing editor of *The Free Lance-Star* of Fredericksburg, Va., summed it up: "Five or ten years ago, your focus could be pretty much solely on content and the question always was, 'Is this a good story?' Now I have to think, 'Is this a story that will connect with my readers' particular lifestyles?' That's marketing, and it's something I never had to think about before."[10]

Unrelenting pressure for constantly higher profits has created a heightened newsroom vulnerability to budget cuts despite the fact that many news organizations were already making world-class profits. Managers have slashed newsroom and travel budgets. At broadcast outlets, canned video and wire copy have increasingly been substituted for original work. Reporters and editors have been stretched thinner, with many people and bureaus eliminated. Serious news has been slashed and dumbed down to appeal to the lowest common denominator. Journalistic standards have also slipped, and news has become more homogenized.

On the other hand, observers such as Michael Arlen and Robert Samuelson contend that the proliferation of news outlets makes for sufficient diversity of news and opinion. Ronald Reagan's Federal Communications Commission used that argument in killing the Fairness Doctrine. The same rationale was spelled out in a headline in *The Washington Post* after the Viacom/CBS betrothal. It said: "CLAP IF YOU LOVE MEGA-TV—WITHOUT CONGLOMERATES, YOU CAN WAVE GOODBYE TO FREE, HIGH-QUALITY SHOWS." Reporter Paul Farhi wrote: "Now is the time to root for the big guys, the conglomerates, the mega-studio..." (The Washington Post Company itself owns six television stations plus *Newsweek*, a paper mill and many other properties.) Viacom's big profits, he said, were "exactly what CBS—and the other broadcast networks—need most these days....Viacom sees the CBS network as the anchor store of a huge mall—one in which Viacom owns all the stores."[11]

Missing from such assessments of media mergers has been any hint of their aggressive nature. Knowing how Sumner Redstone operated Viacom would provide some clues as to what CBS faces now that the purchase has received government approval. His *modus operandi* is to use all his corporate subsidiaries to promote the product of one. Thus, he says, "When you can make a movie for an average cost of $10 million and then cross promote and sell it off of magazines, books, products, television shows—out of your own company—the profit is enormous." Author Robert McChesney said that was the way Redstone promoted the *Rugrats* movie based on its Nickelodeon TV program in 1998. McChesney speculates as to how well the Beavis and Butt-Head movie might have done if CBS stations had helped promote it.[12] Even before the merger, CBS was acquiring Web enterprises in exchange for promotional time on the network.

More important were the vibes that Redstone sent through CBS News warrens before the merger was consummated. At a conference in China after he had announced the big purchase, he was asked about the delicate intersection of journalism with the worldwide holdings of his. "Journalistic integrity," he said, "must prevail in the final analysis. But that doesn't mean that journalistic integrity should be exercised in a way that is unnecessarily offensive to the countries in which you operate." So in essence, he agreed with Time Warner's Levin, News Corporation's Murdoch, GE's Welch and Disney's Eisner that commerce comes before conscience. That makes it unanimous for the Big Five media merchants.

NOT THE FAULT OF BIG MEDIA?

Reporter Farhi represents many in the media who see nothing wrong with a string of megamergers. In a magazine article, he expanded on his upbeat theme by arguing that despite the size of today's media giants, they are losing market share to the proliferating outlets on cable, satellite, radio and the Internet. He pointed to the steady drop in audiences for evening TV news programs. He added that diversity had actually increased on the radio, pointing out that news-talk stations had grown by a third since 1994. And he said the "alarmists" who contend that bigness means badness had not proven their case. As for conflicts of interest, he said they "may not be the fault of Big Media."[13]

But Farhi failed to address the principal concern about media concentration: its stifling effect on diversity of news and commentary, an essential component of a healthy democracy. He assumed that all significant conflicts of interest would eventually get laundered by being reported. He cited Rupert Murdoch's killing of a book critical of China while he was dickering with Peking for satellite TV contracts there. But Farhi knew very well how news can be squelched by large media firms when they see an economic threat to their properties or profits. He was the first reporter to reveal Bob Dole's $70 billion threat against broadcasters in 1995 while the big telecommunications "reform" bill was being considered by Congress. He was aware that no major news outlet picked up the news and therefore it was never relayed to the general public. He knew that none of the news executives in attendance were apparently interested in tipping a reporter to what appeared to be a high-stakes attempt at blackmailing the media. (See chapter 3 for details.)

From an investor point of view, it would be hard to fault the news business for such lapses. For years, it has been the darling of Wall Street, mainly because of its high profit margins. It is not unusual for TV stations to generate a 50 percent return. Over a 20-year period beginning in 1971, newspapers outpaced other stocks on Wall Street by almost 6-to-1 in appreciated value, according to media analyst John Morton.[14] In 1997 alone, stocks for newspapers, broadcasting and cable as a group grew more than any of the 64 industries tracked by J.P. Morgan Investments. Cable topped the field with an increased value of 79 percent, while broadcasting was third with 58 percent, and newspapers sixth with 49 percent.[15] It was just what the nation's media giants planned when they helped pushed through the Telecommunications Act of 1996. Instead of bringing more competition and lower prices for consumers as the publicity blurbs promised, it brought higher rates and a new wave of mergers due to further relaxation of ownership limits. Although stock prices have risen less rapidly since then, media properties are still among the leaders of the Street.

In 1999, it was radio's turn to top the charts. *Broadcasting and Cable* magazine reported that radio more than doubled its industry-wide values, even beating the rocket-fueled Nasdaq index by 30 percent. The top two companies were TCI Satellite, a creation of AT&T's Liberty Media Group, with a gain of 987 percent, and Valuevision, a TV shopping network purchased by NBC, with an increase of 716 percent for the year. Not all media firms were that successful. Disney's valuation dropped 3 percent, and Washington Post Company stock fell 5 percent.[16] But even when they fall, media stocks can offer more stability than high-flying tech stocks in volatile times.

RECORD PROFITS ARE NOT ENOUGH

In today's business climate, though, record profits are not enough. If a particular company doesn't meet the advance estimates of Wall Street experts, and sometimes even if it does, the Street may signal a sell-off. The people who ultimately control media fortunes are not the Ted Turners and Michael Eisners and Rupert Murdochs. They are the hard-nosed money managers of such dull sounding outfits as Fidelity Management & Research, Capital Research & Management, Putnam Investment Management and Janus Capital, the big four, plus a few more large funds. According to John M. Higgins and Price Colman, "These are the Wall Street Media Mafia, the money men and women who dictate how much a company is worth and who can influence everything, including how much capital Viacom Inc. can raise, whether Time Warner Inc. can afford a particular takeover or whether CBS Corp. executives' stock options are worth millions or nothing." This group has the power to rock a stock the way it did to Viacom after turning sour on the firm's video rental operations, causing its price to fall 63 percent.[17]

These market movers also swing their weight on national policy issues. That point was accentuated in the bitter dispute in May 2000 between Time Warner and Disney over access of Disney programs to Time Warner's vast cable systems. The dispute caused William Kennard, head of the Federal Communications Commission at the time, to warn that government might have to act to assure open access. That prompted Laura Martin of Credit Suisse First Boston to comment: "If the government mandates open access, I'll downgrade every cable stock."[18]

The leverage of this clique has been good for business but not for an informed public. The result is newstainment, a product designed to cost less and attract large audiences. The emphasis is on items with strong emotional appeal, especially intimate personal stories. Perhaps the epitome of this kind of journalism was ABC's "interview" with 6-year-old Elian Gonzalez, the survivor of a shipwreck that had killed his mother in 1999 and whose ultimate fate turned into a torrid political issue. In March 2000, Diane Sawyer managed to win exclusive rights to trap the confused boy into some innocent comments that were replayed for three days on *Good Morning America* and then on *20/20* as Cuban-Americans in Miami and elsewhere struggled to prevent his return to a communist Cuba.

As the pressure to produce such stuff grows, so does the tendency to shade the truth and mix in a little fakery here and there. First, it appears in gray areas, such as fabricated "photo illustrations" in news-magazines and newspapers. In some cases, entire stories are falsified. TV examples have ranged from CBS's recreation of the Beirut kidnapping of AP reporter Terry Anderson to the infamous fabrication of truck fires on *Dateline*.

Throughout these controversies and others, media officials have insisted that their sole aim is to find and present news. TV news-magazines have denied that their entertainment divisions had any role in determining subjects or how they were treated. The falseness of such claims was finally documented in a court case involving former NBC correspondent Arthur Kent, who had gained fame during the Gulf War as "the SCUD stud." After a dispute over getting his segments on *Dateline*, he was fired. He later sued the network for breach of contract, fraud and defamation. He claimed that the "news-magazine" took its orders from NBC's entertainment division in

Burbank, Calif. Testimony in the case supported his claims, and he won a multi-million-dollar settlement. Kent summed up network policy: "Program only stories you can sell. Promotion policy becomes editorial policy. Entertainment in Burbank steers news in New York." The same philosophy also governs network evening news programs.

CBS officials got a different kind of comeuppance. Their handling of the tobacco exposé was turned into a popular Hollywood film, *The Insider,* in November 1999. The movie drove home what the public was beginning to see quite clearly: that business calls the shots for the news business.

The final blow for CBS: the producer was competitor Disney, whose ABC network was no stranger to similar humiliation. An added irony: By that time, CBS had been taken over by another entertainment firm, National Entertainment, alias Viacom.

Was this the type of self-regulation Gerald Levin had in mind when he said media firms were more important than government? In the absence of a vigorous anti-trust policy for years, here was one entertainment conglomerate effectively disciplining another through the power of public ridicule. If so, how long will this type of peer review survive in an era of so many joint media ventures?

Prospects are not good.

CHAPTER II

Downsizing News of the Nation and World

There are moral rights which limit the editor's privilege of exclusion...

The Hutchins Commission

As the House of Representatives voted on articles of impeachment for William Jefferson Clinton, millions of Americans watched on TV. Those lucky enough to have tickets crowded into the gallery above the House floor and sat in silence as the proceedings ground forward. All the major organizations were fully focused on this historic event.

Then, incredibly, CBS cut away to a pro football game.

In name at least, this was the same CBS that for many years had been synonymous with excellence in news and public affairs programming. The CBS of Edward R. Murrow, Walter Cronkite and the Army-McCarthy hearings. The CBS that owner Bill Paley had built into the Tiffany Network, which for so long had managed to make handsome profits while setting the standards for television news. Marvin Kalb wrote of a time in the 1960s when Paley invited his senior correspondents to a year-end dinner and sketched out future plans for the news operation. "They were impressive, and we all felt proud," Kalb wrote. "Charles Collingwood observed: 'But Bill, that's going to cost you a lot of money.' Mr. Paley responded: 'Don't worry about that. I've got Jack Benny to make money for me. You guys cover the news.'"[1]

Obviously, things had changed radically for CBS by the time the House voted on the Articles of Impeachment. Long before he died, Paley changed his stripes. In 1966, he shocked journalists everywhere when he decided to air reruns of *I Love Lucy* rather than live congressional hearings on Vietnam because *Lucy* was more profitable. That decision led to the resignation of Fred Friendly, president of CBS News, and marked a turning point for the network. The giants of the original cast were gradually replaced by buttoned-down corporate types who had to give quarterly profits a weight they had not had in the past. After all, the networks were publicly held, and stockholders had to be kept happy. In desperate attempts to stem financial weaknesses caused by falling audiences and tougher competition from cable in the late 1990s, CBS had bid a stunning $4 billion for the right to televise American Football Conference games. There were those who wondered if CBS and its then corporate parent, Westinghouse, would gain or lose in the end, especially given the steadily declining ratings of professional football.

It wasn't long before CBS news crews felt the enormity of the gamble. The division got orders from above to slash 300 people from a payroll that already had been pared down by a succession of cuts in the 1980s and early 1990s. It meant cutting costs by 10 percent overall, with aftershocks spreading to every CBS office from Miami to Moscow, though supposedly not felling any senior correspondents. Many full-time job losers were replaced by temporary workers and young, inexperienced people at lower salaries. Yet no other CBS divisions were affected, not even the vast entertainment operations. NBC and ABC had suffered similar cuts earlier and had to make similar choices in programming.

It was all part of today's marching orders for the news business: spare nothing, even our most sacred public obligations, in order to fatten the bottom line. This chapter describes some of the devastating effects of media commercialization and consolidation on the amount and type of news presented to American citizens.

It doesn't matter that media companies often exceed other industries in profits. It doesn't matter that, according to the polls, most Americans have lost faith in journalism and have even begun to question the value of press freedom. And it doesn't matter that the bewhiskered formula of crime, scandal and trivia appears to have lost its punch.

Some media executives seem to be getting the message, but not many. So while profits for most firms go up, news budgets stay the same or go down. While public trust in the news media falls, the media contempt for their obligations rises. And while news organizations continue to push all the hot buttons, audiences for both print and broadcast news keep disappearing. At a time of unprecedented need for people to keep current with social, economic and political change, the institution most capable of supplying that information keeps focusing on the tired notion that "if it bleeds, it leads." The pressure for short-term profits forces journalists to judge news on its emotional appeal rather than its relevance to citizens.

SOFTENING THE NEWS

In order to understand the basic enigma, it is necessary to go back to a 1978 study done by Ruth Clark, a social scientist. Based on her work with focus groups, she published a report entitled, "Changing Needs of Readers." She said newspaper readers wanted "more attention paid to their personal needs, help in understanding and dealing with their own problems in an increasingly complex world, news about their neighbors, not just the big city and Washington..."[2]

Her findings were widely viewed as a call for less serious fare, less government news. Although she did not suggest that hard news be replaced by soft news, that was the way her work was interpreted. She said her focus group had "recognized that editors have a responsibility to inform and educate the public." But that point was lost in the drive to boost news audiences with more glitz, less grits.

Gannett's Al Neuharth gorged on Clark's report in launching *USA Today* in 1982 with its heavy emphasis on color printing, short stories, bland topics and plain puffery. Although his proud baby was roundly dissed by most editors, they were soon mimicking "McPaper" on a massive scale. Within three years, Leo Bogart found that two-thirds of 1,310 daily editors had increased the ratio of features to hard news.

Similar changes were occurring in the television world where the main catalyst was Van Gordon Sauter. He became CBS News president for the second time in 1986, the year Laurence Tisch purchased the network and decided to slash expenses in order to jack up profits.

Media writer Ken Auletta described how Sauter took tabloids and consumer news as models in beefing up the flow of action pictures and stories designed to arouse personal feelings.[3] ABC and NBC soon followed and eventually outSautered Sauter with softer, consumer-oriented material. Each network also redesigned the set and inaugurated special segments, such as "American Agenda," "Solutions" and "A Closer Look" to help bundle the news for better viewership. It was the beginning of the end of serious news reporting on the national networks.

By 1994, Clark and her guinea pigs had second thoughts. She said her focus groups and survey respondents were now saying: "Give us the news—hard news, real news, whether it's national, state, regional or local." But this time, her findings fell on deaf ears except for the word "local." Three years later, a similar warning was ignored. It was a national survey by Clark, Martire & Bartolomeo finding that "71 percent of those polled said they were extremely interested or very interested in world and national news. The only news interests that ranked higher were local news, investigations of important issues and news about the weather."[4] Again, the warning was largely ignored.

NBC's *Nightly News* preferred to take the tabloid approach one step further, totally revamping its style and riding it to the top of the ratings ahead of the longtime leader, ABC's *World News Tonight*. With a flashier format, Tom Brokaw moved out from behind the anchor desk and gave the news standing up. Recurring segments such as "The Fleecing of America," and "In Their Own Words," were packaged with glitzy logos. Major news still got covered, but it was shortened and overtaken by topics that titillate emotions, not feed brains.

Going out and covering a story was being replaced by canned video and slick packaging. News lite was pioneered largely by ABC, but was soon embraced by other networks. "When Walter Cronkite was here," said CBS news vice president Joe Peyrommin, "we basically were the wire service of the world. We did a minute-15 on the White House, a minute-15 on the Pentagon a minute-15 on the hearing on the Hill." Under the new approach, he said, "We spend longer periods of time on social issues, consumer issues and health issues, issues that are important to the viewer."[5]

Soft news became especially welcome on local television, where polls show that Americans get most of their news. Surveys by Rocky

Mountain Media Watch, a nonprofit group of volunteers, have revealed high "mayhem" levels at many stations, including ones owned and operated by national networks. After examining 100 local television newscasts around the country on February 26, 1997, the group reported that 43 percent of the content featured violence, such as crime, war, terrorism or disaster. At stations in Detroit, Washington and Los Angeles, the mayhem content hemorrhaged to 75 percent. At 15 stations, commercials consumed more airtime than news.

By 1998, however, there were signs that the message to the media symbolized by Monica was finally starting to get through to some community TV stations. Whether it was the negative public reaction to the orgiastic Lewinsky treatment or some other factor, serious journalism began making a comeback in some places, at least according to the Project for Excellence in Journalism. It found that both tabloid and quality approaches could bring financial success. Its report in the *Columbia Journalism Review* apparently got noticed. Only a year later, the Project spotted a new glimmer, reporting that going tabloid was no longer a guarantee of success. It said stations with the poorest quality news programming were twice as likely to fail. Quality was defined as having a broad range of topics and a focus on the significant that is locally relevant, a definition that might include national and international topics as well as local ones.[6] But the news about quality journalism travels slowly in the news business.

JUNK FOOD JOURNALISM

The urge to entertain people rather than inform them is not a recent thing. Yellow journalism reached a heyday more than a century ago. But until the big merger period of the middle 1980s, it was largely confined to big-city tabloids and supermarket scandal sheets. Since then, even the best news organizations have cheapened their main product. In the early 1990s, the criminal and civil trials of football star O.J. Simpson took over broadcast and printed news. He was later replaced by the likes of Paula Jones, Monica Lewinsky and Elian Gonzalez.

Every year, the Organization of News Ombudsmen selects the year's top ten "Junk Food Stories," then reports the winners in the annual book of self-censored news stories published by Project Censored. In 1998, the top ten Junk Food Stories had to compete with the saturation coverage of Lewinsky and impeachment. But still managing to get plenty of attention were the Spice Girls, the movie Titanic, British Royals, JonBenet Ramsay, John Glenn's space flight, Jerry Springer, Viagra and Jerry Seinfeld.[7]

The struggle in newsrooms between journalistic responsibility and the obsession for trivia sometimes plays out in living color. An example occurred in September 1999 when presidential candidate Elizabeth Dole appeared as a guest on ABC's *Good Morning America*. From the start, she clearly wanted to discuss her education policy, but Diane Sawyer wanted to know what she thought about Pat Buchanan's incendiary book, *A Republic, Not an Empire*. Sawyer also inquired about Dole's campaign and fund-raising strategy but refused to discuss education. One of the reasons Dole gave for quitting the race was her failure to get her message out. Sawyer didn't have to cooperate. But she illustrated how the media can degrade public dialogue in the search for excitement.

A similar example occurred on March 28, 1997, the day when House Republican leaders launched an elaborate plan to kill a promising bill to reform campaign finance practices. Although the effort involved considerable intrigue on a subject of front-page interest, *The Washington Post* relegated the story to page 7. It showed how government news is often downgraded even when it offers an extra touch of drama. The front pages in those days were dominated by Paula Jones and Kathleen Willey.

On Feb. 6, 1997, President Clinton submitted his much discussed five-year budget, the first one that balanced in three decades. The historic occasion was an opportunity for news organizations to explain how it might affect average Americans. It was the leading story in the papers. ABC rose to the occasion, spending nearly five minutes on its *World News Tonight*, nearly double the usual time for a lead story, with a colorful array of graphics to help viewers understand the details. But CBS could find only 20 seconds, and NBC 30 seconds for it. The latter network added another three and a half minutes for a friendly interview with House Budget Committee Chairman John Kasich, R-Ohio, who took time to criticize the White House plan without having read it. Yet all three networks carried full reports from the Simpson murder trial even though nothing unusual occurred that day.

CUTTING STAFFS TO SAVE MONEY

In the above examples, serious news was available but wasn't given adequate attention. In many cases, news reports about government affairs are not even filed. This is especially true in the nation's capital, where much of what happens can have a heavy impact on the lives of millions. At a time when the federal government's role in society is being severely challenged, many news organizations have reduced their ability to do their jobs. The reduction seemed to coincide with the big media mergers of the middle 1980s.

Penn Kimball, a former journalist, noticed what was happening but wasn't sure why. In a book published in 1994, he not only confirmed the decline in serious news coverage but found that big news organizations had sharply reduced their journalistic personnel at key news centers. He reported that all three main networks had cut their staffs in Washington, with CBS hit the hardest. He said CBS and NBC used to have about 30 correspondents each but that the number had been reduced to about a dozen each and that ABC had eliminated five on-air and two off-air reporters in 1992. He said ABC had reduced its full-time congressional correspondents from four to two in a decade.[8]

Behind the cuts, said Kimball, was a sour attitude among bureau chiefs toward news about the nation's capital. He traced it to network executives at New York headquarters. He said the latter think "the American people were tired of Washington long before the flood of Washington scandals." He quoted one former executive producer as saying: "I always got the 'Washington is a joke' speech from local news directors. These people believe that Washington is an irrelevant rat hole where Americans send their money with no results. The credo of local news is that people don't give a damn about government—federal, state, or local—in any form."[9] Kimball quoted Steve Friedman, an ABC network producer, as saying in 1993: "The public is pissed off at the president and at Congress. To cover Washington as a problem solver, as it once was, is not correct. We go where the news is and that's not necessarily Washington....If you don't go with the changes, you go out of business. We intend to stay in business."[10]

By the end of 1999, the big three networks each had only four on-air correspondents to handle all of Congress, the White House, State and Defense, plus a number of off-air reporters who did the real work. Each network also employed a retinue of assistants and camera crews to back up their correspondents. But coverage of regulatory agencies, where laws are implemented down to the personal level, had all but disappeared.

On any particular day, some large news organizations are represented in Congress by very few bodies. A call in October 1999 to Gannett News Service, which watches Capital Hill for more than 90 daily papers, found only one person on duty. Web sites for the House Radio and TV Gallery in December 1999 listed only two correspondents for CNN and one for the *NewsHour with Jim Lehrer*. Compare such numbers to ABC's coverage of millennium celebrations around the world on New Year's Eve. According to one press account, it involved 30 correspondents, 225 producers, 485 engineers, 30 cameras, 400 more from an international pool, plus three backup control rooms manned by 300 people.

Reflecting the squeeze on staffing and the feeling that Washington was irrelevant, network news about Congress declined from an average of 124 stories a month on the three networks in the 1970s to only 42 by 1992, according to Thomas Mann and Norman Ornstein.[11] A study by Carl Sessions Stepp reported that the amount of news from Washington in 10 metropolitan papers from 1988 to 1998 dropped by 34 percent.

Queries made for this book by Rita Colorito found reporters spread thinner because they are often handling more beats, a situation especially noticeable at the departments of defense and education. She observed a tendency of news bureaus to use floating correspondents who may move from a department or agency to Congress and then to the White House to follow a specific development. But she reported that some news organizations that had reduced staffing in Washington in the mid-1990s had added personnel since then.

The common frustration of bureau chiefs in Washington has been spelled out candidly by James Warren of *The Chicago Tribune*, whose company (Tribune Co.) has been widely praised for its high (nearly 30 percent) profit margins and its integration of broadcast, print and Internet news operations into one central desk. In a book essay, he acknowledged that "budgetary reasons" left him unable to replace a good reporter on a family beat, unable to cover regulatory agencies the way he would like and unable to send reporters into the country to interview "real Americans." He estimated that "80 percent of [Washington] reporters cover 15 percent of the news."[12]

EMPHASIS ON MICRO-REPORTING

Meanwhile, there has been an increasing emphasis on regional angles in Washington. A growing army of regional reporters focuses on details of Congress and the bureaucracy that directly affect local areas such as a federal contract to a nearby firm or some legislative pork to benefit a nearby institution. According to Alan M. Schlein, a founder of the Regional Reporters Association, regional reporters now comprise 30 percent of American correspondents in Washington, compared to 60 percent for national ones and 10 percent for miscellaneous others. He estimates that foreign reporters comprise fully half of the Washington news corps.

Even at the community level, where polls show people prefer to get their news, TV reporting about local government has been dropping to nearly the point of invisibility. According to the Consortium for Local Television Surveys, news about government and politics accounted for only 15 percent of local TV newscasts in eight cities in 1996 and 1997. By 1999, their surveys showed that such news accounted for only 11 percent. And much of that was called superficial, such as reporting outside a building where a meeting is taking place but not going to the meeting itself. Forty percent of news time was devoted to crime, calamities and Clinton-Lewinsky. The results caused Marion Just, a Wellesley College professor who took part in the surveys, to say: "If you don't cover what government does, but you [do] cover its mistakes, then you aren't going to create the kinds of citizens who want to take an active role in the political process."[13]

All studies show a steady reduction in serious news. That fact helps explain why so many Americans keep electing and reelecting people to Congress who appear indifferent to opinion polls showing strong public support for action on health care, pension security, environmental protection, campaign abuses, gun control and education. "In far too many cases," says *The Washington Post's* David S. Broder, "inadequate reporting or widespread indifference have left people ignorant of essential information they need to function as citizens."[14]

REPORTERS ADMIT POOR COVERAGE

A confidential mail survey of news correspondents on Capitol Hill for this book confirmed that many major stories are not being reported. For example, 73 percent of those responding noticed an increase in lobbyists, but 82 percent said they do not have enough time to fully report their influence. Ninety-one percent said major stories are not covered because of time constraints, and only about half (56 percent) said the media in general give adequate attention to Congress. On the touchy matter of media budget cuts, 41 percent said their employer had reduced personnel in the past five years, while 14 percent failed to answer. (See Appendix A.) A similar survey of congressional press aides found that 66 percent felt that the media did an adequate job covering their own district but 54 percent felt that the media did not do a good job overall in covering Congress. (See Appendix B.)

Stingy coverage of Congress is part of a larger pattern that extends to political coverage of campaigns and elections. Campaign reporting has been plagued for years by the journalistic tendency to reduce everything to a horse race focusing on strategic factors such as fund raising, poll results and tactics. Even in late 1999 and early 2000 when coverage became unusually extensive, it was plagued by the same problems. A survey of the primary campaigns by the Project for Excellence in Journalism concluded that only 13 percent of the stories were about "things that would actually impact the American public if the candidates were elected."

In 1998, the nadir in political reporting might have been reached in California, where there was a lively race for governor as well as numerous congressional contests. A review by the University of Southern California Annenberg School of Communication reported virtually no coverage by local TV stations to the gubernatorial race. A tally of time on 33 channels reaching 87 percent of the state population showed only 32 one-hundredths of one percent of program time devoted to the campaign. Four years earlier, the total was six times greater but still only 1.8 percent of on-air news time. Of the 1,825 stories analyzed, only 22 percent focused exclusively on the issues.

The TV soundbite symbolizes the changes in political reporting. A survey by Kiku Adatto of the Shorenstein Center clocked political soundbites in 1968 at an average of 42 seconds apiece. By 1988, the time was less than 10 seconds. Since then, soundbites seem to be on their way out completely. Far more common now is the picture of a candidate's lips moving while a journalist boils down what is being said to fewer and fewer seconds. According to Martin Plisser, former political director for CBS, campaign news on the networks during the last month of the 1996 presidential race amounted to even less than in 1960 when the evening shows were only 15 minutes long.[15]

For every major gap in the news, there is missing commentary. That's because most commentators merely react to news and don't do original reporting. The new emphasis on local angles further reduces the likelihood that national political issues will be discussed in newspaper editorial and op-ed pages. A six-week survey of 24 leading newspapers for this book beginning Oct. 1, 1999, confirmed that assumption, though there was no earlier survey to indicate trends.[16] (See Appendices C and D.) At the time, the major issues in the news included the presidential primary campaigns, Reform Party stirrings, Congress's rejection of the Nuclear Test Ban Treaty, and the federal budget battle, particularly how it would affect Medicare and Social Security.

Results showed that national political issues got relatively little attention, particularly in editorials. At the lower end of the scale were three major papers, *The Arizona Republic*, *The Cleveland Plain Dealer* and *The New York Daily News*, with no more than nine editorials on national politics in 37 editions. That compared to 53 in *The New York Times* and 50 in *The Washington Post*, the only papers with more than one editorial and op-ed commentary a day. The closest to them were the *Wall Street Journal*, with 32 and the *Los Angeles Times* with 29. *The Washington Post* topped the field for op-ed commentaries on national issues with 89, followed by the *New York Times* with 77, the *San Diego Union-Tribune* with 67, the *New York Post* with 66 and the *St. Petersburg Times* with 65. Gannett's *USA Today* hit the bottom of the pile, running only six op-ed commentaries and 23 editorials on national topics.

FOREIGN NEWS UNDER THE KNIFE

Most news organizations also have cut back the number of correspondents and bureaus around the world in recent years. One big exception is the Associated Press, with some 140 bureaus worldwide.

Another exception is CNN, with 25 bureaus outside the United States in 1999, according to Eason Jordan, CNN president. With less than half a million viewers on the average in this country, CNN has become a major player in international affairs with key locations in many countries around the world. During the Gulf War, the cable news firm became more than just a news service as government officials here and abroad watched each other through CNN and reacted to every change in the situation. Later, it became an important communication link between the U.S. government and leaders of other nations during the Kosovo operations.

CNN also has become an influential force in this country beyond its numbers. Its screen stays on 24 hours a day in many newsrooms, providing journalists with up-to-the-minute reports on the day's events. It also has a big presence in the offices of elected officials, lobbyists and others. Washington correspondent Larry Lipman of the *Palm Beach (Fla.) Post* calls it a "visual wire service," an electronic version of Associated Press. It's available to 80 million U.S. homes and some 1 billion worldwide.

Despite all this, international reporting has dropped precipitously. According to the Tyndall Report, news time in minutes from foreign bureaus on the three major networks' evening news programs fell by more than half from 1988 to 1998. In almost every year, NBC used foreign bureaus the least, while CBS used them most. The accompanying table shows the total number of minutes for each network for three categories of international news in six-year periods.

Two other surveys confirm the decline in news from the rest of the world. One was the previously mentioned study of 10 metropolitan newspapers by Carl Sessions Stepp, a professor at the University of Maryland. He found a 40 percent drop in international news content over a 35-year period ending in 1999.[17] Five months earlier, the magazine reported another survey concluding that "most dailies have drastically reduced the amount of foreign and national news they publish." It's not because of a shortage of available information. It's the refusal of news outlets to use more than a tiny fraction of the news material supplied by the Associated Press and other services.

Another factor cutting into the use of general world news is the growing interest in trade and finance around the world, as reflected by the growing proportion of international news relating to business

MINUTES OF INTERNATIONAL NEWS
ON TV EVENING NEWS

Type of report:	ABC	CBS	NBC	Total
Stories from foreign bureaus				
1988	1158	1090	1013	3261
1993	1057	752	543	2352
1998	513	647	304	1464
Stories about foreign policy				
1988	597	713	674	1984
1993	590	637	584	1811
1998	508	538	525	1571
Other foreign coverage				
1988	1410	1310	1221	3941
1993	1270	862	712	2844
1998	885	887	605	2377

(Source: *Tyndall Report*, ADT Research, Nov. 3, 1999)

rather than topics of general interest. According to *Editor & Publisher*, that change has been especially pronounced since 1990. As U.S. corporations become more involved abroad and foreign firms become more active in this country, news organizations reflect the trend. To illustrate the new emphasis, news organizations with the most international presence are financially oriented, except for the AP. Topping the list of such firms with foreign bureaus and correspondents is Bloomberg News Service with 78 bureaus, followed by *The Wall Street Journal*, with 37 bureaus.

In fact, economic angles are useful hooks to entice people to follow foreign news. The trick is to localize such news, says Andrew Alexander, Washington bureau chief for Cox Newspapers. He says that when General Motors opened a plant in Shanghai to do what its plant in Dayton, Ohio, was doing, all the chain's papers, not just the one in Dayton, were able to zero in on the consequences of today's trade relations. He says he's always looking for such items to connect with his readers.[18] In 1999, the American Society of Newspaper Editors produced a guidebook for editors entitled *Bringing the World Home: Showing Readers Their Global Connections*. It cites the growing foreign interests of Americans–because of increased immigration, travel, trade and such–and shows how to connect them to the global scene. But a year later, only a third of ASNE's 900 members had requested a copy.

Many journalists contend that the decline in general international news has been simply due to a lack of public interest. Others say it is part of the industry's widespread retrenchment in order to reduce expenses. Collecting such news can be extremely costly, a fact that often leads to overseas layoffs when media companies merge. When the Tribune Company purchased Times Mirror in March 2000, merging of their foreign bureaus was one of the most likely results since they had a total of 31, some in the same places.

Whatever the reason for the decline in foreign staffing and use of international news, there is no question about the consequences. Americans have become less informed about the world around them at a time when world trade and tourism have been growing more than ever. When a sample of citizens was asked by reporters how much of the total U.S. budget goes to foreign assistance, nearly six out of ten responded incorrectly that the government spends more on such aid than on Medicare. The average figure offered was more than six times what the government actually spends. Two-thirds of those interviewed could not even name their U.S. representative or his/her party affiliation, and four out of 10 could not name the vice president.[19]

One reason for so much public ignorance is the small amount of time devoted to non-news public events such as charitable and community projects. In determining whether to renew a station's license, the Federal Communications Commission used to consider how well a station performed its public service obligations: the percentage of program time devoted to non-news public affairs, among other things. Although license renewals more recently have rarely touched on such things, the obligation remains. It is also important to democracy that broadcasters demonstrate a commitment to public dialogue similar to that shown by other media. But a study by the Benton Foundation in

March 2000 of programming in 24 markets found an average of only 1 percent of total time devoted to such activity.

Without more of an effort by news organizations to inform the public about broad national and international events, how can American political leaders have the confidence to know what policies to pursue for the nation's welfare and what policies are preferred by the public at large? An example of the news and knowledge gaps occurred in late 1999 when many Europeans protested strongly against genetically modified food being sold there by American firms. Only after the protests were reported did most Americans learn that they themselves were consuming the same food in large quantities without knowing about the degree of its safety. Actually, the main point of the news stories in the United States was not public safety but the possibility that some U.S. firms might suffer steep losses in sales of food, seed and pesticides to other countries.

HOW REPORTING ALTERS HISTORY

Unfortunately, the record for reporting major news developments has never been good. It seems as if the bigger the news, the poorer the coverage. Here are some examples of how inadequate reporting has altered U.S. events:

- **The Cold War:** During most of the four-and-a-half decades between World War II and the fall of the Berlin Wall and the collapse of the Soviet Union, the American press failed to show how exaggerated were fears of the Soviet Union, thus helping lead both countries into an arms race that they are still trying to pay off. A shadow Cold War continues as Congress seeks to build military defenses to protect the nation against threats that no one has been able to clearly define.

- **Vietnam:** By and large, editors and government officials failed to follow up early correspondent reports signaling the futility of the conflict during the Kennedy administration. It wasn't until 1968 that gruesome pictures on television—along with the end of student deferments—aroused massive anti-war sentiment and led Walter Cronkite to turn against the war. By that time, many of the 58,000 American deaths and millions of other casualties had occurred. A survey that year by *The Boston Globe* showed that not one of the 39 major U.S. dailies advocated withdrawal at a time when thousands of Americans were demonstrating in the streets for an end to the war.

- **Savings and Loans:** Taxpayers lost $145 billion in large measure because of the belated response of the national news media to some excellent reporting at the regional level about the mass corruption of this vital industry. Few in the press recognized the importance of federal deregulation in sowing the seeds of this economic disaster.

- **Watergate:** *The Washington Post* and a few other news organizations stood nearly alone in probing the famous break-in and the subsequent cover-up during the final five months of the 1972 presidential campaign. Had more news organizations put their staffs to work, President Richard Nixon might not have been reelected, and the nation might have avoided two years of investigations and impeachment proceedings.

- **Iran-Contra:** Mainstream news media failed to pick up numerous early news reports indicating a major assault on the Constitution involving the sale of missiles to Iran by the Reagan administration in order to raise money for the Contras in spite of the congressional ban on helping them in their war against the Sandinistas in Nicaragua. A small weekly paper in Lebanon scooped the entire American press.

Among other examples of major breakdowns in reporting was the failure to report 45 years of CIA-connected civil disruptions—including terrorist bombings, attempted coups and assorted mayhem in Italy after World War II—connected with a secret U.S. program called Gladio, which Prime Minister Giulio Andreotti finally acknowledged in 1990. It was part of a U.S. effort to prevent communists from ever getting political control of Italy, an effort that proved lethal to hundreds of innocent Italians and helped establish the CIA's reputation as the prime suspect for almost any subversive act in the world.[20]

CONTINUING NEWS GAPS

The news media continue to have trouble connecting with the American people, often making the problems worse with inadequate reporting and uninformed commentary. Among current voids in the news:

- **The perennial push to build a bigger military establishment,** which already absorbs one-third of the entire federal budget at a time when no nation has the capability to seriously threaten this nation's security by military means. The media have done little reporting on the main reason for such a policy: the fear that Pentagon budget cuts would hurt the economy, mainly because the media themselves depend on it.

- **The war against drug addiction,** which has led to draconian laws and irrational programs that are destroying millions of American lives for minor infractions while the degree of addiction worsens. The media have helped to mislead the nation by failing to adequately report the social consequences and viable alternatives.

- **The war against crime,** which has led to massive prison building and an incarceration rate that leads the world. The media deserves major responsibility because of their unwarranted emphasis on violent crime during an eight-year period when rates were steadily going down.

- **The war against international cooperation,** the widespread political sentiment in this country against American involvement in efforts to control nuclear weapons and pollution, conquer disease and resolve disputes among nations at a time when advances in transportation and communication are making the world into a "global village" with common problems. The media tend to exacerbate the problems with their emphasis on random disasters rather than policies in international news.

- **The failure to provide adequate health protection to all Americans.** This comes at a time when some 45 million are outside the health care system and another 20 million are very dissatisfied with their health plans. Surveys showed that the news media played a major role not only in defeating the Clinton health plan but discouraging consideration of viable alternatives.

- **The failure to reform the system of financing political campaigns.** The news media can see better than any other group the degree to which democratic government is being subverted by wealthy interests and their control of elected officials, but they have failed to fully inform the public about the situation and their own conflicting role as chief beneficiaries of political advertising.

- **The media's own role in the crisis of American democracy.** Journalists like to investigate and analyze other institutions of society, but they have failed to examine their own contributions to the decline of public representation in Washington, as illustrated by the number of polls showing what the public wants compared to the lack of results.

As the new millennium gets under way, the news business itself is facing its own crisis. Fewer people are watching. Statistics released in June 2000 by the Pew Research Center showed a bigger disconnect than ever between Americans and the news. In five years, the proportion of adults saying they watched network TV news regularly dropped from 50 percent to only 30 percent, while the proportion of people reading a newspaper dropped below 50 percent for the first time. Young people have fallen away even more, an ominous sign for the future. Fifteen percent of all ages said they went online each day for news, although such news tends to be a brief version of network and newspaper news. It shouldn't be surprising for those who have been cutting the guts out of the news to see their audiences fade away. What is surprising is their disinterest in changing their ways. They prefer to use their special freedom for even more commercial gain.

CHAPTER III

Exploiting the First Amendment for Profit

Freedom of the press cannot be discussed today solely on the basis of the rights of free expression for the producers of opinion.

The Hutchins Commission

On Oct. 4, 1994, employees of *The Washington Post* were startled by a full-page ad in the paper accusing its editorial page of hiding a conflict of interest. The ad's sponsor, Pacific Telesis Group Inc., a San Francisco Baby Bell, opposed congressional passage of the General Agreement on Tariffs and Trade (GATT). Five days earlier, the paper had urged GATT's approval, claiming that the bill "contains no surprises, no provisions that have not been amply discussed." But, as the ad pointed out, the editorial omitted one important fact: The paper itself stood to profit handsomely from passage of the bill.

In fact, in that very day's paper, the *Post* admitted that the bill included a new concession that allowed three firms, including American Personnel Communications, a *Post* subsidiary, to gain nearly $1.3 billion in federal license fees for wireless telephone technologies in return for an investment of only $400 million. Peter Milius, the writer of the editorial in question, said he had not known of the bill's new provisions beforehand. Several news stories had mentioned the arrangement, but none of the other *Post* editorials urging GATT ratification had cited the paper's corporate link to it. The late Meg Greenfield, who headed the editorial page at the time, acknowledged: "We did make a mistake and we really feel awful about it. Of course, we should have known. We wished we'd known. There's a system for information on these things, and it just broke down." She said the idea that the paper was deliberately being coy about the company's interests was "a bit nutty."

Nutty or not, the affair gave the public a rare glimpse of the hidden world within official Washington where top media executives, far removed from their own news operations and the eyes of the general public, work quietly with legislators, lobbyists, federal agencies and the White House to maximize corporate profits, often in the name of press freedom. This chapter describes how the semi-secret system works, often to the detriment of the democratic process. It also looks at how other businesses have learned to use the sacred words to their commercial advantage.

It was predictable that once a few facts had trickled out about the *Post's* gross error—only because of some hurt feelings by one of the competing firms for the booty—that politicians with any complaint against the *Post*, the press in general or GATT would jump at the opportunity to blast the paper and everyone else in sight. (The other two companies involved were Omnipoint Communications Inc. and Cox Enterprises Inc., the corporate parent of the Atlanta *Constitution* and numerous other media properties.) Texas maverick Ross Perot led the charge by alleging that the *Post* had "cut a deal" worth $2 billion with the White House. Appearing as a guest on *Larry King Live*, Perot called it "the ultimate corruption of our system....The biggest piece of pork ever." Suddenly, the debate over the international treaty took on a new dimension by providing its many opponents, including Ralph Nader and Pat Buchanan, ammunition to defeat the measure.

But some of the charges were wrong. Two years earlier, the Federal Communications Commission (FCC) had offered to issue licenses for a new type of wireless telephone service to compete with cellular phones. In order to encourage "pioneering" innovation, the agency promised to cancel fees for the most creative proposals. After spending what they claimed to be tens of millions of dollars developing the technology, the three firms won the competition and received the licenses. The following year, however, the picture turned around when unsuccessful rivals for the business, Pacific Telesis and Bell Atlantic, complained to Congress about the deal. As a result, legislators became sympathetic and directed the FCC to auction future licenses, an indirect slap at the agency. But the agency went further by billing the winning firms nearly $1.3 billion for the licenses already granted.

ENLISTING INFLUENTIAL LOBBYISTS

The *Post* countered by suing and launching a high-level lobbying campaign led by publisher Donald Graham and Thomas Downey, a former Democratic congressman known for his ties to high places in the Clinton administration and Congress. According to *Post* reporter Howard Kurtz, the White House and Rep. John Dingell, then chairman of the House Commerce Committee, "struck a deal" with the three companies requiring them to pay 85 percent of the estimated average price of licenses in upcoming auctions, or no less than $400 million.[1] However, Dingell, a veteran in the game of one-upmanship, made certain that the deal would stick by inserting it in the very public GATT bill without contacting the companies involved. His idea apparently was to improve prospects for passage by offsetting some of the loss of revenues from lowering tariffs once the bill became law.

But none of the companies were happy. Nor did public exposure of the deal improve its prospects. Thus began a more urgent round of insider lobbying at the highest level. Six weeks later, President Clinton and Sen. Robert J. Dole, R-Kan., agreed on a deal that brought eventual approval. A major part of the agreement, according to *Post* reporter Mike Mills, was a commitment that the administration would work with Congress to make the "pioneer" companies eventually pay more for their licenses than required to under GATT if legislators concluded that the government had not received a fair return from the firms.[2]

Money was not the only thing the "pioneer" companies would pay. They were already paying some stiff penalties in terms of public trust, and they knew it. Few news organizations in the country do more to uphold their journalistic integrity than *The Washington Post*. It not only has some of the strictest standards and guidelines to cover potential ethical problems; it is also one of only a few news organizations that contract with an independent "ombudsman" to investigate and report on potential violations. Appointees are given fixed-year terms guaranteeing their independence from the usual chain of command. But the company also is in business to make a profit for its investors beyond the Graham family, which controls the voting stock. Like other media firms, it thus has a basic conflict of interest that constantly affects its journalistic performance.

After the GATT gaff, Joann Byrd, the paper's ombudsman, offered two lessons in her column: "The paper must report the company's business connection to the news every time it comes up—whether the connection is good for the company or bad for the company. When in doubt, it's insurance for the paper's credibility. And the *Post* needs a failsafe internal communication system."

PROTECTING BMW FROM A CUSTOMER

Unfortunately for the company, the improvements did not arrive in time to prevent another substantial breach of its ethical walls the following year. Like many business firms, the *Post* occasionally joins with others as a friend of the court (*amicus curiae*) in cases deemed important to its business or journalistic operations, particularly when they appear to impinge on the First Amendment. One of these cases involved a defective automobile paint job, a subject that does not immediately suggest such a sacred principle. In this case, BMW's office in the United States was appealing to the Supreme Court to overturn a Tennessee court award of $2 million in punitive damages to the buyer of the car in question. The unusually large award aroused concern in the news business and the business community in general. Joining with the *Post* in a petition as friends of the court on BMW's side were ABC; Dow Jones & Co., owner of *The Wall Street* Journal; the Hearst Corporation; Home Box Office; Knight-Ridder Inc.; the *Los Angeles Times*; NBC; the Providence Journal Company; and Time Inc. Media groups also included the Association of American (book) Publishers, Magazine Publishers of America and National Association of Broadcasters. Groups of journalists lining up as "friends" of BMW included the American Society of Newspaper Editors, the Radio-Television News Directors Association, the Reporters Committee for Freedom of the Press and the Society of Professional Journalists.

The basic worry for the media participants was the potential effect of the court decision on future libel awards. For nearly two decades, news organizations have joined with other business firms in advocating strict limits on court awards for damages due to defective products, mainly because of the potential effects on their own defective work that sometimes leads to large libel awards. CBS, which organized the media's case, argued that "even the strictest due process limitations on punitive awards may not be adequate to protect First Amendment values in (libel) cases."

But when it comes time to exercise their First Amendment duty to inform the public about their role, media firms tend to be reluctant. In nine news stories and editorials on the BMW case in the *Post* while it was pending in 1995 and 1996, the paper disclosed its involvement only once. That came in an editorial *after* the Supreme Court wiped out the $2 million award and after a number of people in Washington had made inquiries about the paper's conflict of interest. The *Post* often editorialized strongly in favor of pending federal legislation to limit damage awards to victims of defective products, and it ran news stories without acknowledging its self-interest. A search of the news produced by other media "friends" of BMW revealed no mention of their participation in the case in their news or commentary.

WHO'S FLEECING WHOM AT NBC?

Two years later, the same problem of disclosing important conflicts of interest to the public entrapped NBC News. In an effort to shore up its sagging audience, the proud-as-a-peacock network decided to launch a sporadic segment on its *Nightly News* to highlight public offenses to taxpayers committed for the most part by the big, bad seldom-advertising federal government. Thus was born *The Fleecing of America*" modeled in part from *It's Your Money*, which ABC news had ridden with success for several years.

The NBC segment for July 17 of that year singled out the owner of a telecommunications company in Cedar Rapids, Iowa, that had won four licenses at a poorly advertised government auction for the rights to public airwaves serving 16 million people with cell phones, beepers, walkie-talkies and other electronic devices. The winning price was only $1 per license. Anchor Tom Brokaw reported that the company's chief executive, Clark McLeod—who said he would have paid up to $200,000 for the licenses—"stands to make a fortune with your help, and you didn't even know about it. Your government gave him the deal of a lifetime. You decide: Is this the fleecing of America?"

But where was NBC's "fleecing" crew when the network and its fellow networks and broadcasters won the right to use the new digital TV channels in 1996 without paying a dime? Each channel contains enough bandwidth to provide six separate channels that can be used, not only for high definition TV (HDTV) broadcasts, but also for subscription services ranging from wireless cable to data transmission. Based on auction revenues for other public airways in recent years, the FCC had estimated that a public sale of the digital spectrum could bring as much as $70 billion to the U.S. Treasury. Instead, the major broadcasters got the rights to a significant—and highly lucrative—chunk of the airwaves for absolutely nothing.

Is it possible that Brokaw & Company did not recognize the parallels between the episode in Cedar Rapids and what happened in Washington? If so, this lack of imagination was apparently shared by other network giants: A data search for "digital TV auction" drew no hits on any of the broadcast networks during a time when Cable News Network (CNN) ran 31 stories in the 16 months in which it was being discussed in Congress. Or did the decision of the networks and the nation's television stations to ignore the congressional debate on digital auctions have more to do with keeping the public eye off the political machinations of their corporate parents, such as General Electric, News Corporation, Westinghouse and Disney?

The approximately 20 million Americans who depend on the broadcast networks for their national and international news each evening had no way of knowing about this gigantic giveaway and how it was engineered. It was just one of many cases where powerful media organizations have cited their First Amendment rights—and continue to invoke them, often in secrecy—to help gain profitable privileges not available to other businesses.

SEEKING TO AVERT GRAND LARCENY

The digital auction issue began heating up in late 1995, when then-Senate Majority Leader Dole announced that he wanted to add auction requirements to the telecommunications reform bill that he and House leaders had nearly completed after a four-year struggle. The law's main aim was to transform the regulated field of broadcasting, cable, satellite, telephone and various personal communication devices into a more competitive market, which would theoretically bring lower consumer prices. The key to Dole's sudden public stand became clearer in a private meeting on Nov. 30 that year, among top broadcasters, legislators and lobbyists, including Fox's Rupert

Murdoch and the heads of other large media conglomerates. According to a report of the meeting six weeks later in *The Washington Post*, Dole asked broadcasters: "Why should I give you a $40 billion giveaway when you're driving my [approval ratings] through the floor on Medicare?" The disgruntled Republican leader later formalized his demand for an auction with a fiery speech in the Senate. He apparently was seeking leverage over news coverage. The major news outlets, however, showed little interest in reporting his move, even failing to pick up the *Post's* report of his bold threat.

After the telecom bill passed the House of Representatives in January 1996, Dole vowed not to let it through the Senate without further discussion of the spectrum auction issue. Finally, Dole convinced other congressional leaders to send a letter to the FCC, asking Chairman Reed Hundt for assurances that, if the bill were passed, Hundt would not allow licenses for use of the spectrum to be handed out until the possibility of an auction received further review on Capitol Hill. Hundt agreed. The bill sailed through the Senate and was signed into law the following month by President Clinton. A still dissatisfied Dole, however, kept agitating for auctions, eventually winning the support of Sen. John McCain, R-Ariz., and a few other legislators equally upset by the deal.

By March, the powerful National Association of Broadcasters (NAB), the industry's chief lobby, had had enough from these few objectors. It supported earlier constitutional claims by NBC president Robert C. Wright that auctions "would be a government taking of broadcasters' ongoing business for sale to someone else." The NAB decided to go around Congress to the "grassroots." It launched a $9.5 million blizzard of devious public service announcements attacking auctions as "a tax on free television" that would force "your favorite shows" off the air. Lawmakers were soon buried under an avalanche of parrot-like pleas to "save free TV." Dole accused broadcasters of "bullying Congress" and misleading the public. But on June 11, 1996, a critical time for the issue, he stepped aside to run for president. A week later, his successor, Louisiana Republican Trent Lott, quietly sealed the deal for broadcasters in defiance of Dole and company. In a letter to the FCC cosigned by Newt Gingrich and other GOP leaders, Lott directed the agency to disregard past agreements and grant broadcasters the new channels without auction by April 1997.

Some say Gingrich had been co-opted by the $4.5 million book offer from HarperCollins, a Murdoch property. Then there was Donald Jones, a wealthy cable entrepreneur and GOP contributor, whom Gingrich allowed to work for months in his office undercover. *The Wall Street Journal* reported that Jones, whose firm included a subscription cyberporn service, spent most of 1995 as a part-time "volunteer" in the speaker's office at a time when key parts of the telecommunications bill were being negotiated. On the Senate side, industry observers suggested that Lott's letter to the FCC marked a high point in the career of Edward O. Fritts, president of the NAB and a long-time friend and classmate of Lott at "Ole Miss" University. But the fact that congressional leaders could hand out such a treasure trove of public property without causing a public uproar was due not so much to expert lobbying as to thin news coverage. As McCain told this author: "In the final analysis, the pressure has to come from the people."

But "the people" were kept pretty much in the dark about what was going on. When network chiefs were asked to explain such sustained silence on a potentially big news story, no one at ABC, CBS or NBC would comment. A press aide to Fritts, the broadcasters' chief lobbyist, claimed that a recent knee operation prevented him from discussing the matter on the phone with this author.

CBS news mentioned the auction issue in one brief segment, and ABC news eventually tackled it after the debate was over. With virtually no broadcast or cable organization except CNN reporting on the matter during the two-year "debate," it fell to the print press to take up the slack. But it too came up short, possibly reflecting many publishers' big stakes in radio and TV. A telling survey of 100 newspapers by Northwestern University researchers found that "every [paper] whose owners got little TV revenue editorialized against the spectrum 'giveaway,' whereas every one with high TV revenues editorialized in favor of giving broadcasters free use of the spectrum."[3]

Even after winning such a monumental gift, as well as gaining further legislative relaxation of limits on the number of radio and television stations that one company can own, broadcasters were hungry for more. Unhappy with the FCC's plan to make them return their (free) analog channels by the year 2006, they rolled Congress once again for a clause inserted into the 1997 tax-budget agreement that added so many conditions for returning the channels that many observers believe the stations will never be given up.

NICKING TAXPAYERS FOR $100 BILLION

These little goodies sent the total take for 1996 and 1997 from the U.S. Treasury well over $100 billion. But nobody in the news business was anxious to add up the figures for taxpayers. There was not even a firm commitment that the broadcasters would fulfill their pledges to legislators about the creative, entrepreneurial uses to which they would put their new properties. Indeed, within a month of receiving the entire gift package, *The Wall Street Journal* reported that, instead of gearing up to offer consumers HDTV programming, "networks are now talking about using just a portion of the high-capacity digital spectrum to offer extra channels of standard TV signals that don't look much different from what is already on."

Still not satisfied, broadcasters continued to fight a long-standing prohibition against duopoly, where two television stations in the same major city are owned by the same company. Efforts to legalize such an arrangement in the 1996 telecom law failed. Along with many newspaper publishers with TV properties, broadcasters had also fought for many years to end a ban on cross-ownership of a major newspaper and television station in the same city. Three years after passage of the law, few stations were close to fulfilling promises of digital programming as they continued lobbying for additional bonanzas.

Radio broadcasters have become equally greedy, despite a wave of station mergers that have far exceeded those in the newspaper and television industries. In April 2000, they even got the U.S. House to vote against opening up some FM airwaves to low-power non-profit stations for churches, schools and community groups. They claimed that there would be too much interference from the 10-to-100-watt stations with existing 100-watt programming, but the FCC said tests revealed no technical problem. The 274-to-110 vote demonstrated once again the power of the broadcast lobby to get what it wants in Congress. National Public Radio sided with the commercial broadcasters.

How do the media get away with such grand larceny? To start with, they are among the biggest cash contributors to congressional candidates, though the facts are not often included in news reports about the influence of money on politics. In the 1995-1996 presidential election cycle, printing and publishing industries contributed a total of $3.8 million, 58 percent of which went to Republican candidates, according to the Center for Responsive Politics. Companies in the TV, movie and music industries added another $7.2 million with Democrats getting 52 percent. If contributions are added to those for telephone, telecom and computer equipment firms, which make up the greater media picture, the total was $23.7 million, with 60 percent going to the Republicans. The four major networks alone contributed $4 million. Much of the money was concentrated on the committees specializing on media matters, particularly the commerce committees of both houses and their telecommunications subcommittees.

Lobbyists for media interests are among the most influential in Washington. In the give and take of political maneuvering, contributions don't count nearly as much as personal contacts. Former members of Congress are the most prized possessions of law and lobby firms. Associations also swing much weight. Few can match the clout of the Newspaper Association of America (NAA) and the National Association of Broadcasters (NAB), which not only have lobbyists on their staffs but stables of independent ones for special assignments. Not far behind is the cable lobby. The NAB is considered by the trade magazine, *Broadcasting & Cable,* as "King of the Hill." That was how the weekly headlined its story about the way broadcasters got what they wanted in telecom booty. For the ultimate in the personal touch, these groups can call on member publishers and broadcasters around the country, who stand ready to trek to the Hill for heavy duty. Among the bigger names working for top media companies have been Bob Dole and George Mitchell, former Republican and Democratic majority leaders; Thomas J. Downey and Vin Weber, former Democratic congressmen; Anthony Podesta, brother of John, longtime staff assistant to Clinton; and Vernon Jordan, a close friend of Clinton with many media clients.

But money and lobbyists account for only a portion of the political power exerted by news organizations. The rest comes from three advantages no other lobby has. One is the power to withhold news about their lobbying when desired, as *The Washington Post* did in the GATT and BMW affairs, and broadcasters did with digital auctions.

The second unique advantage over other lobbies is the power to make or break any politician or bureaucrat. Although instances where a media organization actually campaigns for or against a certain candidate are few, there are enough examples to make legislators and bureaucrats wary of displeasing media interests and willing to solicit their favor. Many in Congress remember well what happened to Dan Glickman, the former congressman from Kansas who later became Clinton's secretary of agriculture. His troubles started in 1992 in Wichita, the main city in his district. The local arm of Multimedia Cablevision, upset by his vote earlier that year in favor of freezing cable rates, flooded its 53 channels with "editorials" against his reelection. The company aired anti-Glickman jabs more than 2,000 times before agreeing under pressure from government regulators to run a few pro-Glickman spots a week before election day. The congressman squeaked by with 52 percent of the vote, compared to 71 percent in the previous election. He lost his seat two years later. Politicians don't survive long by recklessly angering the broadcast industry. Whether broadcasters actually have the power to end a single career—or the willingness to do so—is not so important as the belief of politicians that they do.

The third unique power of the media lobby is its ability to use the First Amendment to obtain commercial favors not available to other businesses. Though an invaluable aid to journalistic freedom, the famous words have been increasingly wielded by media interests—as well as others—to gain competitive advantages and maximize profit. For more than half a century, newspapers have used free-press arguments to win exemptions from laws applying to other businesses, such as sales and advertising taxes in many areas of the country. They have also obtained important exemptions from general prohibitions against monopolistic practices and child labor. (For decades, underage deliverers were called "little merchants" in order to avoid paying employment taxes and worker benefits.)

SHORT-CHANGING NEWS CARRIERS

More recently, as the age of newspaper carriers has risen and the job has become more institutionalized, publishers have kept pressing Congress for exemptions from wage and hour laws dating back to the New Deal. Through intensive lobbying, they managed to sneak some golden words into the 1996 minimum wage increase allowing them to stop paying benefits and taxes for certain carriers and distributors, now mostly adult "independent contractors." (A similar request by other types of businesses failed to win approval.) In a glowing victory statement, John F. Sturm, president of the Newspaper Association of America, heaped praise on many publishers and their law/lobby firms, adding that "this is going to save a lot of newspapers a lot of money in the future."

The power of media firms to get their way in Washington was illustrated in the 1998 campaign to extend the life of copyright protection. As soon as Mickey Mouse got involved, it was no contest. The chief backer of change was the Walt Disney Co., which couldn't bear the thought of its famous mouse character becoming public property in 2003 when its copyright was due to expire. So it sprayed thousands of dollars around Congress—in chunks of $1,000, $5,000 and $10,000— to key legislators. And its chairman, Michael Eisner, personally lobbied for a bill to extend copyrights from 75 to 95 years. The measure was named the Sonny Bono Copyright Term Extension Act. Consumer groups and libraries said the original law was designed to help creators of intellectual property for the public good, not to protect corporate profits. But the clout of Disney and its allies, including Time Warner and other movie makers, proved invincible.

Perhaps the longest running example of special interest lobbying has been the fight by newspaper and magazine publishers for deep discounts on postal rates. It was hard-nosed publishers, not little old ladies, who launched the national crusade against "junk mail" in the early 1950s in order to increase their already substantial postal rate advantages over other distributors of mail advertising. Their claim for special advantages goes back many years when Congress set up preferential rates for subscription periodicals to recognize their "educational, cultural, scientific and informational" value. The words are an indirect reference to the founders' concept that the press has an obligation—along with its freedom—to educate the public. Since then, publishers have spent untold millions trying to protect and expand their rate preferences over straight advertising matter, otherwise known as "junk mail." They leave no doubt that their primary motive has little to do with their constitutional obligations and much to do with profit margins.

IMMUNITY FROM ANTITRUST LAWS

The same attitude lay behind the intensive push for special exemptions from antitrust laws that apply to other types of business. The impetus for it arose when the Justice Department filed a complaint in 1965 charging that a joint operating agreement (JOA) between the *Tucson Citizen* and *The Arizona Daily Star* amounted to profit pooling, price fixing and restraining competition. Beginning in 1940, the two papers, though separately owned, shared advertising, accounting and printing operations, but not news operations. Like other similar arrangements, they theorized that they enjoyed such broad antitrust immunity simply because of the First Amendment. Over the same period, successive administrations in Washington conveniently shied away from challenging such arrangements. It was only after Rep. Morris Udall, D-Ariz., complained that the Republican owners of the *Citizen* were planning to buy the *Daily Star*, the last major Democratic paper in the state, that Democratic Attorney General Nicholas Katzenbach took action. The charges were upheld three years later in U.S. district court and, in March 1969, by the Supreme Court. The latter cited a landmark case involving the AP and the *Chicago Tribune* in 1945 when it said: "Freedom to publish is guaranteed by the Constitution, but freedom to combine to keep others from publishing is not. Freedom of the press from governmental interference under the First Amendment does not sanction repression of that freedom by private interests."[4]

Fired up by the court decision, publishers and their friends stormed Capitol Hill with veiled fists for legislation that would overturn the court decisions. According to authors Morton Mintz and Jerry S. Cohen, "Some senators acknowledged privately that certain powerful publishers had given them crude ultimatums: Support the bill or the publishers would oppose them the next time they were up for reelection."[5] Publishers argued that JOAs made it possible to preserve press freedom to compete in cities where one paper was likely to fail without combining forces with the stronger one. In this period, there were only about three dozen cities left with head-to-head newspaper competition. Forty years earlier, there had been more than 500.

The first bill to authorize JOAs was called The Failing Newspaper Act, later retitled The Newspaper Preservation Act to avoid the negative connotation. Among the leading critics was Stephen Barnett, a law professor at the University of California at Berkeley. At a House hearing on the bill in 1970, he said: "What the publishers really want is not relief from financial hardship, not preservation of the second newspaper and not an economic situation in which the paper can make a decent profit....What the publishers want is protection from competition and the right to pile up monopoly profits."[6]

The refusal of publishers with existing JOAs to disclose their financial data to Congress was cited by Rep. Clark MacGregor, D-Minn., as sufficient reason for denying legislative relief. He knew their profit margins were among the highest of any industry. Sen. Philip Hart, D-Mich., whose committee on monopoly and antitrust held numerous hearings, called the bill "a poverty program for the rich."[7] *The New Yorker* concluded: "Any newspaper that has to be preserved this way might as well be preserved in formaldehyde."[8] But in 1970, the combined weight of the newspaper industry—except for *The New York Times, The Washington Post, The Wall Street Journal* and a few others in opposition—won overwhelming majorities of 64 to 13 in the Senate and 292 to 87 in the House. It showed the power of publishers to gain special privileges denied by the courts.

However, President Nixon's signature was not a sure thing because of his well-known animus for the press and the opposition of his antitrust division. So publishers stepped up the pressure. An example of their leverage over politicians at the time was described by author Ben Bagdikian. He revealed that Richard E. Berlin, president and chief executive officer of the Hearst Corporation, the owner of nine daily papers, ten broadcasting stations, 26 magazines and a book publishing firm, had sent two different letters to Nixon and Richard McLaren, assistant attorney general for antitrust. The one to the president was solicitous: "Many other important publishers and friends of your administration are involved in these arrangements....All of us look to you for assistance." The letter to McLaren was more direct: "Those of us who strongly supported the present administration in the last election are the ones most seriously concerned and endangered by failure to adopt the Newspaper Preservation Act....It therefore seems to me that those newspapers should, at the very least, receive a most friendly consideration."[9] Nixon signed the measure in July 1970 without comment.

Since then, the plan to save failing newspapers through joint operating agreements around the country has itself failed. The critics were proved right. Wealthy publishers were given more years to rake in monopolistic profits, while the number of cities with JOAs dwindled from a peak of 28 to less than half that number by 2000. In the words of reporter Paul Farhi, "The cause of death for many JOA papers over the past 15 years seems more closely akin to homicide than advanced age."[10] And, he added, the Justice Department had shown no interest up to that point in making publishers live up to the deals they made with Congress.

WASHINGTON SEEKS TO LOCK BARN DOOR

That was soon to change in San Francisco, where the weaker of the two papers in a JOA there, the Hearst-owned *Examiner*, decided to purchase the *San Francisco Chronicle* in 1999 and probably close the *Examiner*. However, the U.S. Justice Department surprised the media world by launching a formal investigation and asking the Hearst Corporation for documents relating to its joint operating agreement. Rather than comply, Hearst decided to sell the *Examiner* to a local publisher. In a subsequent civil suit, the paper's publisher acknowledged that he had offered to give city mayor Willie Brown favorable treatment if he would stop opposing the merger of the two papers. Hearst then fired its publisher.

The U.S. Justice Department also filed suit in 1999 in support of the Hawaiian attorney general's own suit to prevent the closing of the afternoon *Honolulu Star-Bulletin*. Its corporate owners, Liberty Newspapers L.P., and Gannett Co., owner of the morning *Honolulu Advertiser*, had announced that they would end their agreement by discontinuing the *Star-Bulletin* after 117 years of publication. The state attorney general had charged that the agreement violated antitrust laws. After an injunction was issued, Gannett appealed on the grounds that it was exempt from such laws because of the Newspaper Preservation Act and because the injunction would violate Gannett's free speech rights.

There is no way to tell whether allowing the natural play of economic factors would have brought a better or worse result in any JOA city. But it is clear that the biggest loser has been the general public because of the loss of genuine newspaper competition in so many areas. The number of major cities with genuine newspaper competition has fallen to only six without San Francisco. They are Boston, Chicago, Denver, Los Angeles, New York and Washington. But Denver may be soon off the list because of a proposed JOA there. Only eight other cities have competing commercial dailies: Green Bay, Wis.; Berlin, N.H.; Wilkes-Barre, Pa.; Trenton, N.J.; Aspen, Colo.; Kingsport, Tenn.; Manassas, Va.; and Pleasanton, Calif.

No city illustrates better than Detroit how much the public—and the press itself—can lose when powerful media firms seek to pile privilege on privilege and profit on profit. And no city better symbolizes the commercial cancer eating away at the news business. In 1989, the city had two strong competing dailies, Gannett's *Detroit News* and Knight-Ridder's *Detroit Free Press*, with a total circulation of more than 1.2 million, more readers per capita than any other major city. That was the year the owners, the nation's two largest newspaper chains, entered into a joint operating agreement—approved by Attorney General Edwin Meese—to stem what they claimed were unquenchable financial losses. Author Bryan Gruley, however, called the deal "a disaster aborning," adding that the losses looked as if they had been part of a rational decision in order to get JOA approval.[11]

The resulting personnel cuts and labor disputes spawned a bitter strike by some 2,500 union members six years later. But the papers, with the help of computer technology, some 1,400 replacement workers and hundreds of returning union members, managed to beat the strike and cripple the local unions. They also appeared to alienate most city residents, as total circulation of the two papers dropped to less than half what it had been. Employment dropped by about 500 from pre-strike levels, as the unions continued their fight in the National Labor Relations Board.

About the only thing that didn't fall were Gannett and Knight-Ridder stock prices. Wall Street swallowed the huge losses in Detroit, confident that expected profits from joint operations would eventually far exceed any losses. As the dwindling band of nervous journalists still working there struggled to restore the integrity and public acceptance of the old *News* and *Free Press*, the odds of succeeding were getting worse. Detroit was an ugly example of the new news business in which budget control is transferred from locally-owned companies to faceless financiers on Wall Street. It showed how publishers had come to use the First Amendment to gain commercial favors such as antitrust exemptions.

One has to almost rue those innocent few words of the Constitution barring Congress from "abridging the freedom of speech, or of the press." The frequency of their use for commercial purposes by news organizations was bound to spark the interest of non-journalistic individuals and groups in using them for their own purposes. Meanwhile, the courts have broadened their interpretation of what is protected well beyond journalism.

The turning point came in two later Supreme Court decisions, both in 1976. One was *Buckley v. Valeo*. In it, the court said that money is essentially speech and that limiting campaign contributions violated the right to speak, although limiting campaign spending was not. The court explained that "the concept that government may restrict the speech of some elements of society in order to enhance the relative voice of others is wholly foreign to the First Amendment." The decision kept open a door that some legislators had been trying to shut against unlimited campaign contributions in the belief that money hopelessly corrupts the democratic system by favoring those with lots of it. According to Robert Schiff, a staff attorney for the Nader-founded Congress Watch, less than one third of 1 percent of the population accounted for all contributions over $200 in the 1996 presidential election.[12]

Differing interpretations of the Buckley decision have dogged efforts to restrict campaign spending ever since. Liberals, who tend to champion the fundamental right of free speech, have argued for restricting political speech if it can't be shared equitably by the poor as well as the rich, while conservatives have wound up backing a fundamental right they rarely had invoked before. The liberal American Civil Liberties Union found itself in bed with such arch-conservatives as Sen. Mitch McConnell, R-Ky., the principal opponent of campaign finance reform plans that limit contributions to federal candidates.

The issue also split media organizations. While many editorial writers and television commentators have argued for campaign reform proposals, many corporate owners and their associations have lined up against them. The constitutional argument was enthusiastically adopted by the broadcast lobby, at least partly because it so nicely shielded broadcasters from accusations that they only wanted to retain ad revenue.

One of the lobby's principal targets was the McCain-Feingold bill, named for Sen. John McCain, R-Ariz., and Sen. Russ Feingold, D-Wis. The measure sought to restrict unlimited funds, known as "soft money," as well as ban "issue advocacy" advertisements aimed at certain candidates without naming them and limit issue ads for two months before a primary or general election. The Center for Responsive Politics calls such ads "the stealth bombers of politics" because "they sneak in without detection to drop their deadly payloads." The bill also sought to provide a small amount of free airtime on television for federal candidates. But it wasn't long before the broadcasters' lobby forced the bill's sponsors to drop the free air. McCain later explained that the idea proved to be "too contentious." In late 1999, the sponsors eventually eliminated the issues ad ban, but the bill still did not pass.

The other key decision of the Supreme Court in 1976 involved the right to advertise prescription prices.[13] It resulted from an order by the Virginia State Board of Pharmacy banning such advertising. The court said such a prohibition violated the right of a drug store to speak. Its decision helped set off an intense debate that has broadened First Amendment protections beyond the traditional realms of political speech to all sorts of commercial activity, to the dismay of individuals and organizations that feel such interpretation stretched the original meaning of the guarantee beyond the point where the authors intended to go.

Author Cass Sunstein is among those who have argued that commercial speech is not equivalent to political speech and should not therefore have the same protection under the Constitution. He says "restrictions on political speech have the distinctive feature of impairing the ordinary channels for political change" whereas restrictions on commercial speech do not. According to Ronald K. L. Collins and David M. Skover, "Yesterday's free speech principles have become today's power principles—for the powerful….In the process, citizen democracy succumbs to corporate democracy."[14]

Since the pharmacy decision, the courts have expanded the principle. Among the decisions have been ones backing the right of a Massachusetts bank to contribute money to defeat a referendum for a progressive income tax and rejecting a Vermont law requiring that milk treated with bovine growth hormone (BGH) be labeled with a blue dot.

INVOKING THE FIRST FOR PHONE FIRMS

The Amendment was even invoked by SBC Communications Inc., formerly Southwestern Bell, to challenge the constitutionality of the 1996 Telecommunications Act that banned such firms from entering the long-distance telephone business dominated by AT&T, Sprint and MCI. Laurence H. Tribe, a Harvard University law professor defending SBC, the world's largest local phone service firm, argued that such restrictions impinge on the firm's "right to engage in protected First Amendment expression."[15] The company's motion cited the Supreme Court's reasoning in the AP and Tucson cases.

For many years, the newspaper lobby used a First Amendment argument to keep telephone companies from electronic publishing. Publishers backed various legislative proposals to implement its theory but have been forced by changing circumstances in the industry to drop them. Author and attorney Bruce Sanford summed up the situation by saying that "many First Amendment cases today, such as the 'must carry' wars between broadcasters and cable operators, can be seen as reducing the amendment to a battle for the bottom line."[16]

By equating speech freedom to corporations and campaign expenditures, the courts have diluted the rights of the great bulk of people who don't fit into these exclusive classes. Instead of championing the First Amendment for individuals, news organizations thus weaken individual speech rights with their own aggressive exploitation of such rights for corporate profit. In the process, citizen democracy is being replaced by corporate democracy.

At the same time, media firms are beginning to bump into new limits on their freedom to profit. Resistance has come in the form of increasing libel awards by juries less trusting of the press than only a decade ago. Author Bruce Sanford cites case after case where judges and juries have socked it to news firms for tactics considered overly intrusive. Among recent adverse decisions were a Supreme Court ruling against allowing media people to enter a private home with police on a raid, an appeals court ruling against CBS for violating the Fourth Amendment prohibition against illegal searches and seizures and a federal judge's decision in New York City that parading a burglary suspect before the cameras of a local television station violated the suspect's constitutional rights.[17]

Like these powerful journalistic groups turned pussy cats, many editors and news directors around the country have been pulling their punches like never before. A 1998 survey by the University of Miami School of Communication found that one-fifth of some 360 local television news directors around the nation declined to air news reports the previous year because of fears of possible lawsuits. It also found that over a three-year period, instances of being sued for libel had grown 8 percent and that lawyers were being consulted more. At the same time, ironically, the directors said they had become more aggressive in their news gathering tactics, increasing their use of hidden cameras and microphones. They explained that added competition from 24-hour news channels was forcing them to use riskier stories in order to attract maximum audiences.

REVISITING A KENNEDY MURDER

The object of concern for leading news firms and journalistic societies in this case was the *Globe* supermarket tabloid, the 15-million-circulation paper that once paid a prostitute to trap sportscaster Frank Gifford. The paper was being sued by a Pakistani-American grape grower in Bakersfield, Calif., over a 1989 account fingering him as the murderer of Robert F. Kennedy. The story and photograph accompanying it were taken from a 1988 book, *The Senator Must Die,* by Robert D. Morrow. The book indicated that Khalid Khawar did the deed with a camera-gun in a plot involving Iranian secret police and the American Mafia despite the fact that Sirhan Sirhan was convicted as the sole murderer and imprisoned for the crime.

The case was essentially a test of whether the broad libel protection granted to the media in the 1964 Sullivan case should be extended beyond public figures to private ones. The key questions were whether Khawar became a public figure by being named in the book and whether a news story derived accurately from a book is protected by the long-standing principle that shields such things as wire service reports and book reviews from libel damages. In district court testimony it was revealed that the *Globe* had made no attempt to do any independent reporting to check the accusations. Of 150 news organizations sent copies of the book for review by Roundtable Publishing Co. of Santa Monica, Calif., including most of those backing the tabloid in its court battle, only the *Globe* published anything about it. During the trial, L. Fletcher Prouty, a former CIA official, whose name was on the book's forward, disavowed the book and said it contained numerous falsehoods.

Khawar's attorney, Francis C.J. Pizzulli, alleged that the story contained numerous errors. A photograph in the book was blown up and altered by the *Globe* to show a large arrow pointing to Khawar, a freelance photographer on stage with Kennedy even though the murder was actually committed in a room behind the stage where, according to other photos, Khawar was not in the vicinity. Khawar said that after the story was published, he received death threats, and his family cars were vandalized. A district court jury ruled that while it was a neutral report, it had been published with malice and reckless disregard of whether the defamatory statements were true or false. The court ordered the *Globe* to pay Khawar $1.1 million. The *Globe's* appeal to the California Court of Appeal for the Second District was joined by the *creme de la creme* of the mainstream press including: The New York Times Company, Harper's Magazine Foundation, The Hearst Corporation, Newsweek Inc., Associated Press, Ziff-Davis Publishing Company, Donrey Media Group, ABC, CBS, NBC, King World Productions, the *Los Angeles Times*, McClatchy Newspapers Inc. and Copley Press Inc. Also backing the *Globe* were the American Civil Liberties Union, the California Newspaper Publishers Association, the Association of American (book) Publishers plus journalism groups including the Society of Professional Journalists, the Reporters Committee for Freedom of the Press and the Radio-Television News Directors Association.

The appeals court agreed with the lower court, and the *Globe* then went to the California Supreme Court, where the original decision was affirmed in November 1998. Among those questioning the wisdom of siding with the *Globe* was Mike Wallace of *60 Minutes* and Howard Kurtz, media writer for *The Washington Post*. Wallace said on the air in May of that year: "I know damned well that I would never in a million years have been permitted to put on *60 Minutes* what the *Globe* put in their magazine." Kurtz added: "I don't think we should apologize for the worst excesses in our business. I think we should blow the whistle on them. And I'm kind of embarrassed that so many of these news organizations have embraced this behavior by the *Globe*." After the California court denied the *Globe's* appeal, and the paper petitioned the U. S. Supreme Court, all media participants bailed out. The top court rejected the case in 1999, ten years after the defamatory story about Khawar was published. The decision was not widely reported.

SUPPORTING MURDER INSTRUCTIONS

Many of the same media organizations quietly lined up behind an equally undeserving defendant claiming First Amendment protection. It involved the publisher of a 1983 book of murder instructions called *Hit Man: A Technical Manual for Independent Contractors*. The publisher, Paladin Enterprises Inc. of Boulder, Colo., and Peter Lund, its chief executive, stood accused of "aiding and abetting" a gory triple murder in Silver Spring, Md., in 1993 because the contract killer bought the book beforehand and followed many of its instructions. Paladin and Lund contended that they had the freedom to print such material without being held financially responsible for what anybody did after reading it. But Howard Siegel of Rockville, Md., the attorney for relatives of the victims, disagreed. "The First Amendment," he said, "has nothing to do with this case. It's a matter of aiding and abetting a crime." The murder victims were Mildred Horn; Trevor Horn, her 8-year-old quadriplegic son; and Janice Saunders, the boy's nurse. The adults were shot meticulously in the eyes to minimize blood loss, and the son died when his breathing tube was yanked away.

In 1996, Lawrence Horn, the father of Trevor and ex-husband of Mildred, was sentenced to life in prison for hiring James E. Perry to do the deeds. Trial testimony indicated that Horn ordered the killings in order to get $2 million awarded to the boy in settlement for his injuries. Perry was sentenced to death. Testimony showed that he had purchased the book with a rubber check about a year before the murders and followed some two dozen of its instructions. The suit sought an unspecified amount of damages from Paladin and Lund.

All previous suits accusing publishers of aiding and abetting a violent crime had failed on First Amendment grounds. But after this case was thrown out of district court on the same grounds and appealed, the Fourth U.S. Circuit Court of Appeals ruled that Paladin may be liable because "speech that constitutes criminal aiding and abetting (a crime) does not enjoy the protection of the First Amendment... where, as here, the defendant has the specific purpose of assisting and encouraging the commission of such conduct and the alleged assistance and encouragement takes a form other than abstract advocacy."

After Paladin appealed to the Supreme Court, media lawyers assembled a similar group of leading journalistic "friends" to back its case. Among them were ABC, the E.W. Scripps Co., the National Association of Broadcasters, NBC, the Newspaper Association of America, Primedia Inc., the Radio-Television News Directors Association, the Reporters Committee for Freedom of the Press, the Society of Professional Journalists, the Thomas Jefferson Center for the Protection of Free Expression, Viacom Inc. and the Washington Post Company. In 1998, the nation's top court refused, and a trial was scheduled. But one business day before trial in May 1999, Paladin agreed to a multi-million-dollar settlement. Here again, the media "friends of the court" stole into the night with little publicity.

While leading media and journalist organizations have been trying to champion the cause of those who publish murder instructions and sell damaged cars, they have lost interest in fighting secret public records and meetings, military secrecy and subpoenas for reporters' notes and tapes. Two decades ago, a subpoena for a reporter's notes would have created a furor among journalists. But when more than a half dozen subpoenas for notes and tapes were issued in recent years, there was hardly a complaint from leading journalistic organizations. Felicity Barringer of *The New York Times* explained: "Facing increasingly aggressive prosecutors and operating in an environment more hostile to the journalists, a fresh generation of news media lawyers has decided that negotiation does more good than confrontation."

Media leaders seem to be more interested in exploiting the First Amendment for profit than using the sacred words to break through the censors at the CIA, FBI, Defense Department and other bastions of secrecy on behalf of the general public. Some genuine investigative journalism is still being done. One was the 1999 disclosure of long-secret documents about the U.S. role in engineering the anti-democratic military coup in Chile in 1973. Another was the exposure of President Clinton's wholesale use of the Lincoln bedroom for political "thank yous."

But these stories were not the work of news organizations. The first was from the National Security Archives, a private non-profit group. The other came from the Center for Public Integrity, a similar organization. As such groups proliferate and with Ralph Nader groups still scooping the press on occasion, members of the media and public have reason to wonder what has happened to that once-proud institution, the American free press.

As its reputation for enterprising journalism fades, its drive to cash in on government favors never stops. In May 2000, the FCC finally succumbed to years of media pressure by agreeing to ease two of the few remaining limits on media concentration. One was the rule prohibiting one company from owning both a daily paper and a TV station in the same city. Media firms that would benefit included the (Chicago) Tribune Co., with its purchase of the (Los Angeles) Times Mirror Co.; Cox Enterprises Inc.; E. W. Scripps Co.; Hearst Corp.; and others. The other rule to be relaxed barred one firm from owning more than one TV network. The chief beneficiary here would be Viacom (half-owner of UPN network) with its purchase of CBS.

CHAPTER IV

Trashing Washington for Media Purposes

There is a point at which tolerance must cease. That is when…
the strict use of democratic methods among men not fully aware of
their meaning tends to throw power into the hands of the enemies
of the democratic state.

The Hutchins Commission

"MANY AMERICANS VIEW WASHINGTON AS A MESS AND JUST TUNE IT OUT," read the front-page headline in *The Wall Street Journal* on June 4, 1997. The article described a $1.5 billion Congressional measure to fight youth crime and noted one particular lawmaker, Rep. Jane Harman, D-Calif., who had not heard from a single voter back home before the vote. The story said the lack of public response was leaving legislators unable to tell what voters wanted, calling it "the year of the great disconnect." What the article did not say was that news outlets in Harman's Los Angeles district had done nothing to inform constituents about the bill. How could they react to a measure about which they knew nothing?

When C-SPAN's call-in show highlighted the *Journal* story that morning, the reaction was surprising. Instead of focusing on public apathy, the *Journal's* target, nearly every caller as well as the show's two guest legislators from the House of Representatives criticized the news media rather than public apathy. The response seemed to say that people do care but are not getting the information they want.

The *Journal* article was part of a constant stream of news and comment that has ridiculed and downgraded Washington and government in recent years. The following month, the big theme in *The Washington Post* Style section was "Dullsville," the title of a photo/print spread dominating the front page. It tagged Washington "snooze city." Reporter Howard Kurtz quoted columnist Walter Shapiro of *USA Today* as saying: "I cannot recall a period in which government has been more irrelevant....Nothing is going to happen in Washington that affects anyone's life for years."[1]

These attitudes are typical of Washington journalists. As a result, news of relevance to the public is often dismissed as boring, compared to the personal antics of politicians. The period in 1997 that so bored these leading journalists included the final fling of the Supreme Court for the year, with decisions on the terminally ill and Internet pornography among others that, according to the same *Post*, "set benchmarks for the next century." Other events included the congressional struggles over Medicare, juvenile crime and gun control. What made the period boring for reporters was the absence of any new scandal.

But what turned off journalists could turn on millions of people if reporters did more digging into serious national issues and tried harder to make them interesting. In a democratic system, criticism of government is healthy. So is skepticism. But when they turn into a constant knee-jerk attack on government as an institution and rampant disrespect for all elected officials, the consequences can be dangerous for a free society. The risk grows when the privately owned press with virtually no limit on its power encourages the notion that self-government is irrelevant or evil.

This chapter describes how the bash-government syndrome has been promoted, usually unconsciously, by news organizations looking for more excitement than government activities and international developments seem to possess on the surface. And it suggests how such attitudes are eating away at the foundations of democracy.

Anti-government attitudes have a long tradition on these shores, beginning in colonial days. In the fight for liberty against British oppressors, the press was pivotal in galvanizing support for the American Revolution. On the eve of hostilities, the Continental Congress urged towns to denounce publishers who printed views sympathetic to the crown. As a result, angry mobs destroyed many Tory presses. But once independence was obtained, leading publishers resorted to political patronage, so they tended to cover events to please their sponsoring politicians.

The lowest point for the press came in 1798. Facing the possibility of war with France, Congress passed the Sedition Act making it a crime to "write, print, utter or publish...any false, scandalous and malicious writing against the government, Congress, or the president." While it was in force, publishers shied away from denigrating the political establishment for fear of fines or imprisonment. But when Thomas Jefferson became president, he pardoned all victims of the law and saw that it was repealed.

In the early 1800s, the big issue became federalism, the division of authority between central government and the states, a concept promoted by Secretary of the Treasury Alexander Hamilton. With government funds, he supported newspapers with pro-federalist views. Criticism of government remained relatively subdued until early in the 20th century when a new breed of journalist emerged.

"Muckraker" was a term first used by President Theodore Roosevelt in a 1906 speech in which he cited the character in John Bunyan's *Pilgrim's Progress*, as "the man who would look no way but downward, with a muckrake in his hands." Roosevelt suggested that muckrakers, though "indispensable to the well-being of society," should "know when to stop raking the muck," a remark that echoed all the way to coverage of the impeachment scandal in 1998. One of the journalists Roosevelt was alluding to was Lincoln Steffens, who called the Senate "a chamber of traitors." However, Roosevelt was careful to praise those who exposed corruption in politics, business and society. He eventually conceded that newsmen are "just as much public servants as are the men in government service themselves."[2]

TRUMPING UP SUSPICIONS

It was the great Red Scare, however, that forever changed the way government and the news media interact. Press encouragement of anti-communist actions began with the government raids in the 1920s against trade unions and continued to some degree all the way through the Cold War. The overblown fear of infiltration or invasion by communists owed more to the press and politicians than to the Kremlin. In the early days, the Justice Department planted stories in newspapers about a vast Moscow-directed plot to overthrow the U.S. government. Urged on by government press releases warning of a Bolshevik menace, newspapers ran stories forecasting imminent communist invasions of Europe, Asia and America. Editorial writers pointed accusatory fingers at Democrats who backed trade unions and the right to strike. Support for labor and consumer groups was often equated with communist sympathy.

In the 1930s and 1940s, the situation was ripe for the rise of an early prototype of today's Washington bashers: the Rev. Charles E. Coughlin. The Radio Priest, as he was known, charged that government was doing more to help itself and big business than it was the poor. One of the first voices outside politics and the establishment news media to reach a vast audience with attacks on government, Coughlin attracted an estimated 30 million listeners nationwide and received 80,000 letters a week. He finally became so shrill and anti-Semitic that radio stations dropped him.

Despite fierce press opposition, Franklin D. Roosevelt's New Deal brought the nation out of the Great Depression and restored some faith that government served a public good through such programs as Social Security and public welfare. Victory in World War II also enhanced the prestige of Washington. But President Harry Truman, still obsessed by the communist threat, cast suspicion on government bureaucrats by establishing "loyalty boards" to screen political views of federal employees.

In the early 1950s, the demagogic mantel shifted to Sen. Joseph McCarthy, R-Wis., who saw the Cold War as an opportunity to further boost the Republican Party as anti-communist. At one point he claimed 205 State Department employees were "known communists," part of a massive communist infiltration of government, academia, the clergy and the press. He said he had documents to prove it. His failure to produce them didn't seem to matter at first. The media eagerly spread his torrent of allegations. As a result of the national mania, many innocent people were hounded out of their jobs and marked for life. Some private organizations, particularly Catholic clubs and veterans organizations, helped by compiling lists of suspects. According to author Garry Wills, these private efforts accounted for more victims of McCarthyism than did official agencies.[3] Many in the media joined in the redbaiting, conducting their own investigations and casting aspersions on progressive politicians and organizations. *The New York Times* purged members of its own staff who had any ties to suspect organizations.

With so much suspicion in the air, it became increasingly difficult to maintain faith in government. President Dwight D. Eisenhower stood by silently as McCarthy tried to whip the country into a paranoid frenzy. Only when McCarthy accused the U.S. Army of being disloyal in 1954 did Eisenhower finally order an investigation. As objections grew about McCarthy's conduct, television proved to be his undoing. First, the hearings exposed his ruthlessness. Then Edward R. Murrow, the legendary CBS journalist, produced his hard-hitting "Examination of Joseph R. McCarthy." The end came when the Senate voted to censure him. Thoroughly disgraced, the senator died three years later.

The press itself shared in the disgrace. In a unique period of introspection following McCarthy's demise, much of the news business agreed that it had been used by McCarthy and his supporters in Congress, with their numerous hearings into the alleged communist menace. What emerged was a general agreement among journalists to tighten standards to prevent unsubstantiated allegations about people from being broadly circulated without thorough investigation. Belatedly, the press learned a lesson after playing along with trumped-up fears of communism since the early 1920s.

BIG GOVERNMENT TARGETED

But the lesson did not muzzle the politicians and their sounding boards for long. The enemy began to shift from disloyalty to "big government." Conservative think tanks and journals, such as William F. Buckley's *National Review*, sprang up with a principal focus on reducing the size of government. In 1957, Ayn Rand published her novel *Atlas Shrugged*, which painted government as an inefficient, meddling and corrupt force and advocated a *laissez-faire* society. Rand continues to inspire young libertarians to this day. A Library of Congress study in 1991 deemed her book the second most influential one in America after the Bible.

The failure of strong efforts to dislodge Democrats from their control of Congress in the 1970s led many Republicans to revive anti-New Deal slogans about government waste, red tape and over-regulation in efforts to upset incumbent politicians, particularly those running for Congress. These were the seeds of today's anti-Washington fervor. Democratic candidates for office also adopted the slogans with effectiveness.

By 1976, with Gerald Ford, Nixon's handpicked replacement running for reelection as president, the situation was ripe for a peanut farmer from Georgia to ride the theme to the White House. When complaining about the "bloated bureaucracy," Jimmy Carter had the advantage of being a true outsider, having won the Georgia governorship with the same approach. As columnist E.J. Dionne observed, "The bias of the system was toward insurgents. Carter…understood that his lack of national stature and Washington experience was thus an asset, not a liability."[4]

Once ensconced on Pennsylvania Avenue, however, Carter was no longer an outsider. In the words of columnist Chris Matthews, "Carter's mistake was to allow his anti-Washington posture, which was so formidable on the campaign trail, to hinder his effectiveness in the capital. It's one thing to run against institutions; it's another to declare war against the people you have to work with."[5] Carter's famous comments about the public's "malaise" and "crisis of confidence" dampened whatever rapport he had with the press at that point.

In 1980, it was Ronald Reagan's turn to play the game. He did so with vigor, adding a few historic *bon mots*, such as the "puzzle palaces on the Potomac" and "get government off the backs of the people." It was Reagan who said: "Government is part of the problem, not the solution." He promised to reduce the size of "big government" and eliminate those perennial villains: "waste, fraud and abuse." In eight years as president, he failed to accomplish those missions but he continued to get away with anti-Washington themes. In speeches around the country, he liked to quote his chief of staff Donald Regan as saying they were "leaving the beltway and going out where the real people are."[6]

The outsider role didn't work for Democrats Walter Mondale or Michael Dukakis in the 1980s, but Arkansan Bill Clinton won with it over George Bush in 1992. Bob Dole's campaign against Clinton in the 1996 presidential campaign was hampered by the fact that his long senate career prevented him from using anti-Washington verbiage effectively. Four years later, it was Texas Gov. George W. Bush's turn to exploit his outside-the-beltway status against Vice President Al Gore even though both had grown up in the nation's capital. In order to offset his own history, Gore decided in the fall of 1999 to move his campaign headquarters to Nashville, the home city of the Gore family.

FROM SKEPTICISM TO CYNICISM

In the meantime, what was once a healthy skepticism of the federal government has turned into widespread cynicism. Members of the press, who are taught to be suspicious of authority, have not only repeated the many barbs but, like *The Wall Street Journal*, have added to the fervor. The fact that government buys little advertising has added to the fearlessness of reporters in attacking it. Politicians, even those already holding federal office, have found that taking potshots at Washington, regardless of which party is in charge, can pay off at the ballot box. Business interests have been especially enthusiastic members of the chorus because of their inherent dislike of regulations. Conservatives continue to lead the battle to downsize and denigrate the national government while seeking to build the power of individual states. The fact that their social initiatives affecting abortions, teen-age pregnancies, drug enforcement and other matters have added to federal powers has not blunted their drive.

After three decades of anti-Washington slogans, Republicans were finally able to oust the Democrats from control of Congress in 1994. They were helped by a series of minor scandals magnified by the media. One involved 83 members with overdrafts at the House bank; another amounted to petty thievery at the House post office, which led to a prison term for Democratic speaker Dan Rostenkowski, D-Ill. Polls showed public support of Congress plummeting to near-record lows. The winning ploy for Republicans was their carefully crafted "Contract With America," with many of its goals designed to reduce the power of Washington.

But Republicans made the same mistake Jimmy Carter did. In their efforts to pass the "Contract" items in 1995, they forgot to stop fighting against Washington once they were in power. They thought they could risk shutting down the government entirely in their efforts to gain their primary objective: getting the upper hand over President Clinton. The climax came in December 1995, when Republican leaders and Clinton failed to reach agreement on the budget. As news reports told of national parks closing and 770,000 government workers being furloughed, the Grand Old Party suddenly realized that it had lost a bigger battle, for the minds and hearts of American citizens. It was a bitter lesson, reflected in the loss of five House seats in the next congressional election, followed by an eight-seat loss in 1998 and the resignation of Speaker Newt Gingrich.

But politicians and pundits continued to trash government, often straying well beyond the line between political criticism and downright contempt for a functioning democracy. A steady diet of ridicule can be a good attention getter. But the cumulative effect of TV segments like ABC's "It's Your Money" and NBC's "The Fleecing of America" that focus constantly on government waste and errors leaves an impression that government can do nothing right, regardless of which party is in power.

Damage can also be done by well-meaning reporters investigating economic conditions around the country. That is what Donald L. Barlett and James B. Steele did for *The Philadelphia Inquirer* in 1991 and 1996. The results were two highly praised series that became best-selling books, *America: What Went Wrong?* and *America: Who Stole the Dream?* Their principal findings: The average American is not sharing in the economic prosperity enjoyed by the wealthy few because of tax, trade and immigration policies. They interviewed residents of city after city where local factories had moved abroad.

So far so good. But then they asked: "Who is responsible?" Their simple answer: "Washington policy makers." They mentioned a few lobbies but little about their influence on Congress and the White House, regardless of the party in control. They didn't explain how or why "Washington policy makers" had so utterly failed the people who keep electing them. They didn't explain because they didn't include the nation's capital among their places to investigate. Like countless others in the media, they also didn't look in the mirror to see the press's own role in all this. So they wound up spoiling a good journalistic effort by adding more confusion than enlightenment to the anti-Washington attitudes.

RADIO LEADS WASHINGTON BASHING

Government bashing has become the main theme of talk radio. The unchallenged master is Rush Limbaugh with his self-styled "Excellence in Broadcasting Network" of more than 650 radio stations. Each day for three hours, he dishes out sharp-edged chatter based on his view of the news. In January 1995, he was made an honorary member of the Republican freshman class in Congress in recognition of his work in the previous fall's historic election.

Not one to rest on his laurels, he acted like a man on a mission. Despite helping put Congress in the control of Republicans he seemed to grow even angrier at the federal government. He got so worked up the next month in a discussion with listeners that he offered a solemn prediction. "The second American revolution," he warned, "is just about—I got my fingers about a quarter of an inch apart—is just about that far away. Because these people are sick and tired of a bunch of bureaucrats in Washington driving into town and telling them what they can and can't do with their land."[7] One of "these people" seemed to be Limbaugh himself.

Two months later, the world heard about another of "these people." On April 19, the day celebrated each year in Massachusetts as Patriot's Day to mark the beginning of the American Revolution in Lexington and Concord, a truck bomb blew up in front of the Alfred P. Murrah Federal Building in Oklahoma City, killing 169 people, including 30 children in a day-care center. It was the biggest domestic terrorist attack in the country's history, destroying the regional offices of 14 government agencies and departments. Through a lucky coincidence, Timothy McVeigh, a Gulf War veteran, was quickly arrested and charged with setting the bomb. Later, Terry Nichols was also implicated.

One of the first callers to Limbaugh's show after the disaster sought to link him with the bombers. "Rush," said a caller named Richard, "you're their poster boy.…You give them credence to go out and do what they do." Limbaugh didn't take long to lash back. He blamed George McGovern "and other liberals" for trying "to put shackles on the ankles of FBI investigators" in order to limit domestic intelligence gathering in the 1960s and 1970s. "Make no mistake," he added, "the liberals intend to use this tragedy for their own political gain." He then turned on the mainstream media, his second favorite whipping boy, blaming it for "irresponsible attempts to categorize and demonize those who had nothing to do with this....There is absolutely no connection between these nuts and mainstream conservatism in America today."[8] The same Limbaugh who took personal credit for the 1994 Republican capture of Congress was now saying he had no effect on his listeners when it came to fomenting violence.

Limbaugh later condemned the bombing, adding: "Since the beginning of our nation, citizens have been debating the size, scope and role of the federal government. Now, suddenly in 1995, it is claimed that this two-century-old argument caused the Oklahoma tragedy....My audiences are mainstream Americans, and they lay blame solely on the criminals who committed this crime. And that's as far as the blame will go."[9]

Although there was no way to directly link the bombers to what Limbaugh said, he could not—no matter how hard he tried—duck the likelihood that his words about revolution and his often-stated contempt for the national government were influencing people who are vulnerable to irresponsible and inflammatory talk.

In speaking about revolution, Limbaugh was echoing his good friend Newt Gingrich, then the House speaker who often talked about revamping government. In 1991, Gingrich told *The Los Angeles Times Magazine:* "I'm not interested in preserving the status quo; I want to overthrow it." Like Limbaugh, Gingrich also reacted defensively to questions about the Oklahoma bombing. In answer to a reporter, he said it was "grotesque" to suggest that his anti-government talk had fostered extremism.

SPREADING HATRED ON THE AIR

President Clinton, for one, was not convinced. In a speech at Minneapolis five days after the bombing, he suggested that hot rhetoric on the radio was helping to engender violence against government by hate groups. "We hear so many loud and angry voices in America today whose sole goal seems to be to keep some people as paranoid as possible and the rest of us all too upset with each other," he said. "They spread hate. They leave the impression that, by their very words, violence is acceptable."

He didn't name names, but if he had done so, the list would have been long. Sure to have been on the list would be Chuck Baker, a talk show host on KVOR in Colorado Springs, Colo., who followed Limbaugh's show each day with his own three hours. Like Limbaugh, he blamed Washington or liberals for almost everything. "The federal government," he said on one occasion, "has started a war against our people. But we are turning our weapons against them....Shoot the sons of bitches." He has also advocated bringing in private militia groups to kill members of Congress whom Baker considers traitors and "slimeballs."[10] On one occasion, when a caller suggested an armed intervention in Washington, Baker replied: "Am I advocating the overthrow of this government?...I'm advocating the cleansing....It's provided for in the Constitution....It's well within my right under free speech."[11]

One of Baker's listeners, Francisco Duran, heard those words as his own marching orders. He left his job and drove to Washington Oct. 29, 1994, where he fired more than two dozen bullets from a semi-automatic rifle at the White House in an attempt to kill the president. He was wrestled to the sidewalk by passersby and arrested. According to authors Robert L. Hilliard and Michael C. Keith, Duran was a big fan of right-wing radio pontificators, including Limbaugh and Baker, and was active in the militia. Baker's reaction to Duran's acts was: "So what if the jerk, the wacko, the creep, this piece of crap shot up the White House? If he thinks I or Rush Limbaugh are the reason he went out there, the man needs psychiatric counseling."[12]

Another soldier in the war is G. Gordon Liddy, who has one of the largest audiences in the talk radio field. The convicted Watergate burglar has a long record of angry words for the federal government, particularly the Clintons. He once said he used cardboard figures of the Clintons for target practice. During his time in the Nixon White House, he took a facetious remark by presidential aide Jeb Magruder seriously—that it "would be nice if we could get rid of columnist Jack Anderson"—and began making plans to actually kill him, only to be pulled away before he went too far. He later said he would have considered the assassination "justifiable homicide" because Anderson had once disclosed classified information. As for agents of the Bureau of Alcohol, Tobacco and Firearms, he has advised his listeners to be ready to "defend yourself and your rights with deadly force...head shots, head shots—kill the sons of bitches." After the arrest of Duran, Liddy told a reporter: "I accept no responsibility for somebody shooting up the White House....I don't believe I'm fueling the lunatic fringe." This from a man who once told his listeners how to build a bomb using ammonium nitrate, diesel fuel and dynamite, not unlike the one used by McVeigh.

Despite all this, Liddy commands respect from his fellow talk show hosts. After the Oklahoma bombing, the National Association of Talk Radio Hosts decided to give its coveted First Amendment award to him. The decision led House Minority Leader Dick Gephardt, D-Mo., to tell the group: "You do not have to honor hateful speech in order to uphold Gordon Liddy's right to utter it."

Among other widely heard radio talkers with similar views are:

- **Spencer Hughes**, based in San Francisco, who defended McVeigh by asking: "Is he supposed to break down on his hands and knees and 'boo-hoo-hoo, it's horrible what happened?'"[13]

- **James "Bo" Gritz**, the most decorated Green Beret commander in Vietnam, who was so close to extremist leaders that he served as negotiator between federal agents and those inside Randy Weaver's Idaho compound and later the Freemen in Jordan, Mont. He denounced the Oklahoma bombing but praised its technique, calling it a "Rembrandt...a masterpiece of science and art put together."[14] Gritz's program, *Hour of the Time*, is reported to have been a favorite of McVeigh's.

- **Linda Thompson**, who urged an armed march by militias on Washington a year before the Oklahoma tragedy. She reportedly said: "Let's take guns to Washington, D.C., take U.S. senators and congressmen into custody, hold them for trial and, if necessary, execute them. We've got to hang those bastards in Washington."[15]

WACO AND RUBY RIDGE

What upset McVeigh and Nichols, as well as many other people across the entire political spectrum, was the government's conduct at Waco, Texas, where 74 men, women and children of the Branch Davidian cult died in a fire on April 15, 1995, after a protracted assault by federal agents. Linda Thompson said McVeigh and Nichols had watched the tapes of her video, "Waco: The Big Lie," before planning to blow up the Murrah building. Another major irritant was the shootout at Ruby Ridge, Idaho, where tax-delinquent Randy Weaver's wife and son were shot to death by FBI agents in a standoff in 1992. Gritz urged the killing of government "tyrants" responsible for the siege against Weaver, a white supremacist, who became a martyr to right-wingers after the assault on his home. Gritz even sought to prepare his listeners by conducting a training course in the use of weapons.[16]

In the eyes of these agitators, the government has no right to enforce the laws or collect back taxes. As political reactionaries, they are thoroughly contemptuous of the federal government. Most of them rant against liberals and Democrats with the implication that only Republicans can solve the nation's problems. Few have any qualms about passing on rumors. As a result, their programs are riddled with falsehoods that are never corrected. Callers who offer opposing views risk being ridiculed or abruptly cut off.

Millions of gun owners have joined the bash-Washington brigade. Most outspoken has been Wayne La Pierre, executive vice president of the National Rifle Association. In a letter to members dealing with federal legislation in 1994, he said: "It doesn't matter to [members of Congress] that the semi-auto ban gives jack-booted government thugs more power to take away our constitutional rights, break in our doors, seize our guns, destroy our property and even injure or kill us."[17]

But it is a mistake to assume that anger at government comes only from the right. Michael Kelley, writing after the Oklahoma bombing, referred to "fusion paranoia" shared by both the left and right, a version of the old "Us versus Them." He described the Us as the American people and the Them as those who control them, "an elite comprising the forces of the state, the money-political-legal class and the producers of news and entertainment in the mass media."[18]

Media conglomerates have been doing their bit to fan the flames. They have sponsored some of the more strident voices and aired many of them on their stations. The steady drumbeat of such content—found in all news outlets—feeds on public anger, much of which flows from ignorance. According to author Susan Tolchin, "Less knowledgeable Americans are more likely to believe that government makes every problem worse." These are the people who know the least about their representatives and the way government operates. Polls confirm an increasing lack of awareness of events in Washington and the world.

News ignorance is the mother of citizen apathy, a disinterest in wanting to know about the surrounding world. Such an attitude is behind the steady decline in audiences for newspapers and network evening news shows, especially in the last decade. The evening TV news audience has dropped by a half, leaving only 20 million people to divide up among the three networks by the century's end. Circulation of daily newspapers dropped from 62.5 million in 1990 to 56.2 million in 1998, while the population went up.

Many of the dropouts from the audience for newspapers and network news have moved to cable and the Internet, while others have become grazers, absorbing whatever news falls into their line of vision or hearing as they go about their daily rituals. At the same time, the number of places serving up news tidbits has multiplied rapidly. Thanks to the Internet and cable TV, news details are more available than ever for those who want them. But the trend is toward less formal, hit-or-miss consumption of news. For many, the leading anchorman is Jay Leno.

FLIGHT OF THE YOUNGER SET

Young people have been leaving the major media faster than older adults. In 1965, Gallup reported that two-thirds of Americans under age 35 said they had "read a newspaper yesterday." By 1990, that figure was less than one-third. Voting rates have dropped more for younger people than for older ones. As a result, younger Americans are less well represented than older ones in Washington. And they are paying for it. The 50 million 18-to30-year-olds who make up "Generation X" in advertising parlance were ignored in the 1997 budget offering nearly $100 billion in targeted tax cuts that went mostly to Baby Boomers and the elderly.

When the Pew Center asked in 1996 why people were watching less network news, 48 percent said they were too busy. Another 29 percent claimed they had no readily available TV set or were critical of coverage. Others said they had no interest or got their news elsewhere. Yet the claim to have too little time didn't ring true in a year when the average viewing time for television was more than 16 hours a week.

Reasons for not following network news sound like the ones people give for not voting. In fact, they are linked. And the link is ominous. Despite the so-called Motor Voter Law in 1993, which made it easier to register, and despite the availability of much useful information for people who want to look for it, less than half the eligible voters turned out for the 1996 presidential election. It was the lowest turnout since 1924. Two years later, only 36 percent bothered to vote in the congressional elections. That left a total of 119 million people who were eligible to vote but did not do so.

Voting rates in the United States are lower than in all other advanced nations. Curtis Gans, director of The Committee for the Study of the American Electorate, links the steady drop in American voting to a "prevailing cynicism" about government that has been building since Vietnam. "The media," he said, "look for a hidden agenda in everything the government does, which projects a cynicism onto the electorate." Among other reasons he cites for voter apathy are: "The malling of America, the decline of community, children being brought up in two-wage earner homes where parents don't have the time or interest to vote, shifts in values to consumerism [and] a decline in the quality of education."

But the biggest factor is the press (radio, TV, newspapers, magazines, books, cable, satellite, Internet). As the main channels of communication between the people and government, the national news media are more influential than any other force in determining whether people vote—and how they vote—in national elections. According to interviews with non-voters for a book, 57 percent follow what's going on in government and public affairs some or most of the time, but almost half (48 percent) say the media get in the way of society solving its problems. Little more than a third were registered to vote.[19]

As interest in the news and knowledge of public affairs decline, people inevitably become more vulnerable to demagogues, such as Limbaugh and Liddy, and to fears and theories that more knowledgeable people would consider unreasonable. For example, many talk show hosts were playing on unfounded fears of a United Nations takeover of U.S. parkland in 1997. Largely due to the uproar they created, the U.S. House of Representatives voted to reject a long-established U.N. program that designated certain nature preserves and cultural attractions such as Yellowstone National Park as "world class." The action in July of that year blocked the Interior Department from spending $750,000, mostly for environmental research in connection with a forthcoming world convention on the biosphere. Earlier, the House had voted to cut funds from the Pentagon budget for similar purposes.

In another case of media-driven paranoia, most of the nation's elderly became innocent victims. In 1986, Congress passed a catastrophic health care bill with a slight increase in Medicare premiums to pay for it. But news stories focusing on complaints by the American Association of Retired Persons and others generated a backlash on Capitol Hill. Congress quickly repealed the law, which had passed by large margins. Afterward, polls continued to show a large majority of the public and the elderly in favor of the measure. Apparently they had not understood how small the costs would be.

OPPORTUNITIES FOR MISCHIEF

Some people might consider such episodes examples of a healthy democracy responding to an aroused citizenry. But with the great mass of Americans out to lunch, the danger grows that incomplete reporting can interact with unrepresentative politicians to gain unfair advantages over a trusting, disinterested majority. When demagogues employ falsehoods or baseless fears, they can help create a media tyranny in the name of democracy. Daniel Webster saw the problem in 1837, when he warned that the greatest danger to democracy would come not from beyond the borders but from "inattention of the people to the concerns of their government, from carelessness and neglect."

As public awareness falls, it creates a vast empty space between the public and its representatives in government, a space that gets filled by special interests. Against a total of 535 members of Congress stands an army of 17,500 lobbyists, many of whom can create a flood of "grassroots" messages almost overnight, often in lockstep with a few partisan commentators in the media. Some degree of true representation still exists, but legislators spend increasing time meeting with lobbyists and begging for contributions rather than legislating. Almost all of this work is done in secret, out of the range of TV cameras.

Legislation to "reform" the Food and Drug Administration was a case in point. Fashioned almost completely by representatives of drug and medical device manufacturers to gut regulations on health and safety, the bill (S.830) was sent to the Senate floor in July 1997 without public hearings or input from consumer groups that year. Yet it passed by a vote of 98 to 2 and was merged with a House bill to become law. It allows device makers to form their own safety-review committees and cuts in half the number of tests required of drug makers. Such undemocratic actions used to be rare. Now they are common. A big reason is the declining interest of the press in reporting them. The effect is to leave the public more uninformed and alienated from government.

Lawmaking is rapidly being reduced to balancing one special-interest lobby against another. As a result, nearly every piece of legislation winds up looking like a Christmas tree, a compromise laden with goodies for those with the most clout rather than on the basis of what may be needed to correct an important public problem. The proposal to raise the minimum wage in 1996 got watered down so much with trinkets for everyone that the final law didn't please anyone. Efforts to complete the job in 1999 ran into the same bottleneck. Many politicians—as well as journalists—like to blame legislative gridlock on competing political parties or the fact that one party controls Congress and the other the presidency. But it is more often due to tensions between competing special interests.

Another reason for such legislative limbo is the difficulty journalists have in detecting and reporting such maneuvering. Much of the wheeling and dealing goes on behind closed doors for fear that exposure would stop the process. When journalists get frozen out, there is no way for the general public to know what is happening to their interests. That is one reason why so many (91 percent) journalists covering Congress say major stories go unreported, according to the survey in the previous chapter.

Yet in all the discussions about public ignorance and apathy, the press receives the least attention. That's because it controls the discussion. At the same time, it has a constitutional obligation to educate and inform citizens about the workings of democracy. If the press doesn't adequately report what public representatives are doing, how can the people cast intelligent ballots? If the press chooses not to discuss a certain topic of importance, how can people know what to think? If the press chooses frivolous instead of relevant news, how can people know what to oppose or support?

While waiting for the news media to have second thoughts, some politicians and journalists have acknowledged their own. In 1992, columnist George Will said: "There is a kind of scorched-earth, pillage-and-burn conservatism that is always at a rolling boil, and which boils down to a brute animus against government. Those who subscribe to this vigorous but unsubtle faith have had jolly fun in the early 1990s as public esteem for government, and especially for Congress, has plummeted....Patriotism properly understood simply is not compatible with contempt for the institutions that put American democracy on display."[20] Four years later, House Majority Leader Dick Armey, a career Washington basher while on the federal payroll, told *The Washington Post*: "I regret what I'm sure is the part I've had in it—that we've reinforced the myth that they're all a bunch of crooks up here."[21]

Interviews in the same year by *The Washington Post* with more than two dozen public officials, including Bill Clinton and Bob Dole, showed "a loss of social trust among Americans and the dramatic decline in confidence in the integrity of government and politicians." Most respondents felt that public cynicism was "both severe in intensity and stronger than it once was."[22]

THE WALL STREET BULLY

What rarely is mentioned in such reports is the fundamental role of the media themselves in creating such views. As *The Wall Street Journal* did in the article cited at the start of this chapter, today's news corps tends to ignore or dismiss the way it helps promote the very situation it implicitly deplores in news reports and commentary. The *Journal* itself is the most prominent example as the daily paper with the most circulation—1.8 million as of March 31, 2000—and rated by the *Columbia Journalism Review* as the third best newspaper in the country. Media organizations have the undisputed right to make comments freely as long they don't violate the laws of libel, slander and national security. But there is a point where legitimate comment can become destructive to the very freedoms that allow open comments in the first place. That point arrives when the commentary comes without letup from such a powerful force as the *Journal* and when it is "unfair (and) riddled with errors—distortions and outright falsehoods of every kind and stripe." The quoted words are from an article in the *Columbia Journalism Review* in 1996 by Trudy Lieberman, an investigative reporter for *Consumer Reports*. When errors are pointed out, she added, the newspaper often avoids or delays setting the record straight.

More important than the errors cited by Lieberman and others, however, have been the number of times the editorial page has altered history because of its close ties to conservative politicians. Among the occasions cited by Lieberman were several prospective Supreme Court justices, whose nominations were dropped shortly after being dive bombed by *Journal* editors. Then there's the suicide of Vincent Foster, another *Journal* target, whose briefcase contained a note saying *Journal* "editors lie without consequence." The paper has filled five large volumes with anti-Clinton attacks, books that it peddles from its editorial page with an 800 number. The paper justifies its rabid partisanship by stating: "It doesn't hurt these columns to be one of the only two or three conservative voices left in the American media. In a business sense, we don't mind having a 90 percent intellectual market share."[23]

The reaction to Lieberman's article by Robert Bartley, editor of the editorial page, was angry. In a letter to the *Review*, he disagreed with some of the accusations and explained that the reason he would not talk with Lieberman was because "I do not trust her not to distort whatever I say." He then launched an all-out assault on the credibility of Lieberman and Consumers Union through articles and editorials. They helped illustrate the hoary maxim that one should never argue with someone who buys ink by the barrel.

The 2000 census illustrated how Washington bashing can disrupt the proper functioning of government. None of the previous decennial censuses met the degree of objections raised by this one. Soon after the long-form questionnaires were mailed out, a crescendo of complaints mostly from critics of the Clinton administration—and echoed in the media—alleging invasions of privacy and focusing largely on questions about race, income and number of bathrooms. Republican presidential hopeful George W. Bush suggested that people not fill out the form even though it was legally required. Then the Senate, which had earlier approved census plans, passed a resolution urging "that no American will be prosecuted, fined or in any way harassed by the federal government" for not complying with census demands. Overshadowed by news reports was the fact that the data were needed in order to redefine electoral districts, plan welfare budgets, calculate cost-of-living indexes and the like. Also not often mentioned in the discussion about privacy was the fact that much more personal information was already available through private business firms.

At a time when the government cannot even conduct a census because of anti-government hostility, what is the future of self-government? Author Garry Wills says the tradition "that asks us to love our country by hating our government, that turns our founding fathers into unfounders, that glamorizes frontier settlers in order to demean what they settled, that obliges us to despise the very people we vote for…belittles America."[24]

CHAPTER V

Narrowing Political Debate for Profit

Public debate through the usual editorial triumph over an absent and misrepresented opponent is a luxury which a democracy can no longer afford.

The Hutchins Commission

For several years, Jim Hightower was riding high as an independent radio voice for ABC's stable of talkers. The former editor of the rambunctious *Texas Observer* clearly enjoyed needling big corporations like Nike and Reebok for tolerating devastating working conditions in their shoe and clothing factories in Southeast Asia. His folksy liberalism helped build up more than 100 client stations.

But in 1995, ABC canceled the show. The reason, according to his agent Betsy Moon, was his failure to capture enough of the top hundred markets. "Advertisers," she said, "want provocative people who can talk about issues that divide us. As an economic populist, Jim talks about issues that unite us but which are sensitive to advertisers." She added that there were no other economic populists on talk radio, although a few list themselves as liberals.

Peter Laufer, a radio veteran and author, confirmed her reasoning: "Many station owners and operators, understandably, are more comfortable with a host who embraces the business world with no questions asked....Certainly, Nike would rather have a talk show host who believes in unrestricted world trade selling its shoes than hear its commercials adjacent to Jim Hightower as the talk show populist draws attention to the company's factories in Malaysia, saying working conditions there violate baseline health and safety standards and workers make in a day less than the minimum hourly wage in the United States."[1]

Laufer told of a station manager who was considering adding Hightower to his programming but was worried about the potential dampening effect it might have on advertisers. "Can we find out what he's going to talk about in advance?" he asked. It was not so much the possibility of a direct conflict with a Nike ad but the fear that having such a blunt talker would dissuade advertisers in general from joining such a format without knowing what Hightower's next target would be.

Charles Grodin illustrated the same point on television. As one of the few liberal commentators on that sensitive medium, he suffered a similar fate. In 1997, NBC canceled his eponymous CNBC show, in which he interviewed people in the studio, because, as *Variety* wrote, "the network finally got fed up with [his] nightly denunciation of the capitalist system."[2] Six weeks later, he was back, but finally departed in November 1999, saying he was returning to Hollywood as a movie actor.

Despite the perennial claim that the news media heavily favor liberal views, the record shows just the opposite. That is largely because conservative pundits tend to be more acceptable to advertisers than liberal ones and because media owners and managers don't want to taunt advertisers and prefer to hire those who agree with their own predominantly conservative opinions. This chapter shows how extensively all major sectors of the news media favor conservative points of view and how this imbalance discriminates against at least half of the electorate with different views. The result is a far cry from the democratic requirement for a full and fair public forum.

'DON'T READ THE STUFF'

Yet claims of liberal bias appear almost daily in the news media, especially from conservative politicians. Bob Dole, the Republican presidential nominee in 1996, knew well how to arouse the 9,000 people in the coliseum of Southern Methodist University. Get them worked up about media bias. "We've got to stop the liberal bias in this country," he shouted. "Don't read the stuff. Don't watch television.

Don't let them make up your mind for you." Then he added the kicker: "We're not going to let the media steal this election.... The country belongs to the people, not *The New York Times*."

As his listeners went wild, yelling and stamping their feet, reporter Katherine Q. Seelye might have wondered if she would be physically assaulted the way Dan Rather and Mike Wallace had been at previous political conventions. But she made it out and filed the story for her paper, *The New York Times*, which led with Dole's remarks on the front page. Ironically for such a complainer about bias, Dole not only got big headlines but was the most frequent guest on weekend talk shows during the campaign.

His boffo performance was typical of the hit-and-run tactics of political media bashers over the years. Four years earlier, the Republican rallying cry was: "Annoy the media, vote for Bush," a slogan that still lives on bumper stickers around the country. The bias charge has been thrown around as long as there has been a political press.

During Franklin Roosevelt's regime, Democrats were the chief critics of the press. Roosevelt was vehemently opposed by newspaper publishers before each of his election landslides and consistently received hostile coverage. But Republicans soon took the offense, dominating the anti-press forces ever since. Returning war hero Dwight Eisenhower joined the chorus of press bashers despite the fact that publishers played a key role getting him nominated for president. During the Republican convention in 1952, he fired a broadside at "the liberal media," thus setting the pattern that continues to this day. He also set the tone for his running mate, Richard Nixon, who was confronted a few weeks later by news reports about a secret "millionaire's fund" for his private use. Any qualms about his place on the ticket were removed by the positive public reaction to his masterful "Checkers" speech. The close call helped form Nixon's strong animosity toward the fourth estate for the rest of his political career.

Yet it was the press itself that helped the Nixon crew delay and squelch important details of the story. A study of 31 major newspapers showed that only 9 of the 28 papers endorsing the Republican ticket put the story on their front page at the earliest opportunity while all three pro-Adlai Stevenson papers did so. A similar fund for Stevenson got just the opposite play, with all but five papers running it on the front page.[3]

Although Stevenson had more reason to claim bias and complain about a "one-party press," it was the Republicans, not the Democrats, who latched onto the political potential of press bashing. Barry Goldwater took up the cudgels in the 1964 Republican convention in San Francisco with his complaint about "the Eastern liberal press." Nixon's own bitter memories emerged full-blown in a 1969 speech by his vice president, Spiro Agnew, and written by William Safire, a White House ghost writer. Agnew lashed out at "a small band of network commentators and self-appointed analysts...who enjoy a right of instant rebuttal to every presidential address but more importantly wield a free hand in selecting, presenting and interpreting the great issues in our nation." Agnew also targeted unnamed "nattering nabobs of negativism" of the "Eastern media elite, " while Safire went on to join the ranks of those he bashed so eloquently.

The fighting words marked the beginning of a holy war of sorts against the infidels who hold the power to determine the news and set the national agenda. People from any political perspective who felt that they were being treated unfairly finally had a way to discredit news or comment they didn't like. At long last, the press was on the defensive, a position that has done little to diminish its overall power. By reporting the charges without trying to refute them, news organizations essentially invite the public to agree with the allegations regardless of the evidence.

THE INTIMIDATION FACTOR

Most of the news establishment appeared to still be in a defensive posture in June 1972 when *The Washington Post* reported what President Nixon called "a third-rate burglary" at the Watergate residential complex in Washington. Despite the widespread impression of a gung-ho press digging out the Watergate story, which still prevails, most news organizations were slow to follow the disclosures that made *Post* reporters into heroes for budding journalists and into media stars later portrayed by Robert Redford and Dustin Hoffman in the movie, "All the President's Men." The apathy of many news organizations— along with the administration's damage control efforts essentially gave the "unindicted coconspirator" a free ride to reelection. But according to Ben Bagdikian, a former editor at the *Post* and a longtime critic of the trade, the slow reaction of the mainstream press was largely "The Fruits of Agnewism," the title of an article he wrote for the *Columbia Journalism Review*.[4] After checking Watergate stories in 30 daily papers around the country, he concluded that their fear of being accused of bias was behind much of the reluctance to accept the early *Post* stories or do any reporting of their own. Television networks also dragged their feet.

It wasn't until well after Nixon's reelection that the story commanded full media attention, ending with his resignation under threat of impeachment two years later. Ironically, while the press was congratulating itself, many Nixon supporters were blaming it for his troubles. Henry Grunwald, managing editor of *Time*, wrote a cover story about the "success and backlash" of the press's performance on Watergate. "At the very moment of its triumph," he said, "the press has become a villain to many, for Watergate has also focused attention on journalism's weaknesses."[5]

Those charging the press with being liberal usually base their claim on surveys showing that working journalists vote Democratic in large numbers. Two frequently cited studies on that point were done in 1981 and 1982 by S. Robert Lichter, a social scientist at George Washington University, and two others.[6] They concluded that journalists tended to be liberals and social elites, with better education and more advantaged backgrounds than the average American. Other data have shown that journalists are more likely to be in favor of affirmative action, favor choice on abortion and be less religious than the average American.

It is not surprising that journalists tend to vote Democratic, as Lichter and cohorts have shown. A poll of 139 Washington journalists in 1996 by the Roper Center and the nonprofit Freedom Forum found that 89 percent of the Washington journalists responding had voted for Bill Clinton four years earlier, 7 percent chose George Bush and 2 percent preferred Ross Perot. The results compared to the popular vote that year of 43 percent for Clinton, 38 percent for Bush and 2 percent for Perot. When asked to state their political orientation, 61 percent of the Washington journalists placed it left of center and only 9 percent to the right. Similar surveys going back to the 1930s have shown about a 4 to 1 preference for Democratic presidents.

But to imply, as Lichter and others have, that journalists slant their work to fit alleged liberal or elitist views is to stretch the available facts. A middle-class upbringing and a college education do not inevitably produce a political liberal. More commonly, such a background spawns a vested interest in the status quo. One of the few who have sought to respond to the Lichter charges was Herbert J. Gans, a sociology professor at Columbia University. He noted that the authors had not considered "a sizable number of studies in which social-science researchers...found that (journalists') personal political beliefs are irrelevant or virtually so to the way they covered the news."[7]

Years later, Robert Lichter softened his stance, finally acknowledging that "evidence that journalists hold certain beliefs or come from certain backgrounds does not in itself demonstrate that those beliefs or backgrounds shape their coverage."[8] He claimed there are too many other variables at work to make a direct connection. But his shift has not stopped others from assuming a close correlation between possible personal and reportorial bias. Nor has Lichter himself always followed his own advice. He and others have continued to cite the data without interpreting them, thus implying a direct connection when there may be none.

DIFFERENT PICTURE EMERGING

In fact, a more recent study indicates that there has been an influx of political conservatives in the news business. A 1998 project by David Croteau, a professor of sociology at Virginia Commonwealth University, found that on social issues, 57 percent of journalists were in the center, and on economic issues 64 percent lined up in the center. He also found them more favorably disposed than the general public toward business.[9]

Missing from the bias charges has been any real understanding of journalism's practicalities, a vocation that few of these experts can claim. It should not be surprising that journalists, like other people, might occasionally allow their background and views to affect their work. But three offsetting factors greatly reduce that possibility. The first is the fact of employment. Once upon a time, news organizations were run by editors likely to be notoriously independent. However, in the past generation, nearly every such firm has come under the domination of conservative business types. As a result, left-leaning journalists who want to get ahead these days soon quit or learn to muzzle any tendency to inject their personal views into their work, especially if their views diverge significantly from those in the executive suites. Most people are smart enough not to unduly upset those who control their promotion prospects and paycheck. More likely is a tendency to cheerlead the business establishment.

The second factor involves journalism's standards of objectivity and fairness. Even though those standards have slipped considerably in recent years, almost all practitioners still try to meet them, knowing that failing to do so could mean losing their jobs and their credibility as journalists. As one writer, Richard M. Cohen, put it: "Every news organization has a culture, defined by its reward system. That's the unofficial rulebook by which cub reporters are promoted to become cynical, seasoned tough guys. It's called giving the folks who sign the paychecks what they want, and it has nothing to do with coverage of politics and government."[10]

A third factor is the absence of strong political feelings among reporters and news executives. Veteran reporter Robert Parry speaks for almost all when he says: "I have never known a single (editor or producer) to consciously promote liberalism. Indeed, whatever their private opinions, they seemed far more inclined to bend over backward to appease conservatives."[11] There is strong pressure to be apolitical. When Leonard Downie Jr. assumed the post of executive editor of *The Washington Post*, he went so far as to announce he would no longer vote in political elections.

It wasn't long after Agnew that media bashing became steady work for an army of political conservatives. The first was Reed Irvine, a middle-level bureaucrat at the Federal Reserve Board. Within weeks of Agnew's blast, he and several friends formed the prototype conservative media watchdog group that he impishly called Accuracy in Media (AIM). He cited "a feeling by many that there was a need to call the media to task."[12] Richard Mellon Scaife, a right-wing heir to the Mellon fortune, was one of the financial angels. Irvine and friends were soon soliciting members, publishing newsletters and reports, running a stable of lecturers on conservative topics, firing off angry letters and op-ed pieces to newspapers and commenting daily on the radio. His complaints about a 13-part PBS series on the Vietnam War led to the public network's airing an hour-long taped

AIM response. He insisted that "the news media helped lose the war" for the United States.[13]

NEW TYPES OF PRESSURE TACTICS

Later, Irvine added two new dimensions to media bashing. One was to take out full-page ads in major papers, particularly *The Washington Post*, calling attention to examples of alleged unfairness or neglect. Another was to buy a few shares in media firms, particularly the Washington Post Company, in order to raise a fuss at their annual meetings about the treatment of certain issues.

In answer to the question, "How do you know the media are biased?" his organization's Web site says (inaccurately): "All the major media surveys for the past 20 years have shown that 80 to 90 percent of the mainstream media consistently vote for Democrats." In answer to the question, "But how do you know the media's political opinions influence their reporting," it quotes only former CBS commentator Bernard Goldberg, who once wrote a newspaper article claiming that liberal bias "comes naturally to most reporters." Although Irvine claims to champion accuracy, he finds the lack of accuracy always on the other side of the political ledger.

Irvine's group also has had a substantial, though unmeasured and unreported, influence on national affairs. During the Cold War, he gained attention by branding certain journalists as communist dupes for stories he deemed to be anti-American or anti-business. Among those accused of being communist dupes was *New York Times* correspondent Harrison Salisbury, after a wartime visit to North Vietnam. Irvine felt the same way about Walter Cronkite, whose chief offenses appeared to be his 1946-1948 tour of duty as CBS bureau chief in Moscow and his change of mind in 1968 about the Vietnam War.

In 1982, Irvine repeatedly lambasted *The New York Times* for spreading "disinformation" about U.S.-trained death squads in Central America. He demanded that the paper dismiss its El Salvador correspondent Ray Bonner after his report about the massacre of civilians at El Mozote. Irvine labeled Bonner "worth a division to the communists" and accused him of "conveying guerrilla propaganda." Irvine had a secret advantage in the affair. Each year for nearly two decades he had met annually in confidence with *Times* publisher Arthur L. (Punch) Sulzberger. The paper eventually pulled its punches and fired

Bonner.[14] Years later, after a truth commission convincingly confirmed Bonner's stories, the paper rehired him while Irvine continued to argue vehemently over the number of peasants killed.

Irvine had the gadfly business pretty much to himself until 1987 when two young conservatives formed separate media monitoring groups that were to have an even more profound effect on the press and the nation. One was Robert Lichter, who with his wife Linda, a teacher of sociology, organized the Center for Media and Public Affairs. The other was L. Brent Bozell III, a former finance chairman for presidential aspirant and sometime journalist Pat Buchanan. He started the Media Research Center. The stated purpose of both groups was, like Irvine's, to fight "liberal bias" with research-based reports but also, without actually saying so, to alter national policy by electing more conservatives. Both purposes have helped them attract millions in grant money from predominantly conservative individuals and business foundations, such as Scaife, the Coors Foundation and the John M. Olin Foundation.

The same year saw a group of liberal journalists start a newsletter called *Extra!* as part of an organization formed the year before with the acronym FAIR (Fairness & Accuracy in Reporting). Their aim was to offer "constructive criticism in an effort to correct media balance." In the first issue of the newsletter, executive director Jeff Cohen objected to groups like AIM "harassing journalists who uncovered unpleasant truths about poverty, inequality, government corruption or U.S. military and nuclear policy." Instead of "reporters, editors and producers as our enemy," he said, the villain is "the increasing concentration of the American media in fewer and fewer corporate hands." Its newsletter seeks to put the lie to conservative claims of liberal bias in news and commentary. It also has syndicated commentary by radio and tried to build a network of activists.

But it has had far less impact than its conservative cousins, largely because of its comparatively minuscule funding. As of 1999, federal tax filings showed FAIR with assets of only $385,000 and income of $964,000. Lichter's group, by comparison, had $1.8 million in assets and $935,000 income. Bozell's group held $4.0 million in assets and took in $7.0 million in income. And Irvine's group had $4 million in assets and $2.0 million income. That makes a 10-to-1 advantage for conservatives in propaganda clout.

ETHICS VS. POLITICS

Bozell's Media Research Center, the largest of the groups, conducts a continuous propaganda blitz through newsletters, press releases, books, radio commentary, speakers, weekly newspaper columns, guests for talk shows, even bumper stickers saying: "I'm Fed Up With the Liberal News Media." Its inventory of news programs totals more than 160,000 hours on some 25,000 videotapes, including not only network news programs but TV news magazines and weekend talk shows. The organization also runs the Conservative News Service, "an online primary news source for citizens, news organizations and broadcasters who put a higher premium on balance than spin." The Gingrich ethics case was an example of the Center's approach to the news: It preferred to focus on the ethics of the Florida couple who recorded the speaker's conference call, which violated his agreement with the Ethics Committee, rather than the basic charges against him, which it felt got excessive play.

Its political aim was demonstrated in 1996, when the Center set up shop at both the Democratic and Republican conventions, where it produced and delivered daily newsletters, faxes and "CyberAlert" e-mails to key media contacts as well as talk radio. Its *MediaNomics* newsletter boiled down the whole tobacco-and-health issue to a matter of news bias: "MEDIA BALANCE UP IN SMOKE: HOW THE MEDIA ARE DISTORTING THE TOBACCO ISSUE." The Center also maintains a blacklist of more than two-dozen "media stars" on "the starting lineup of the pro-Clinton press corps."

Asked about changes that have occurred since his group was formed, Bozell said the proportion of Americans believing the media are biased has doubled to more than 50 percent, and news itself is less biased.[15] In 1998, the group broadened its appeal and financial base by forming the Parents Television Council to combat what it sees as excessive sex, violence and foul language in TV programs.

Lichter's Center for Media and Public Affairs has carved a niche for itself by applying social science tools to news analysis in order to determine political bias. It has taped almost all national news programs since its founding. Even the late-night laugh-a-minute shows are boiled down to the number of slurs against political figures, a dubious honor that Clinton has won hands down. And networks are compared even down to the size of their soundbites.

Over the years, Lichter has gained more credibility than the rest, mostly because of his pseudo-scientific analyses of the news and his comparatively restrained commentary. He has become a regular fixture on talk shows and has attracted support from many respected figures, including David Gergen and Paul W. McCracken, who sit on the board of directors. A press corps that was somewhat suspicious at the beginning soon began to circulate nearly everything he produced without questioning his methods or the validity of the findings.

By being creative and quotable, Lichter and his fellow crusaders on the right have gone a long way toward accomplishing their goals of discrediting the news media and ridiculing those who disagree with their own political and economic views. They and their political allies have played a big role in creating the massive public distrust of the news media and the intimidating atmosphere in many newsrooms that prevents many journalists from probing very far into areas that might upset the right wing.

PROBLEMATIC METHODS

But their methods of study and analysis have gained more credibility than they deserve. A printed explanation of Lichter's research method, for example, uses such vague terms as "an initial qualitative examination," "reliable coding decisions" and "predetermined decision rules which guide the assignment of each piece of information to its appropriate category." Area college students are recruited to determine whether an item of information is a statement of fact, which is not counted in a study, or an opinion, which is counted. Statements considered neutral are eliminated, distorting the analysis from the start. Thus, in a study of Gulf War news, 5,666 out of 5,915 statements were eliminated, leaving only 249 for study.[16]

A 1999 comparison of campaign coverage for father and son Bush alleged that the three main networks were unfair to the senior Bush in 1992 because they produced "twice as many economic stories as they had the year before, and more than 90 percent of that coverage was negative."[17] In fact, the nation was struggling to emerge from a serious recession as President Bush was running for reelection, a newsworthy situation that couldn't help but result in coverage unfavorable to his administration. Like many other findings of the Center, this one raised questions about how so many political variables could be measured so precisely and how neutral statements could be ignored without distorting the results.

The basic flaw in the system appears to be its inability—anyone's inability—to separate fact from opinion in a precise way. It is the same dilemma that infected the Center's April 1995 *Newswatch* report headlined: "MEDIA WON'T SIGN ON TO G.O.P. CONTRACT." The first problem is the headline, the implication that a news corps that "won't" endorse a political promotion is therefore unfair. The more important problem is the text that said: "Researchers found that criticism outweighed praise for GOP policies by margins of…3-to-2 in news stories at eight major media outlets." It added that "the harshest coverage was directed at policies on abortion, school lunches and funding for the arts and humanities." But since such policies went against public wishes, as shown by polls at the time, stories reporting those poll results or quoting someone noting them could have been negative without being biased.

The personal bias of researchers is another problem. Interestingly, Lichter questions how experienced reporters can keep their own political opinions from unduly influencing their work but doesn't question his own ability or that of his young researchers to do the same. According to Everette Dennis, a professor of communications at Fordham Business School, Lichter also has not been responsive to requests from social scientists to do secondary analyses to confirm the validity of his methods, a common practice in academic circles. Lichter declined several requests from the author for a telephone interview.

GOING AFTER PBS

One of the main targets of these groups has been the alleged liberal bias of the Public Broadcasting Service, the organization that aired William Buckley's *Firing Line* for nearly three decades and gave the right-wing *McLaughlin Group* its start. The Heritage Foundation and the Center for Popular Culture have led a holy war to defund public television, a cause dating back to the first Reagan budget. One result was a 1992 law requiring PBS to review its programming each year for "objectivity and balance." PBS has managed to keep its annual government subsidy throughout the combat, but its journalistic zeal and balance has faded over the years with the exception of *Frontline*.

When Erwin Knoll, the liberal editor of *The Progressive* and regular on a panel for the *NewsHour With Jim Lehrer*, died in 1994, he was eventually replaced by Patrick McGuigan, the ultra-conservative editorial page editor of *The Daily Oklahoman*, which the *Columbia Journalism Review* in 1999 called "the worst newspaper in America." McGuigan, a Christian Coalition activist in Washington before becoming editor, was named to the panel after MacNeil/Lehrer Productions had sold a majority interest to Liberty Media, which was controlled by conservative John C. Malone, a man whom Vice President Gore once called "the Darth Vader of telecommunications." In explaining the heavily conservative tinge of the panel, Robin MacNeil said: "We're trying to reflect what we see as the landscape of American opinion, and you can't pretend the weight is on the Left....There's not much Left left in this country."[18]

Even before right-wing pressures reached such a point, mainstream news organizations were already reluctant to investigate sensitive topics important to public policy. In 1987, Seymour Hersh, the prize-winning muckraker of My Lai and other national embarrassments, listed a few prominent examples. Asked to assess the role of the press in Watergate and Iran-Contra, he mentioned Nixon's bombing of Cambodia, the wiretapping of 17 American citizens by Henry Kissinger, CIA assistance in the overthrow of President Allende in Chile and added: "If the press had been able to break any of these stories in 1971, we might have saved Nixon from himself. He might have been afraid to do some of the things he did in 1972, and this would have changed the course of history."[19]

From the first Iran-Contra stories, reporters found great difficulty digging facts from stonewalling Reagan officials such as Elliott Abrams and Robert McFarlane and getting their stories used. Robert Parry, an Associated Press reporter who was the first to report Oliver North's role in the Iran-Contra connection, later described the resulting reluctance of editors to fully staff the story at both the wire service and at *Newsweek*, where he later worked: "I confronted editors whose reactions ranged from fearful to openly hostile. Other reporters who worked the same territory experienced similar problems."[20] They included free-lancers Jefferson Morley and Tina Rosenberg, who wrote: "Administration pressure created an atmosphere in which reporters were reluctant to publish sound stories for fear of being attacked."[21] Parry describes such attacks by saying: "A story critical of a Contra atrocity in Nicaragua, for instance, could mean State Department 'public diplomacy' officials visiting your bureau chief to complain about your shoddy work, your bias and your suspect loyalties—arguments against you that might be reprised by Accuracy in Media, *The Washington Times* and a host of conservative magazines....Mainstream journalists lived with a constant career dread of being labeled 'liberal.' To be so branded opened a journalist to relentless attack by well-funded right-wing media 'watchdog' groups and other conservative operatives. It guaranteed that a reporter's career would be at least damaged, maybe ended."[22]

One of the main victims of the Iran-Contra affair was Lawrence Walsh, the Republican prosecutor. While George Bush and Ronald Reagan managed to escape indictment, and most of the prosecuted aides eventually were pardoned by Bush, Walsh found himself under relentless attack by administration officials, media watch groups and the press itself. The ultimate blow for him was the way the news media greeted his final report in January 1994. Without reading it to mine the rich vein of newsworthy nuggets from George Bush's diaries, CIA documents and Caspar Weinberger's long-withheld notes, most reporters dismissed it like an old hat and painted Walsh as the villain. According to author-researchers Malcolm Byrne and Peter Kornbluh, it was the press itself that helped turn the affair upside down by turning the miscreants into martyrs and the prosecutor into an ogre. They said the press did it "by failing to adequately investigate Iran-Contra in the first place and by providing an uncritical and even deferential vehicle for former Reagan administration officials to attack Walsh" and by blurring "the distinction between villain and victim, lies and dishonesty, criminality and the rule of law."[23]

COUNTING FEEDING FRENZIES

Journalistic fear of reporting facts that might arouse media attackers from the right has had a sweeping effect on political reporting ever since the charges of "liberal bias" became common. It helps explain the political disparity in "feeding frenzies" found by Larry Sabato in his book of the same name. Of the 36 cases he and his students studied over four decades, Democrats were the victims in twice as many cases as Republicans. Since publication of the book in 1991, that margin has grown. Of the political frenzies discussed in Chapter X, not counting the Clintons directly, the frequency of Democratic victims was more than three-to-one.

In the past two years alone, there could be no comparison between the amount of space and time devoted to Clinton's personal problems and the amount given to numerous Republican miscreants including Newt Gingrich's ethics battle, especially compared to former speaker Jim Wright's. One of the most underplayed stories of all was the discovery of Gingrich's love affair with a Hill staffer while he was regularly lambasting Clinton for the Lewinsky affair. Despite the massive hypocrisy quotient, the 1999 Gingrich divorce proceedings were treated like a non-event. The only reports in *The Washington Post* were in its gossip column.

Another example of soft treatment for a vulnerable Republican involved Rudolph Giuliani, New York City's mayor, who openly consorted with one female city employee, then another while casting aspersions about First Lady Hillary Clinton, his opponent in the 2000 senatorial race. For a whole year, the tabloid *New York Daily News* and *New York Post*, which had almost daily fun with Bill Clinton's woman problems, remained silent about Giuliani's latest affair. The *Post* even had incriminating photographs which it withheld for 10 days until the mayor held a press conference in May to announce the end of his marriage. He still blamed the media for much of his troubles before bowing out of the political race.

Right-wingers continued to complain all during President Clinton's time in office that the press was too easy on him. Yet the frequent source of their charges, the Center for Media and Public Affairs, found 1,053 stories about the Lewinsky affair taking up 29 hours of airtime on network evening news shows in only eight months ending in September 1998. The Center said the total was more than all White House scandal stories since Clinton took office and more than for Watergate and Iran-Contra, which involved constitutional violations.

In the case of alleged Chinese spying for nuclear secrets, it seemed to be a matter of too much information too soon. Few issues received more headlines in recent years than the allegations of Chinese spying, the subject of highly publicized congressional hearings. The 700-page report released on May 25, 1999, engulfed the press for weeks. But coverage was still not enough for the Media Research Center's Bozell or *Wall Street Journal* editorial page editors. In an article headlined "NETWORKS COVER PRO WRESTLING OVER CHINESE ESPIONAGE," Bozell deplored what he considered scant coverage on the morning news-entertainment shows. He said: "ABC's *Good Morning America* aired a total of three minutes on the report—compared to eight minutes on professional wrestling. NBC's *Today* gave professional wrestling triple the time it gave Chinese espionage." Only Fox gave the Cox report enough coverage to suit Bozell.[24] As it turned out, the alleged failure to give more attention to the spying allegations proved to be eminently justified at the time. According to Washington journalist Bill Messler, the Cox report was based on two stories published that spring by *The New York Times*[25] by James Risen and Jeff Gerth, the latter of Whitewater fame. The *Times* claimed that Wen Ho Lee had transferred "millions of lines of secret computer codes to help China design nuclear weapons." Yet, wrote Messler, the facts emerging since then showed "no evidence" to back up the claims.[26] The following month, the *Times* appeared to recant in an article by science reporter William Broad, saying there was not enough evidence to show that espionage had helped China's nuclear weapons program. Three months later, five experts on the subject at Stanford University, hardly a liberal stronghold, accused the Cox committee of presenting "no evidence or foundation" for the allegations. In December 1999, Lee was finally indicted, not for spying, but for illegally downloading secret data on his computer. Whatever happens to Lee cannot justify the absence of facts to back up the early coverage.

ARMY OF THINK TANKS

Meanwhile, a growing network of think tanks has also been promoting the conservative point of view from their bases in the Washington area. Like the media monitoring groups, most essentially act as surrogate lobbies for the business establishment by furnishing authoritative spokespeople for talk shows and quotations for use by print media. The process amounts to simple barter: The expert gives the newspaper reporter a quick and easy sentence or two, and the reporter provides a whiff of fame and a platform for expounding a hidden message that may or may not be understood by the reporter or the final consumer of information. Such a relationship often builds into a close bond that can tip the balance of news and opinion for or against a broad point of view.

The playing field is dominated by four large organizations whose names have become familiar to the public: the center-right Brookings Institution and the out-and-out conservative Heritage Foundation, American Enterprise Institute and Cato Institute. A 1997 data search by Michael Dolny of citations in the news found that TV mentions for the big four equaled the total for 20 others he studied, including the RAND Corporation, the Council on Foreign Relations and the Center for Strategic and International Studies. He also discovered that conservative and centrist ones accounted for 87 percent of all media citations, with left-leaning ones accounting for the rest, such as the Urban Institute, Economic Policy Institute and Institute for Policy Studies.[27] With their nonprofit tax status and appearance as quasi-universities, these groups add to their impact by appearing to be nonpartisan.

This makes it important for a journalist to put some perspective on their prolific output. But the conservative groups, such as Heritage and AEI, are rarely identified as such, while Brookings is often called "liberal" because it was once headed by Kermit Gordon, a veteran of Lyndon Johnson's "Great Society." By 1984, even *Fortune* magazine noticed a significant change in an article entitled, "Brookings Tilts Right."[28] Like many others, it has become dominated by former officials of Republican administrations. And like most others, it is funded by large business firms, wealthy individuals and business foundations, including media firms such as Time Warner and the Washington Post Company.

Adding to the problems are some embarrassing media connections. In 1997, Fox's Rupert Murdoch joined the board of directors of the Cato Institute, where John C. Malone, president of Tele-Communications Inc. (TCI), the nation's largest cable network that is now part of AT&T, was already a member. Murdoch was also a director of Philip Morris, a large contributor to Cato at the time.

Perhaps the most influential think tank over the past generation has been the Heritage Foundation, which was formed in 1973. Its biggest *coup* came just as the Reagan administration took office in January 1981 with publication of its 1,000-page book, *Mandate for*

Leadership. It quickly became more important than the federal budget as gung-ho Reaganites began using it as a blueprint for promoting their programs in Congress. Heritage's papers and studies, often quoted in the media, became instrumental in pushing expanded defense spending, cutbacks on various social programs and deregulation of numerous industries, from airlines to trucking to banking. Summing up in 1996, its annual report proclaimed: "Heritage has been involved in crafting almost every piece of major legislation to move through Congress....We've in effect become Congress's unofficial research arm....We truly have become an extension of the congressional staff, but on our own terms and according to our own agenda."

One of its major efforts has been the campaign to privatize Social Security to please its many business donors. Although the idea has not yet been approved, key politicians including President Clinton have expressed support. Along with the Cato Institute, Heritage has managed to get media and public acceptance of the false notion that the system is bankrupt. News organizations have enthusiastically quoted representatives of these and other conservative groups without challenging their reasoning.

Guest appearances on TV are one measure of an organization's influence. A survey of guests on ABC's *Nightline* from 1985 to 1988 showed heavy use of officials from the Reagan administration and "distinguished fellows" from many conservative think tanks. Few were from public interest groups, civil rights organizations or organized labor. Anchor Ted Koppel maintained that the imbalance merely reflected the fact that the Reagan administration was in power. A follow-up study of the *MacNeil/Lehrer NewsHour* in 1989 showed a similar pattern. Dominating the field were representatives from the conservative American Enterprise Institute and Center for Strategic and International Studies.[29]

FEAR OF BEING LABELED

All this favoritism toward conservative and business interests has had its effect on journalists and what they present as news and commentary. So has the fear of being criticized for being "liberally biased" when they are not. The powerful forces pushing the media to the right have succeeded to an impressive degree. By 1994, it was clearly noticeable to Reese Cleghorn, dean of the University of Maryland's College of Journalism. He said journalists "have been shifting to the right for decades" in their choice of tools for their daily work. By that he meant that they had come to avoid such terms as "radical" and "arch-conservative" and "reactionary," preferring instead such terms as "conservative" and "liberal." The journalists' attempt to be objective, he added, "has made them captives of other people's ideology."[30] Since Cleghorn's article appeared, the shift has continued. It is illustrated every time Mike Kinsley, Geraldine Ferraro or Bill Press is introduced as "from the left" on CNN's *Crossfire* though they are all political moderates.

The same conservative pattern applies to the weekend talk shows. While the Sunday network programs clearly seek to present a political balance, they often pitch rightward merely in the preponderance of moderates and absence of many voices from left of center. The left itself disappeared from the screen long ago. Strong liberals such as Ralph Nader, Noam Chomsky, Norman Solomon and Jeff Cohen are rarely seen or heard. They would clearly be a threat to many sponsors.

A study by Ruth Fort of preprinted schedules for ABC, CBS, NBC and Fox guest appearances for eight Sundays in October and November 1999 confirmed the rightward slant. Although each network made an effort to have political balance, it didn't always turn out that way. In single appearances, rather than joint ones, Republican/conservatives topped the listings 12 to 5, while CBS's *Face the Nation* presented foursomes of Republican/conservatives on each of two Sundays with no one in opposition. In addition, former prosecutor Kenneth Starr was scheduled on two programs. Fort also found a heavy preference for challengers in each major party, with four appearances by Sen. John McCain to two for Texas Gov. George W. Bush, and four appearances by former New Jersey Democratic Sen. Bill Bradley (or his former basketball colleagues) against one appearance by Vice President Al Gore. On Nov. 13, it was a full court press for Bradley, with each network listing two to four former professional basketball players running interference for Bradley. The final score that day was Bradley 10, Gore 0.

As for newspapers, one way to gain a perspective on their political slant is to follow their editorial endorsements for president over the years. Endorsements tend to reflect the politics of publishers, since they hire the editors. According to data from *Editor & Publisher* mag-

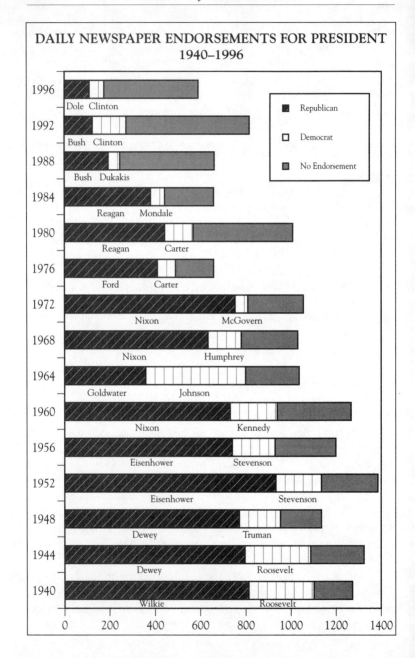

DAILY NEWSPAPER ENDORSEMENTS FOR PRESIDENT 1940–1996

azine on the 15 presidential elections since 1940, Republican nominees won the most newspaper endorsements in all but two races, Lyndon Johnson in 1964 and Bill Clinton in 1992, both of whom won election. In six elections, the newspaper favorite lost, each time to a Democrat. The biggest change over the years has been the steady increase in the number of papers choosing not to endorse any presidential candidate. From a proportion of only 13 percent in 1940, the neutral attitude grew to 70 percent in 1996. The most logical explanation for this shift is the growing corporatization of newspapers and the consequent need to avoid upsetting audiences and advertisers by taking sides as politics becomes increasingly partisan. (See accompanying chart and Appendix F.)

PUNDITS LEANING RIGHT

So-called op-ed pages tend to reflect the editorials. That's because they are usually run by the same person. Only three of the top 19 columnists (claiming 100 clients or more) on the accompanying list can be described as liberals: William Raspberry, Molly Ivins and Mary McGrory. On the basis of client numbers, the liberal portion equals approximately 18 percent of the total, while 17 percent could be considered political moderates and 65 percent were conservative. That's a 3 to 1 advantage for conservatives over liberals. Right-wing pundit Cal Thomas tops the field with 537 newspapers by his own count. Next on the list is George Will, with close to 450, Ellen Goodman, with 420, and Mona Charen, with 400. (See accompanying table on the next page.) The New York Times News Service distributes the paper's columns—including those of William Safire, Anthony Lewis, Maureen Dowd, John Herbert, Gail Collins and Thomas Friedman—to approximately 600 clients but does not keep score of the number of columns actually published. Several syndicates and individuals declined to reveal numbers of clients, so the list cannot be considered complete. It must be noted that some figures may not be accurate because of the tendency of sources to exaggerate, and the fact that actual publication varies greatly.

(Keys to political views: C—conservative;
M—moderate; L—liberal)

ESTIMATED CLIENTS OF POLITICAL COLUMNISTS

Cal Thomas [C]	537	John Leo [C]	120
George Will [C]	450	Mary McGrory [L]	120
Ellen Goodman [M]	420	Charles Krauthammer [C]	100
Mona Charen [C]	400	Ariana Huffington [C]	100
William Raspberry [L]	300	Anne Coulter [C]	100
David Broder [M]	300	Garry Wills [M]	100
William Buckley [C]	300	Richard Cohen [L]	70
Molly Ivins [L]	300	Armstrong Williams [C]	50
Morton Kondrake [C]	250	Henry Kissinger [C]	50
Ben Wattenberg [C]	250	Bill Press [L]	50
James Kilpatrick [C]	200	Jesse Jackson [L]	50
Tony Snow [C]	200	Matthew Miller [M]	50
Robert Novak [C]	150		

(Sources: Washington Post Writers Group; Los Angeles Times Syndicate; Universal Press Syndicate, *Editor & Publisher*, May 8, 1999; and individual sources, December 1999. Other syndicates declined to provide requested data.)

RADIO'S HEAVY RIGHT TILT

No part of the media is more conservative politically than talk radio. Both radio and the Internet lend themselves to unfiltered discourse with all the rumors, irrationality, errors and excesses that go with it. Talk radio got started in earnest only 14 years ago and has grown to 1,350 stations, according to *Talkers* magazine. Of the 14 most popular hosts who comment politically, all but two, Howard Stern and Tom Stephan, were conservatives of varying degrees, from mild to extreme. They represent a total audience of approximately 70 million, according to *Talkers* magazine's interpretation of Arbitron figures for people who tune in at least once a week. (See table) According to the magazine, nearly all on the list have lost listeners in the past few years.

(Asterisk denotes conservatives, from mild to extreme)

RADIO AUDIENCES FOR TOP 15
POLITICAL COMMENTATORS

Talker	Total Audience
Paul Harvey	23,000,000*
Rush Limbaugh	14,250,000*
Dr. Laura Schlessinger	14,250,000*
Howard Stern	9,250,000
Art Bell	5,500,000*
Don Imus	5,000,000*
Jim Bohannon	5,000,000
G. Gordon Liddy	3,250,000*
Neil Boortz	1,750,000*
Mike Gallagher	1,750,000*
Michael Reagan	1,750,000*
Tom Leykis	1,750,000*
Doug Stephan	1,750,000*
Tom Joyner	1,750,000*
Bob Grant	1,250,000*
Total	**91,250,000**

(Sources: The Talk Radio Research Project, based on analysis of Arbitron samplings of weekly audiences by *Talkers* magazine, fall 1999. Figures for Harvey are based on industry sources in 1999. Harvey presents news and comments, but does not take calls from listeners. Asterisk denotes all shades of conservatives. Schlessinger specializes in personal advice but also offers socio-political commentary)

This may be partly due to competition from an influx of hosts who specialize in health, financial and consumer fields and partly due to declining political interest.

According to the survey, the co-leaders, with 14.25 million listeners each, were Rush Limbaugh and personal advice expert "Dr." Laura

Schlessinger—a doctor without a medical degree. The latter frequently sprinkles right-wing political comments into her personal advice. Al Peterson, talk radio editor of *Radio & Records* magazine, estimated that totals for Limbaugh and Schlessinger were actually closer to 20 million each and that the figures for others were also on the low side. If newscaster Paul Harvey's 23-million listeners (estimated by Peterson) to his conservative-flavored newscasts and right-wing commentary were added, they would bring the total for 15 commentators to over 90 million, with all but 10 million on the political right. A sampling of the top 100 talkers listed by *Talkers* indicated that conservatives outnumber others by a ratio of about 20 to 1.

The Internet is marked by a refreshing variety of viewpoints except in the chat rooms where reactionary views predominate. Because of the creation of many Web sites by media firms and the importance of corporate advertising, however, the Internet's political coloration increasingly mirrors big media, a change spurred by the pending AOL/Time Warner merger. With the growing domination of the busiest sites on the Web by a few large firms, the outlook is for a narrowing of public discussion, not the open forum that was so widely expected.

The news media have drifted so far to the right that some persistent critics are eating their words. Even Brent Bozell acknowledges the press has lost some liberal bias. And William Kristol, editor of *The Weekly Standard*, said in 1995: "I admit it, the liberal media were never that powerful, and the whole thing was often used as an excuse by conservatives for conservative failures." Pat Buchanan confessed, "The truth is I've gotten fairer, more comprehensive coverage of my ideas than I ever imagined I would receive....For heaven sakes, we kid about the liberal media, but every Republican on earth does that."[31]

But there has been no backtracking from the political preferences of advertisers. The profit-oriented earthmover that flattened Jim Hightower also pushed pacifist Colman McCarthy and First Amendment guru Nat Hentoff out of the *Washington Post* and added Michael Kelley, an in-your-face right-winger claiming to be a Democrat, and Michael Kinsley, editor of Microsoft's *Slate*. Some formerly liberal journalists, notably pundit David Horowitz and ABC's John Stossel, even switched sides, managing to spike up their own bottom lines as a result.

No matter how the political lineup of media commentary is measured, its heavy list to the right is a long way from the fairly even split between Democrats and Republicans and between liberals and conservatives at the polling booths. And it is a far cry from the fair and open debate implicitly guaranteed by the Constitution.

CHAPTER VI

Tailoring National Politics to Media Needs

To the press with its present scope and equipment attaches an unprecedented power.

The Hutchins Commission

A few weeks before the 2000 New Hampshire primary, Sen. John McCain, R-Ariz., and former Sen. Bill Bradley, D-N.J., made an unusual deal. They would meet to jointly promote the idea of campaign finance reform, a favorite theme of theirs in the race for the presidential nomination of their parties. Their campaign staffs had determined that the affair would resonate positively among reporters, who bit hard for the promotional gimmick. So hard, in fact, that it seemed to wound the pouty editorial writers at *The Wall Street Journal*.

One thing that apparently bothered the *Journal* writers was the prospect of more publicity for reform, which they strongly opposed. Also disturbing them was the artificial nature of the affair, which they called a "Media Self-Love-In," the title of the paper's editorial. They said "the media are holding their own election...voting for themselves by staging...a made-for-TV event." They noted Ted Koppel's plans for a special *Nightline* edition on ABC and Cokie Roberts's plan to interview the two candidates on her ABC Sunday talk show with Sam Donaldson. "The media," said the *Journal*, wants (*sic*) to help [McCain] or Bill Bradley become president; then they will help the media become the overwhelming arbiter of what the political system spends its energies on. The only loser is democracy."[1]

There was no one to point out another overwhelming arbiter at work, the *Journal* itself. As the paper with the largest circulation in the nation, it serves as a "bible" for conservative political forces, especially in Washington, where it frequently gets its way. It is also an important cog in the media machine that is reshaping the way the nation chooses candidates, passes laws and shapes the judicial system. This chapter describes how politics and the political process are being changed more to fit media needs than those of the electorate.

The public has already noticed some of the changes, and it doesn't like them. A poll by Rasmussen Research in 1997 showed that by a 3-to-1 margin, Americans believed "that if reporters liked one candidate more than another, that candidate is likely to win, even if the other candidate raised more money." It also found that 59 percent of respondents distrust the news media so much that they would place restrictions on newspaper coverage even though they would violate the First Amendment. Only 22 percent thought public financing of campaigns was a better option. By a 2-to-1 margin, people thought third party candidates would win more often if they received coverage equal to other candidates. Forty-five percent said newspapers should be required to give free advertising to candidates.

Candidate debates are also undergoing major changes as they increasingly fall under the control of the media, particularly television. Once conducted mostly by the League of Women Voters, most debates are now contracted in advance to individual news organizations with exclusivity that blocks others from full access to candidates for interviews and news. NBC ran the Iowa Republican debates in December 1999 and an exclusive debate between Gore and Bradley on *Meet the Press* the following Sunday. And CNN won the right to three debates in New Hampshire and Arizona. C-SPAN, which used to carry such debates live, was reduced to taped snippets supplied by the commercial networks. Clearly, the media prefer to offer debates than free time for candidates to use as they wish because debates are likely to get higher ratings and can be controlled better by media forces.

Media influence has been especially evident in presidential races. In the 2000 primary contest, money and status helped put Texas Gov. George W. Bush and Vice President Albert Gore into early leads for the Republican and Democratic nominations, respectively. Bush and Gore also got much help from early stories anointing them as frontrunners.

Then came a rush of reports casting them in an unfavorable light while favoring their leading opponents, McCain and Bradley. The extra push helped McCain beat Bush handily in New Hampshire and a few other states, but he soon flamed out with his attack on the Christian right, a major voting bloc for Republicans. Bradley won no state and later bowed out.

Bush's and Gore's big war chests clearly helped them grab the lion's share of attention. Bush set all-time records for amounts raised, with a total of $37 million in hand more than a year before the election and nearly $70 million before the New Hampshire primary. For that reason, he decided to reject federal matching funds amounting to $66 million to each party nominee in the general election because he didn't want to be limited to such a level of spending.

THE ULTIMATE ARBITER

But money is only one of several major factors weighed by the news media in reporting and analyzing primary and election contests. Others include campaign strategy, poll standings, personality and debating skills. The biggest determinant is rarely mentioned, the press itself: how it reports and assesses the campaign, which themes it chooses to emphasize and which to ignore. A review of presidential campaigns shows the growing power of the news media to decide who runs for office, who wins and what it all means.

Over the years, the so-called Fourth Estate has played an influential role in American politics, particularly in choosing a president. Wendell Wilkie's rise to become the Republican nominee to oppose Roosevelt in 1944 was essentially the work of Henry Luce, founder and head of Time Inc. And the clamor for Gen. Dwight Eisenhower to run for president after World War II was led by the nation's editorial writers.

However, party officials always kept the upper hand. That was particularly true in 1952, when Sen. Estes Kefauver, D-Tenn., rode headlines about his organized crime hearings to defeat President Harry Truman in the New Hampshire primary and in 11 of the next 12 primaries. The victories plus Kefauver's lead in the polls helped convince Truman not to seek a second term as president. Yet the convention, under firm party control, nominated Illinois Gov. Adlai Stevenson.

The process took three roll calls, the last time it required more than one.

Media muscle was also a key factor in 1968 when journalists interpreted Eugene McCarthy's 42-to-52 percent *loss* to President Johnson in New Hampshire as a dramatic *victory*. News reports to that effect were seen as the principal factor behind Johnson's surprise decision to discontinue his reelection campaign. Later that year, when the Democratic convention was upstaged by bloody street rioting, the repeated scenes on television helped greatly in sealing the fate of Hubert Humphrey's bid to defeat Richard Nixon.

That year marked the end of traditional conventions and party apparatuses. Party influence was diminishing. The funeral was arranged by the McGovern-Fraser Commission, which was charged with reviewing the nominating system and making recommendations. Echoing many pundits and others, its report the next year urged more "popular participation" through binding state primaries and open caucuses rather than "preferential" primaries and handpicked delegates. By the next election, three-fourths of the Democratic delegates to the national convention were selected in binding primary elections instead of by party officials. Republicans followed suit, effectively ending the practice of picking nominees in smoke-filled rooms. It was hailed as a major step toward more democracy.

But a funny thing happened on the way to future national conventions. Instead of having the nomination determined primarily by convention delegates, the selection process shifted even more to the press. Party reformers didn't intend to give away the store, nor did news organizations immediately realize they had it. According to Thomas E. Patterson, who wrote the definitive book on the subject, "not a single editorial, analysis piece, or news story about the press's power in the new system appeared in the prestige media when the McGovern-Fraser reforms were adopted."[2]

Gradually, the media began taking over the tasks of party conventions by reporting candidate messages, evaluating the various contestants and even declaring victors before the conventions did. Journalists didn't quite control the nomination process, but they made it impossible for a candidate to win without them.

Even the choice of New Hampshire, a state with barely 1 percent of the nation's population, as the key testing ground was a decision of

the news media, according to Martin Plisser, longtime political director of CBS News. He says the three major networks "created the modern New Hampshire primary...for their own purposes." He says they
"converted this once marginal political event...into a unique showcase and proving ground for aspiring presidents."[3] Making the Granite
State even more of an odd choice was the fact that it was dominated
by one statewide news organization, *The Manchester Union-Leader*,
owned and run for many years by an eccentric right-winger named
William Loeb, long noted for his front-page editorial ramblings with
heavy use of capital letters.

TURNING LOSERS INTO WINNERS

Thus, 1972 was the first year that the presidential nominating
process was turned over to state voters. Some of the first indications of
what that could mean to voters and candidates came in the New
Hampshire Democratic primary where Sen. Edmund Muskie of Maine
and Sen. George McGovern of South Dakota were leading contenders
in the race to oppose President Nixon's reelection bid.

Just 12 days before the New Hampshire primary, Loeb starting firing from his front-page perch. Under a headline reading, "SENATOR
MUSKIE INSULTS FRANCO-AMERICANS" was an editorial calling attention to a mysterious letter inside the paper containing what
Loeb said were "derogatory remarks emanating from the Muskie camp
about the Franco-Americans in New Hampshire and Maine—remarks
which the senator found amusing." The crudely written letter said a
man traveling with Muskie had referred to "Cannocks," a slang term
correctly spelled "Cannuck," for French-Canadians, who make up a
large part of the population in New Hampshire.[4]

The tempest prompted Muskie to take the next flight to
Manchester from Florida, where he had been campaigning. Just hours
before he addressed the matter from an open truck in downtown
Manchester during a light snow the next morning, Loeb struck again,
this time with "a guest editorial" from *Newsweek* and *Women's Wear
Daily* saying Muskie's wife liked to tell dirty jokes, smoke cigarettes,
chew gum and preferred two drinks before dinner. As the senator
attempted to defend his wife, cameras showed him brushing his eyes
either to clear the snow or remove tears. The incident—repeated over

and over on TV—led to a nearly unanimous decision of pundits that the senator was too weak to be president.

As Muskie's poll numbers started dipping, *Washington Post* columnist David Broder declared that the candidate would have to win at least 50 percent of the Democratic votes "in order to claim victory." Five days later, R.W. Apple of *The New York Times* repeated the figure. So when Muskie wound up with 46 percent to McGovern's 37 percent, the news media declared the latter the real winner. From that point on, Muskie was written off, and McGovern won the nomination.

Journalists expanded their influence over the election process in subsequent campaigns. Jimmy Carter benefited greatly from a *New York Times* story on him in October 1975 as he began to barnstorm around the country with little attempt to court party operatives. The press also played a big part in Ronald Reagan's come-from-behind victory in the 1980 New Hampshire primary, which was considered home territory for rival George Bush, who had a summer home in nearby Maine. The crucial point came when Reagan reared up at a local editor during a candidate debate, declaring: "I'm paying for this microphone..." The polls immediately showed a 15 point drop for Bush and an equal gain for Reagan, a margin undoubtedly enhanced by constant repetition of the incident on TV.

On the Democratic side, it was Sen. Edward Kennedy, D-Mass., who saw a huge lead in the polls over incumbent President Carter go down the drain after an unusually hesitant performance in a TV interview with Roger Mudd, portions of which were repeated many times. By this time, it was clear that old-fashioned politicking among voters was being replaced by the need for favorable media coverage. Yet many journalists downplay their importance.

INFLUENCE EVEN BY DEFAULT

In a book reviewing the 1980 election, CBS commentator Jeff Greenfield declared that "television and the media made almost no difference in the outcome" of the campaign." Yet on the same page, he concluded that the media had failed "to recognize the nature of the campaign" because of a "fascination with itself as a political force..." He added: "The failure to recognize the enduring political terrain of American politics by the media, and its obsession with the mechanics, both distorted the nature of the 1980 elections and deprived citizens of a sense of connection to the campaign."[5]

In the 1984 race, when GOP primaries were no longer a factor for incumbent Reagan running for reelection, Democrat Walter Mondale won 49 percent of the votes in the Iowa contest to Hart's 16 percent. But reporters and commentators took a liking to Sen. Gary Hart, D-Colo., giving him enough of a boost to win the New Hampshire primary and six states on "Super Tuesday." But Mondale eventually turned the race around, thanks largely to his famous made-for-TV debate quip to Hart based on a Wendy's commercial: "Where's the beef?"

In 1988, polls showed Vice President Bush leading Sen. Robert Dole, R-Kan. But when he finished third in Iowa behind Dole and television evangelist Pat Robertson, the press collectively declared Bush finished, sending his poll numbers tumbling. The key incident helping Bush recover occurred later in a televised debate in New Hampshire when Dole refused to sign a written pledge not to raise taxes. After TV news producers finished playing that scene, Bush went on to win the primary there and the eventual nomination.

On the Democratic side, a front-page cartoon in the *Des Moines Register* in May 1987, a year before the primary season, helped set the stage. The seven candidates—Bruce Babbitt, Michael Dukakis, Richard Gephardt, Albert Gore, Gary Hart, Jesse Jackson and Paul Simon—were depicted as the Seven Dwarfs of Disney fame, a label that stuck to them through much of the campaign. In the election campaign, the two defining moments were the repeated TV image of Dukakis posing awkwardly in an army tank and the Willie Horton ads, constantly repeated on TV news shows, linking the Democratic nominee to a convicted rapist.

In the 1992 Democratic primary to pick a rival to President Bush, the key factor again turned out to be TV, particularly the appearance of Bill and Hillary Clinton on *60 Minutes* in January before the New Hampshire primary. The CBS interview by Steve Croft was generally credited as the turning point because of the way it projected Clinton's fabled charisma in counteracting the scandal stories in the press, especially in New York City. Talk radio also played a big role when Clinton turned to it as he began to get negative press coverage because of the Gennifer Flowers accusations.

Media manipulation of the nominating process reached a peak in 1996. News crews took over the New Hampshire primary so completely that they outnumbered voters at numerous candidate appearances. *The New York Times* described a photo opportunity for Lamar Alexander at a meat market, where its reporter counted 37 other journalists, 11 TV cameras, 13 still cameras, eight boom microphones and one butcher. *The Washington Post* pointed out a scene where Republican Pat Buchanan was scheduled to address workers at a lumberyard. "When reporters arrived," said the *Post*, "they found a sea of 300 media people and only a handful of lumbermen." CBS alone had some 200 staffers in the state.

The same media saturation occurred in Iowa that year. The *Post's* Howard Kurtz summed it up: "Finally, in the wake of the Iowa caucuses, one all-important group will have its say in the presidential campaign. The media. We make the rules. Sure, the voters play a walk-on role. But the real stars are those who read the electoral tea leaves. Forget about who gets the most votes in the early primaries. That's for wimps. The question is who triumphed in the arcane game of expectations, and therefore can be said to possess 'Big Mo,' as George Bush once called it, as opposed to Little Mo, or worse, No Mo. The momentum was awarded to Sen. Bob Dole last night as CNN projected him the winner at 8 p.m. EST, even before the Iowa voting had begun, based on a technique called 'entrance polls.'"[6]

Then came the analyses. After projecting Dole as the clear winner, CNN analyst William Schneider said: "He didn't get the big victory he needed." Fox analyst Tony Snow wondered if Dole was electable. NBC's Tom Brokaw called him a "weak" front-runner. The candidates were also doing their own spinning. The whole primary and election process was becoming an entertainment serial for media exploitation.

MEDIA TO CONVENTIONS: DROP DEAD

One of the clear losers is the quadrennial convention itself. As an institution, it has turned into little more than a public relations show with no mystery as to who the top nominee will be after all the primaries and caucuses. In an effort to restore some of the convention's importance in 1996, the Republicans set up their own TV production set, with anchors and skyboxes to air nightly programs for TV. It was enough to turn off anyone looking for news. The one most turned off was Ted Koppel, ABC's anchor for *Nightline* who walked out after two days. Although convention chiefs were stunned at what they saw as an insult, it illustrated what most journalists had come to feel—bored.

Koppel explained to viewers: "For the past couple of days, like all the other reporters out here in San Diego, we have been telling you the obvious, the very thing, in fact, that the Republicans themselves have been telling us: This convention is more of an infomercial than a news event. Nothing surprising has happened. Nothing surprising is anticipated....Frankly, we expect the Democratic convention in Chicago to be much the same." He added that part of his staff would remain in case something newsworthy happened. Actually, Dole's choice of Jack Kemp as running mate was news, though it wasn't the kind of news the media wanted. The same complaint has been made about every recent convention regardless of party. The ideal type of "convention" news for today's media occurred in the middle of the 1996 Democratic convention when a tabloid paper caught Dick Morris, Clinton's close political adviser, with a hooker. No event at either party's convention topped that for headlines.

News values and Nielsen ratings had submerged any sense of journalistic obligation to report political events that people should know as citizens. It was the overnight ratings that sent Koppel packing. After the first night, they dropped 20 percent below what they had been four years earlier, then plummeted more the next night. It marked the end of intensive media presence at national conventions. Network coverage was already down to one hour per evening. For the year 2000, news organizations except for PBS, CNN, and C–SPAN, were planning still further cuts, while the political parties struggled to find ways to connect with voters without boring the news corps or the public.

Such plans illustrate how extensively the news business has transformed the nation's political business and why so many Americans have been tuning out such affairs. Said Peter Jennings of Koppel's copout: "I don't think ultimately anybody will benefit from this, the media or the party. I think the Republicans will not benefit...because this managed convention, I think, contributes to the suspicion people have that the party is just trying to use them. We, on the other hand, are in danger...of contributing to the negativity in politics today."[7]

The facts bore out Jennings on negativity, a quality compounded by the media tendency to treat so many candidates for high office, especially those in a primary, as misguided if not wacky. The "Seven Dwarfs" label was still bouncing around ten years later when CNN political analyst William Schneider applied it this time to Republicans seeking the White House. Such labeling had become especially effective in coloring the political scene.

The serious side gets downplayed. Position papers by candidates rarely get more than a brief mention by a news corps more interested in horse-race issues such as who has raised and spent the most money, what is their strategy and who is ahead in the polls. The horse-race aspect can be fascinating news, but it can lead to major distortions of the full picture. Thus, it was largely George W. Bush's record-setting money raising, not his political philosophy, that drew the massive news coverage in 1999. Elizabeth Dole said her decision to quit was due to her inability to get her message through the media, but she also had problems raising enough money and winning press attention, which might have helped her raise money and poll standings.

News coverage is often a reflection of a candidate's place in the polls, and vice versa. Some polls are even conducted before a candidate has time to get any message to the public. Such was the case in the Iowa straw poll of August 1999. Although McCain had gotten considerable publicity by that time, he hadn't entered the Iowa race, and his ratings were in single digits. He soon corrected that with the help of headlines about his efforts to promote campaign finance reform. There was no mention of his two major dilutions of the proposal in order to please broadcasters. McCain deftly parlayed the publicity to a Web site that funneled some $2 million in contributions to his campaign fund.

By 1999, cable talk shows had become essential for presidential candidates. What CNN talkmeister Larry King started in 1992—by giving Ross Perot a platform to announce his presidential candidacy— blossomed into an almost continuous parade of candidates across the cable screens of MSNBC, CNBC, CNN and Fox. Coverage of non-horse-race issues blossomed in mainstream news outlets because of some newsworthy events, including Bush's visit to Bob Jones University, McCain's swipe at Jerry Falwell and Pat Robertson and Bradley's personal attack on Gore. As a result, voting rates in early primary states jumped far ahead of 1996 figures. It showed that genuine news can have a positive effect on voter turnout and the representative system.

THE POWER OF REPETITION

Controlling what people see and hear is the ultimate power. By deciding whether to carry a live event, broadcasters can decide whether an issue lives or dies. Adding to that power is the ability to repeat key scenes over and over. The requirements of the media, especially TV, are helping to make politics little more than another sideshow arranged primarily to fill the needs of their business. More than ever, politicians must gear their campaigns to what the media consider newsworthy, not what may be useful to potential voters.

Confusing the picture more for the public has been the steady decline in reporting about politics up to the 1999-2000 primary campaign. In 1996, TV coverage of presidential politics fell 50 percent below what it had been four years earlier, according to the Center for Media and Public Affairs. It said both the proportion of television news time devoted to campaigning and the time provided to candidates dropped. On-camera voice time of candidates also dwindled, allowing journalists more time to interpret what the candidates say. It also gives journalists more power to set their own themes.

Slashing the time for the candidates' own words fits into the media focus on strategy over policy. A study of *New York Times* front-page headlines from 1960 to 1992 by Thomas Patterson showed a marked increase in strategy themes as opposed to policy themes after 1968, the last convention that operated under the old party rules. Politicians have to devote increasing energy to creating gimmicks for media attention rather than focusing on substantive policy.

No matter how hard candidates try, their reward may be no more than a yawn from the news crews. That was the most common assessment of the 1996 presidential primary and election campaign. "Wake Me When It's Over" was the headline on Howard Kurtz's summation in the *American Journalism Review*. It was a play on the title of a book on the 1984 campaign by Jack Germond and Jules Witcover. "Boring" was the word most frequently used by reporters to describe the campaign while it was going on, thus adding to the chance it would indeed be so. Journalists were playing a growing role in determining whether a candidate, issue or campaign was boring. Such attitudes seemed to have a dampening effect on voter participation that year when it reached the lowest point since 1924. It raises the question of whether the news media have an obligation to go beyond the prevailing definition of newsworthiness when it comes to reporting politics.

The horse-race syndrome has been encouraged by the McGovern-Fraser reforms. Kathleen Hall Jamieson, dean of the Annenberg School of Communications, found that from 1977 to 1997, there was "a fundamental change in the distribution of media coverage from issue-based stories to ones that emphasize who is ahead and who is behind, and the strategies and tactics of campaigning necessary to position a candidate to get ahead or stay ahead."[8] But the change has also been due to the increased influence of the news media in the electoral process. While the public has gained more direct involvement in choosing presidential candidates in the primary system, the press seems to have gained more power to influence public choices.

Adding to the media influence was the elimination of the Fairness Doctrine by Nixon regulators in 1987 at the insistence of broadcasters. Removal of the rules designed to open on-air political discussions—though not news or debate programs—handed TV and radio hosts additional freedom to do and say what they pleased without giving opposing voices a chance to be heard.

HOW THE MEDIA DOMINATE CONGRESS

The press has also gained power to influence lawmaking though its power is used sporadically. Witness the media's pivotal role in the budget battles between Congress and the White House from 1995 on. Flushed from their historic takeover of the House and Senate in 1994, Republican leaders felt that they could shutdown the government with impunity the following year in order to force their priorities on Clinton. They had gotten away with relatively positive coverage of the Contract despite its mixed results. What they didn't realize was that closing parks and furloughing workers would crash through the news barrier that surrounds so much in Congress, causing the media to incur great damage to their image. As a result, their slim majorities in Congress were shaved in both the 1996 and 1998 elections, sending them into a defensive posture for fear of losing another battle of headlines. While conservative pundits such as Robert Novak kept urging them not to back down in their confrontations with the White House, especially in the fall of 1999, Republicans caved in on almost every major issue of contention for fear of more unfavorable headlines. The elephant in the room was not the GOP mascot but the power of the press when it got aroused from its usual torpor on the Hill.

The turning point in the shift of power from Congress to the media came when the House agreed to let TV cameras into its chambers in 1979. It led to a bizarre scene when Rep. John Seiberling, R-Ohio, rushed to take advantage of the new dynamics. Although the chamber was empty of other legislators, he assembled a collection of easels and charts for a speech that consumed nearly one hour before the C-SPAN cameras. They were the same cameras that backbencher Newt Gingrich used to such advantage—often without a legislator in the chamber—in parlaying his ability to speak into the speakership. Speeches were given to empty chambers before TV cameras arrived. For decades a member had to give a speech to get it in the Congressional Record. But rules were changed to permit a member to be recognized and ask immediately for permission to "revise and extend my remarks," allowing a written statement to be printed in the Record without being delivered.

TV cameras have changed nearly every aspect of congressional affairs. What used to be called press conferences have turned into "events" featuring live witnesses and props to dramatize preplanned points, not to interact with reporters. As one close observer of the scene has remarked, "You don't get elected if you don't like cameras." Veteran Capitol Hill reporter Richard Sammon observed that "in the past decade, the national interest…has clearly taken more of a back seat to the aggressive political interests of lawmakers and their quest for greater publicity and credit in the news media."[9] Never has that point been clearer than it was during the battles of the budget, most of which were fought via prop-filled news conferences.

Even the decision to hold committee hearings is media driven. The purpose is often not so much to find a basis for legislating as to seek press attention for a partisan purpose. Another purpose is to shake down big money lobbies that are more likely to give generously if their interests are threatened, facetiously or not, by legislative initiatives. The fate of a legislative issue depends increasingly on: (1) how high the issue is on the media scale of attention, (2) how the matter rates in opinion polls, (3) how strong the pressure of private interests is in contributions and lobbying, and (4) how a propaganda advantage can be obtained for one party or another. What's best for the country rarely makes the list.

As the amount of serious reporting about government and the world becomes scarcer, competition among legislators for attention becomes fiercer. Gingrich once related why he became such a publicity hound while climbing the ladder of success in the House of Representatives. "Part of the reason I use strong language," he said, "is because you all pick it up....You guys want to cover nine seconds; I'll give you nine seconds, because that is the competitive requirement....I've simply tried to learn my half of your business."[10] Three years later, the Georgia cracker found out that living by the sword means dying by it. His political star-power was at least partly extinguished by overexposure.

Other party leaders have also been losing power while the news corps has gained it. Norman Ornstein of the American Enterprise Institute points out that TV has helped transform Congress from a closed system with inside rewards from party leaders to an open arena where the power to punish or reward politicians now comes from outside the system. "Rewards now come automatically as members get more leverage on television than they do by working within the system," he says. "They can set their own agenda by fitting into the press's own priorities. It means that the more strident politicians get the most TV exposure, thus skewing the debate more to the extreme of either side. Political success is now determined more by who gets on TV than by what that person knows or does."[11]

Never was that clearer than during the final impeachment presentations on the floor of the House Dec. 18, 1998. Not long after the charges were read, the networks decided that the proceedings were too dull and repetitive (of the Judiciary Committee hearings) for an American audience. They began interviewing such impeachment authorities as Rep. Mary Bono, R-Calif., widow of Sonny, plus fellow journalists. Then they cut away completely to their regular programming. The media turned the solemn occasion into a soap opera starring politicians and celebrities, then turned it off because it didn't rise to their sit-com standards. *The New York Times* captured the essence the next day: "TALKING HEADS ON NETWORK TV UPSTAGE THOSE IN THE HOUSE."

The same pattern was repeated a month later at the Senate trial. Although the networks again began carrying the proceedings live, CBS switched after 90 minutes to soaps, to be followed shortly afterward by the other networks. During the trial, politicians fled *en masse* from the Senate chamber to the waiting cameras to sell their individual views. That weekend, a record one-fifth of the U.S. Senate appeared on TV talk shows. Anyone wanting to follow the details could do so on PBS, C-SPAN, CNN and other cable channels. But the networks with the bulk of the audiences made it clear that they, not Congress, were in charge, and that the biggest political event in many years was not worth their full attention.

IMAGING REPLACING LAWMAKING

Legislating itself is being increasingly replaced by the pursuit of media images. One measure of that is the number of public laws passed. According to the Thomas Web site, the number passed averaged 620 per Congress from 1973 through 1988 but went down steadily down from 713 for the Congress that year to a low of 333 for 1995-6. The number rose to 394 in 1997-8 only to tumble in the first half of the 106th Congress to only 144, indicating a total of only 288 for both sessions.

At the same time, the makeup of the press gallery has been shifting substantially. As stated earlier in this book, there has been a huge influx of regional reporters who focus primarily on federal contracts and other narrow issues of interest to hometown audiences rather than broader issues. Leland Schwartz, founder and editor of States News Service, said the pool of such reporters has grown at least ten-fold since his outfit opened in 1973. Such reporting tends to focus on narrow areas such as personal behavior, junkets taken and money spent rather than on broader matters affecting all Americans.

On the other hand, localizing can make Washington news more relevant and even increase coverage. A study by the *American Journalism Review* indicated that localizing statehouse coverage has meant more emphasis on news of city and county.[12] The absence of a correspondent in Washington or a state capital does not mean that news services cannot fill the gap. But it reduces the media's ability to do a sufficient job.

By failing to cover Washington as much as before, the news media belittle the legislative process. Reducing the flow of such information to citizens through media channels has the effect of surrounding elected representatives with an increasing veil of silence that allows them greater freedom to deal with special interests in secrecy, thus distorting the lines of public representation built into the Constitution. Gaps in the news about Congress also help increase the clout of large campaign contributors who often double as lobbyists seeking favors for their clients.

When asked in a confidential mailed survey for this book whether the media have gained influence in Congress in recent years, 70 percent of congressional press aides who responded said yes. When asked whether Congress or the media were ultimately more powerful, most chose the media. (See Appendix B.)

Such responses, though no doubt self-serving, help explain why leaders of Congress so often hold press conferences both before and after a major vote and why 38 percent of congressional press aides responding to the survey said they check with reporters before arranging a public hearing. The data also explain why members try to keep their many contacts with lobbyists and big contributors as private as possible, far from cameras and probing pencils. Although overall coverage has been falling, there is always a chance that a probing reporter will find an item unfavorable to a legislator. The business of Congress has always been a struggle to balance the nation's needs with the personal needs of legislators to get reelected. Now that reelection is so much in the hands of the media, that is where so much of their attention goes.

A decade earlier, these changes were not so easy to detect. In 1992, *The Washington Post* ombudsman wrote about what he saw as "The Growing Irrelevance of Journalists." Under the headline, however, he sang a different tune, quoting from a study indicating that 72 percent of all the TV time devoted to the 1992 election campaign was supplied by news people and only 15 percent by the candidates. He concluded that "journalists—not politicians and not the people—dominate the conversations of democracy in the United States."[13]

Even in 1995, when *Los Angeles Times* reporter William Eaton left the congressional press galleries to take up a university post, the media were not as dominant as they are today. He says C-SPAN made Congress more accessible to the public than ever before. Up to that point, he adds, Congress was more in control. He even maintains that the press "hardly influenced the outcome" of Clinton's losing battle to get his health care bill passed, a view not shared by many media critics.[14]

MEDIA ROLE AT WHITE HOUSE

It's a close race now between Congress and the White House as to which is more beholden to the news media. From JFK to Clinton, presidents have become increasingly influenced by the press and increasingly skilled at exploiting it. A glimpse behind the curtain was revealed in a White House Bulletin in May of 1992 revealing staffers obsessed by media concerns. Saying "all policies are developed and presented with the media reaction in mind," it quoted one assistant as saying that the media have "incredible power, far beyond what professors teach in college." Another was quoted as saying: "A lot of every day is spent on anticipating how the press will cover (an event or policy), how they are going to evaluate it and what kind of analysis they are going to give it."[15]

Gearing political activities to suit the press is not just to polish the president's image. Bill Moyers, former press assistant to Lyndon Johnson, said the problem goes "to the ultimate question of how does the president shape the issues and interpret them to people—how, in fact, does he lead."[16]

Even the Supreme Court, the mysterious institution that sits far above the daily fray, is becoming shaped by the media. The late Justice William J. Brennan summed it up by saying: "[T]hrough the press, the court receives the tacit and accumulated experience of the nation, and…the court needs the medium of the press to fulfill this task of instructing and inspiring."[17]

Various justices have acknowledged being influenced by the media. Edward Lazarus, a former clerk to Justice Harry Blackmun, provided rare glimpses of the deep concern of the justices about the media in his 1999 book, *Closed Chambers*. He described a "Greenhouse

Effect," named for Linda Greenhouse, a *New York Times* reporter whose court reporting won her a Pulitzer Prize. Lazarus defined it as the effort by some justices to look good in her influential reports.[18] Lazarus described ways in which conservative Justice Anthony Kennedy sought approval from the sometimes liberal *Times* and an occasion when Blackmun seemed to change his vote because of a *Times* editorial.[19]

FAULTY POLLS AND FAULTY POLLSTERS

Adding to the media's influence is the public opinion survey. Polling has become such an integral part of journalism that nearly every major news organization now has a joint arrangement with others. The leading ones are: ABC/*Washington Post*, with International Communications Research; CBS/*New York Times*, with the Election Surveys Unit of CBS; *Los Angeles Times*, Times Poll; NBC/*Wall Street Journal*, with Peter D. Hart Research Associates; and *USA Today*/CNN/Gallup, with The Gallup Organization. Hardly a day goes by without a poll about a politician or issue. No candidate for a major office these days can afford to be without a polling expert to test campaign themes on potential voters. For both politicians and the press, polls have added to their political power to determine events.

For the news business, polls provide the opportunity for exclusive news about who's up and who's down and by how many percentage points. They also help set the tone of political discussion and determine which issues get attention, again with precise-seeming measurements. It all looks very scientific with the mentions of the margins of errors. But the data shield a growing mixture of uncontrollable variables that can skew the results but are rarely discussed. Perhaps the biggest problems are the choice of words in the questions and the interpretations given to interview responses. Other problems include the refusal of people to participate and their dishonesty in saying whether they voted or not.

If polls were run by a public institution, they would be subject to rigorous scrutiny for such defects that might seriously distort the results. But political polling has been co-opted by the news business, which shows little interest in conducting a thorough examination, largely because of the embarrassing defects that might be revealed. One of the few authorities who has analyzed the subject in recent years, Slavko Splichal, says polls play a stronger role than they deserve. He counts five "major objections" to such widespread use of them: They "presuppose that each individual has, or must have, an opinion about everything; that opinions could be statistically sampled; that individual opinions have an equal value;...that opinions extracted from respondents are their true opinions; [and] that there exists in society a consensus about which questions are important and therefore must be put to the respondents."[20]

An example of how polls can be manipulated to affect national affairs occurred in 1994 when GOP pollster Frank Luntz devised the "Contract With America" for Gingrich and his band of Republican "revolutionaries." The ploy worked wonders in getting media attention and putting them in control of Congress for the first time in 48 years. But reporters showed little interest in questioning Luntz's methodology and the validity of his work. Three years later, after the largely unfulfilled Contract had been forgotten and the Republicans had lost some of their congressional majority, Luntz gained an unusual distinction: formal chastisement by his polling peers in the American Association for Public Opinion Research (AAPOR). The reason: his earlier refusal to disclose his methods in creating the Contract. In contrast to his claims that all items in the Contract had at least 60 percent public approval, his polling had been done merely to determine the most saleable language to describe the ten Contract items. This belated revelation implied that the American people, the news media and the GOP had been sold a bill of goods.

Apparently unaware of these facts, *Brill's Content* hired Luntz to poll public views on the news business in 2000, failing to identify either his professional censure or his partisan leanings. Part of the problem for the critical journalism magazine was the failure of the censure news to get the prominence it deserved. A Dow Jones data search for print and broadcast coverage of the April 23, 1997, release from AAPOR showed that only two news outlets, *The Washington Post* and the Albany (N.Y.) *Times Union*, ran the news. By failing to be more candid about such major poll defects, the news media add to the power of pollsters to mislead the nation.

The timing of polls can also be a problem. By the time President Clinton announced his big health plan on Sept. 23, 1993, numerous polls were already featuring public views about parts of the plan that had been leaked to the press. Under banner headlines the next day was an article citing a *Washington Post*/ABC News poll claiming that 56 percent of the public already approved the Clinton plan, compared to 43 percent in an earlier poll days before. The story went on to warn of "a counterattack designed to erode confidence" and "tough questions" that could threaten the plan. The timing of this poll did more to set the tone of discussion about the health care plan than later polls after more facts were known. By publicizing largely uninformed public views of a plan that had not yet been presented in detail, the newspaper couldn't help tilting the balance of opinion before many of the facts had been presented.

But the biggest problem with polls may be the growing ignorance of people who answer the questions about political affairs. This is another topic that does not much interest media pulse takers because of the negative effect it might have on their work. What little data are available indicate that public knowledge of candidates and issues has been falling steadily since the early 1950s. The Pew Center for the Public and the Press has occasionally separated poll respondents by the degree of their knowledge of a particular issue being polled. But few others have attempted to do so.

DROPPING NAMES AND RUBBING ELBOWS

In addition to the use of news and polls, the media wield political power by hobnobbing with big wheels of business, law, government and society far beyond the contacts required to practice good journalism. One cannot read any autobiographical work of a journalist— whether it be Walter Lippmann, Joseph Alsop, Drew Pearson, James Reston, Walter Cronkite, Henry Grunwald, Ben Bradlee, Sally Quinn or Katherine Graham—without seeing one big name dropped after another in describing the privileged life of the author. There's rarely a mention of the conflicts of interest in getting so familiar with news sources and how the conflicts compromised the journalist's work. That's partly because the boundaries of this shadowy world inevitably get blurred as the cocktails get passed and the dinner favors exchanged. Contacts made at such affairs provide the basis for much of the high-level maneuvering—and lobbying—that gets done in the nation's capital in the name of the public interest.

Washington's pecking order fits perfectly into the needs of jour-nalists, lobbyists, government officials and assorted celebrities, includ-ing journalistic ones. On the press side are dozens of organizations designed to mix the breeds and spread good cheer, including the National Press Club, the Gridiron Club and assorted correspondents associations. The social whirl includes numerous White House parties for journalists, press parties for politicians, formal state dinners and even nights in the Lincoln Bedroom. That's where Rush Limbaugh sacked out when Bush was president and where CNN's Ted Turner, ABC executive producer Richard Kaplan and dozens more camped out while Clinton was president. Every formal White House dinner includes a gaggle of working journalists and their bosses sucking up to the powers that be. Much of the nation's business gets done at such affairs with members of the media often not sure whether they are wearing the hat of host, guest or working journalist.

This confusion of camaraderie upset the late Meg Greenfield, the longtime editorial editor of *The Washington Post.* In 1997, two years before she died, she wrote a column asking: "Have our journalists and political leaders and just about everyone else whose head is above the trench in public life succumbed to the lure of celebrity?" Her answer was yes, including herself, a fact she deplored in print but obviously also enjoyed.[21] At her memorial service, some 500 people, including many from the top ranks of lobbyists, political leaders and publicists attended.

Yet isn't journalism supposed to be set apart from all the rest? How can a reporter or editor exercise independent judgment with news and commentary without harming friendships and valuable sources to some degree? The answer is that compromises must be made. But the blending of journalism with business, government and the social whirl has become so complete in recent years that the independence neces-sary for attaining the public's trust and maintaining a free society has all but vanished.

Rarely is there any finger pointing at ethical breaches as there was in January 1994, when a *New York Times* editorial gently chastised journalists who attended a Renaissance weekend along with President Clinton over the year-end holidays. It said media participants had suc-cumbed to "a particularly virulent strain of the Washington insider virus." Yet *Times* people themselves have suffered from the same malady as they quietly exercise their power along with others from lesser organizations. In 1997, when the *National Journal* selected the 25 "most influential journalists" in Washington, it was no surprise that 17 on the list were from just four organizations: *The New York Times*, *Washington Post*, *Wall Street Journal* and *The Los Angeles Times*.

When it comes to running the country, there's no power higher than media power. The nation's capital resembles a media matriarchy under the domain of *Washington Post* grande dame Katherine Graham and the equally unelected social arbiter, Sally Quinn, wife of Ben Bradlee, vice president at large for the *Post*. A glimpse of *Post* power in the cocktail and dinner circuits became duly recorded in a lengthy lament of hers in the paper's Style section just as Republicans were preparing to roast William Jefferson Clinton on the impeachment spit in November 1998. The hostess with the mostest served notice to all that "Beltway Insiders" were mighty unhappy at the unwelcome out-siders who had trashed their town, her town. She identified the unhappy Insiders as "the high-level members of Congress, policymak-ers, lawyers, military brass, diplomats and journalists who have a pro-prietary interest in Washington and identify with it."[22]

It was a calling of the roll of power couples and singles who regu-larly sup and schmooze at the Quinn-Bradley manse. She listed some in her article, much as she had done the year before in a fawning book she wrote about party giving. Among the anointed journalists was *Post* superstar columnist David Broder, who was quoted by Quinn as saying about Clinton: "He came in here and he trashed the place, and it's not his place." (The fact that Clinton was twice elected president gave him no standing with this group.) A sampling of other media stars on her list of the power elite included ABC's Cokie Roberts, wife of columnist Steve Roberts; NBC's Andrea Mitchell, wife of Alan Greenspan, the ruler of all things financial from his post at the Federal Reserve Board; David Gergen, editor-at-large of *U.S. News & World Report*; CNBC's Chris Matthews; PBS's Jim Lehrer; and author Elizabeth Drew. Quinn wrote that these and other bigwigs attending a gala charity event that day constituted "Establishment Washington" and were "all behaving like the pals that they are."[23]

In case those outside the Beltway didn't appreciate the political clout of such Insiders, NBC News and John McCain provided impres-sive proof in April 2000. Shortly after the feisty senator returned to the Senate after his unsuccessful ride in the primaries, the network's *Today* show announced that it had signed an exclusive contract with the ex-prisoner-of-war that involved taking him to Vietnam on a weeklong junket to mark the 25th anniversary of the U.S. defeat there. It was another merger of politics and journalism. NBC—and its defense contractor parent, GE—bought a key politician, and McCain won a unique opportunity to embellish his patriotic credentials for campaigning in behalf of Republican candidates for high office in preparation for his own run for president four years hence.

CHAPTER VII

Trading News Negligence for Political Ads

Our system of freedom, helpless against most forms of press lying, is still more helpless against this close neighbor of the lie, partisan propaganda.

The Hutchins Commission

Harry and Louise keep coming back. The middle-American couple that did so much to kill the 1993 Clinton health care plan through misleading advertisements paid for by insurance companies were reincarnated in the summer of 1999 in an effort to kill a pale image of the original. This time, the pair was transformed into an elderly couple whose female member was named Flo. But the pitch hadn't changed much. After telling about how new medicines had made it possible for her to walk again despite her arthritis, she explained that she wanted Medicare "reform" but only in "the right way." Then came the punch line:

"I don't want big government in my medicine cabinet."

In the fine print of the newspaper version of the ad—the TV ads went by too fast for clear disclosure—the sponsor was identified merely as "Citizens for Better Medicare." The ad seemed logical and appealing. After all, how many seniors don't want "better Medicare," and how many want big government in their medicine cabinet even if it could fit there?

What was this costly new flood of political advertising all about? First, a word from the sponsors. A call to the 800 number in the newspaper ad brought this message: "Thank you for calling the Coalition for Better Medicare. We're the coalition of seniors, patients, care givers, pharmaceutical research companies, health experts and citizens just like you." Callers were then invited to leave their name, address and e-mail address in order to get further information. People who contacted the advertised Web site were told that the Coalition was for a bipartisan approach to Medicare reform proposed by Senators John D. Breaux, D-La., and Bill Frist, R-Tenn. But few details were made available.

What aroused this outpouring of ad dollars from "citizens just like you" in the major media was a proposal by the White House to give about half of the 39 million Medicare beneficiaries 50 percent coverage for prescription drugs in return for increased premiums. The proposal aroused many of the same groups that fought the earlier health plan. The moneybags behind the Coalition belonged mostly to prescription drug makers and the United States Chamber of Commerce. The real reason for their going with Flo—though not stated anywhere—was the prescription drug industry's fear that the White House plan foreshadowed large-scale, discount drug purchasing by the government and that might reduce profits for one of the most lucrative industries.

But there was a bigger reason for such advertising. It was the steady reduction of serious news from Washington, a fact that was leaving gaping holes in the public's knowledge of important matters and the various congressional efforts to deal with them. The growing void presented an enhanced opportunity for affected businesses to use issue (advocacy) advertising to gain public support for their legislative battles without the distraction of divergent news themes. Corporate interests not only could hog the microphone with their dollar power but could frame the debate to suit their needs by emphasizing or distorting the issues they preferred. This chapter describes how the process weakens the democratic system by distorting political discussion for media and business purposes.

The 1999 ad blitz to defeat the prescription drug plan resembled one a year earlier that attacked Democratic plans to allow patients to sue their health maintenance organizations (HMOs). The legislative ban on lawsuits had become a major complaint of patients who suffered from incompetent medical or surgical treatment often attributed to the financial pressure on HMOs to increase profits. News stories, opinion polls and congressional hearings had long indicated widespread public dissatisfaction with the quality of health care by such for-profit organizations. In response, Senate Minority Leader Tom Daschle, D-S.D., and Rep. John Dingell, D-Mich., jointly sponsored a Patients Bill of Rights, which sought, among other things, to eliminate the existing ban on patient lawsuits, provide better access to emergency rooms and require HMOs to disclose more information.

DOCTORS JOIN BUSINESS LOBBY

But a selective advertising campaign by health care businesses, which feared losing the debate in Congress, borrowed the Harry and Louise formula to block the Daschle/Dingell initiative. Although the legislation was not designed to increase costs, opponents claimed that it would. "Make me pay more for health insurance and then expect my vote?" asked a hard-hat worker in one ad. "Forget it!" The Center for Responsive Politics, a nonpartisan research organization, estimated that more than $50 million was spent in 1998 to defeat the prescription drug bill and other legislative efforts to improve health care coverage. Among the larger advertisers were the American Medical Association, the Business Roundtable, the Health Insurance Association of America, the Pharmaceutical Research and Manufacturers Association, the American Association of Health Plans and drug companies such as Pfizer and Eli Lilly. Sympathetic legislators repeated the ad themes to add punch to the campaign, thus reducing the issue to simple slogans with all the distortions they present.

A watered-down version of the Patients Bill of Rights passed both the House and Senate in the summer of 1999, but GOP House leaders, who had fought it, stacked the joint conference committee with opponents of the measure, so it died aborning. It was another victory for industry clout enhanced by skillful advertising. In some issues, Congress is being replaced as the main forum for such discussion by advertisements from powerful special interests with the resources to persuade an increasingly uninformed portion of the public of almost anything. It means an increased likelihood that the forces with the most money and the most persuasive ads will prevail over rationality in national discussions.

Such ads are also being used between election campaigns to attack or praise key lawmakers. For that purpose, the Business Roundtable, a powerful lobby including many firms in the health care industry, launched a unique advertising campaign in December 1999. It sought to reward five Republican senators who had joined with other Republicans in blocking a series of health care reform proposals proposed by Democrats, including the one allowing patients to sue HMOs. All but one of the five were up for reelection. The ads under the banner of "Citizens for Better Medicare" again depicted a construction worker who said: "Congress is working on health care reform. But what's right for you? Senator (fill in blank) has voted for health care reforms that are right for families and employers. Thanks, Senator (fill in blank). Good job." What the ads didn't say was that they were designed more to preserve drug industry profits than to do "what's right for you."

While Congress was still in session, the Democratic Party decided to fight back with its own dollars. It focused on 17 areas around the country with ads criticizing Republicans for failing to approve a bill to allow lawsuits against HMOs and failing to allow the government to subsidize prescription drugs for Medicare patients while at the same time pushing through a large tax cut. The ads were answers to an earlier campaign by Republicans claiming that Democrats were raiding the Social Security trust fund.

To get an idea of why so much of the national debate has switched away from news stories and commentary to advertisements, one needs only consider how the media reported an important study released by the National Coalition on Health Care on May 5, 1999, showing that the number of Americans without health insurance had grown from 38 million at the time of the original Clinton plan to 43 million. That was an increase of 1 million each year.

Yet a data search of big news outlets by the National Press Club library found no mention of the study on the major television networks and only a brief mention by the Associated Press and USA Today. The AP story led with another initiative (by Aetna Inc.) offering a new type of pared-down insurance for workers who had none, a plan that critics said would do little for people with a serious illness.

It was enough to upset Washington Post columnist David S. Broder. Commenting on the lack of attention to the study by politicians and the media, including his own newspaper, he said: "You'd think it would be an issue every presidential candidate would address. Instead, what we hear is silence." He called attention to the last sentence of the report that said: "We continue to ignore this problem at our peril."[1]

PROFITING FROM THEIR OWN NEGLIGENCE

Such press behavior helps explain why politicians and special interests on both sides are turning increasingly to advertising to get their messages across. The press cannot be expected to serve merely as a megaphone for anyone's message, but the failure to report this kind of news encourages greater use of paid announcements by politicians seeking to fill the information void. It's another step in the process of turning political debate in the world's largest democracy into a cacophony of untrustworthy claims with no reliable means of separating truth from fiction or correcting the distortions. Journalistic efforts to monitor political ads rarely focus on this variety. It is ironic that the media are thus profiting from their own journalistic negligence.

Tobacco is another topic where the debate has moved to big-bucks advertising backed by lobbying and campaign contributions. In 1998, the industry faced a proposal by President Clinton to increase federal regulatory authority and to raise some $500 billion over 25 years from an increased federal excise tax on cigarettes. The idea was to discourage youngsters from starting the habit and thus save not only many lives but countless billions in medical costs paid by taxpayers. For a short time, the proposal looked like a winner. But that was before the besieged industry launched a counterattack. Once again, the Chamber of Commerce joined the fray. Both groups stepped up contributions to key members of Congress and started an advertising and lobbying campaign aimed not only at the public but at individual members of Congress who might not be firmly for or against the bill.

Again, the Harry and Louise theme was chosen, this time in the form of a harried waitress with large earrings. What won the battle for the industry this time was having her focus on the tax rather than health issue. In one ad sponsored by the Chamber, she sighs: "I'm no millionaire. I work hard. Why single me out?" *New York Times* reporter Melinda Henneberger credited the waitress ad for defeating the plan by "turning what opponents view as a bill that would discourage teen-age smoking into an assault on working stiffs who cannot afford to pay more for cigarettes."[2]

Sen. Christopher Bond, R-Mo., soon learned how it felt to be a target of such a campaign. He was one of several senators who was considered a likely supporter of the legislation. While visiting his home state, he was confronted by a constituent who said she had seen the ad and would never vote for him again if he supported the proposal. "As people looked at it," Bond told a reporter, "they saw a massive, bloated, tax-and-spend bill. Before the tobacco companies started advertising, no one saw it as a tax bill." It was enough for him to change his mind.[3] President Clinton assailed the industry's campaign as an "absolutely false" attempt to distract attention from its own attempts to mislead the public about the dangers of tobacco.

A relatively small campaign by the American Cancer Society accusing tobacco companies of "lying to the American people for decades" failed to make a dent. Helping defeat the bill, according to the Society, was the industry's ability to hire a lobbyist for each senator. The total cost to the industry was estimated by several authorities at close to $60 million. Efforts to organize a strong counter ad campaign failed. Truth and rationality count for little in the face of such well-financed onslaughts.

Unfortunately, there are almost no federal rules requiring identification of sponsors or contributions for such advertising. A billionaire Texas supporter of George W. Bush demonstrated that fact in March 2000 with $2 million worth of television ads praising Bush's environmental record, which had been the target of some unfavorable stories. The name of the sponsor was given only as "Republicans for Clean Air," arousing suspicions that it was an illegal front group for Bush. After several days of mystery, Dallas investor Sam Wyly 'fessed up to being the culprit. He said his ads were motivated by Bush's decision to deregulate utility companies and encourage alternative forms of power, which Wyly considered to be less polluting. His aim obviously was to provide a boost to Bush on an issue where his Democratic opponent, Al Gore, had better credentials.

EXTRA BONUS FOR ADVERTISERS

Such advertising not only can be extremely effective, but its impact can be enhanced by a type of double bounce. The first bounce is the effect of the ads themselves. The second is the free ride they often get when repeated in the news. It was the constant media repetition of the Willie Horton and Harry and Louise ads that made them so effective. The same syndrome works for candidate ads. It has been the main reason why there has been such a rapid growth of political advertising of all kinds, especially since 1988, the year of the Willie Horton ad.

At a conference to analyze that year's campaign, Paul Taylor, then national political correspondent for *The Washington Post*, concluded that "political advertising set the tone of the 1988 campaign. We didn't do enough to point that out even though ad monitoring went on throughout the period." The main problem, he added, was "the difficulty of finding a way to tell the truth about an ad while continuing to be objective."[4] One of the first campaign consultants to see the value of this phenomenon was Roger Ailes, co-creator of the Willie Horton commercials and later head of Fox News Network. "If you need coverage," he once said, "you attack and you will get coverage."

That fact happens to fit neatly into the mission of Marc Rosenberg, manager of public policy advertising for *The Washington Post*. In speeches to business groups, he emphasizes the potentially big second bounce of such messages: the chance that they will be repeated as news items and thus multiply the value of each dollar spent. He said such advertising in the *Post* has doubled in six years, making the paper the largest recipient of such business in the world. He noted the full-page ad by pornographic magazine publisher Larry Flynt in 1998 seeking "documentary evidence of illicit sexual relations" involving members of Congress as an example of how one ad in one paper led to a flurry of national attention that was far more effective than a mere press release. Rosenberg said most ad campaigns are not purchased nationally but on a "spot" basis in media outlets in key areas.[5]

CONGRESS LOSING CLOUT

Issue advertising is changing the dynamics of political discussion in two basic ways. First it is pushing congressional debate further into the background. Second, it is providing a more effective means for politicians and lobbies to reach potential voters than through a news process that is becoming less and less serious about government affairs. Polls show that political ads now provide as much as 90 percent of the information people get about candidates and that the percentage is still rising.[6]

Further spurring such advertising drives was a decision by the Federal Election Commission in 1995 approving political party expenditures on issue advertising that previously had been limited to ideological interest groups. The agency also endorsed the mixing of hard and soft money for such purposes. But the cost of issue ads is not reported to the Commission. The most widely quoted estimate was one made by the Annenberg Public Policy Center in November 1998. It calculated a total of about $340 million for most of the 1997-1998 election cycle, a figure that had doubled from four years earlier. At that rate, the amount in 1999-2000 could total close to $1 billion. (In June 2000, Congress decided to require that big donors to some nonprofit groups be identified, but the long-term effect was not clear.)

When Congress neared the end of its session in 1998, both parties prepared to continue some of their arguments through advertising campaigns after adjournment. In early October, at the height of the impeachment buildup, the Republican National Committee launched a $37 million series of ads in 57 congressional districts not to exploit the scandal but to counteract the charge that it had been a "do-nothing" Congress. Republicans said they were merely copying what President Clinton and the AFL-CIO did in 1996. With only $12 million to play with in 1998, Democrats were at a disadvantage, but they were able to slash the Republican margin in the House by five votes.

A year later, the main issue was saving Social Security, a cause that Democrats felt they owned because it was they who had created and passed the program. But Republicans, believing that the best defense is a good offense, launched a series of radio ads in targeted districts contending that Democratic members from those areas were using Social Security funds to pay the government's current bills. It was the same charge that Democrats had used against Republicans. In the past, such charges were pretty much confined to the realm of reporters and political pundits.

Meanwhile, the U.S. Chamber of Commerce was growing more determined than ever to separate pro-business politicians from anti-business ones through more extensive advertising in key races. Chamber officials said they were reacting to increased spending by organized labor even though the amount spent each year by business interests usually is ten times the labor total.

The 1998 congressional campaign was marked by a new intensity of attack ads across the country. And many of them were highly negative. *The Washington Post* found numerous Republicans using the Clinton scandals to attack their opponents, but most were "relying on old-fashioned ideological warfare and attempts at demonization." Some Democrats, on the other hand, chose House Speaker Newt Gingrich, R-Ga., as their bogeyman. Among the charges in the New York senate race were that Republican Sen. Alphonse M. D'Amato was "like a bully taking lunch money from hungry kids" and that his Democratic opponent, Rep. Charles E. Schumer was "soft on child pornographers and violent criminals." The common themes for Republicans were crime and taxes; for Democrats, they were gun control and Medicare. The latter was a reference to the 1996 legislative effort by Republicans to slow the program's costs, an effort that Democrats used with success in that year's congressional elections.

PROTECTING MOTHER'S MILK

Another ad battle broke out as the 1999 session of Congress was winding down a full year before the next congressional elections. Republicans again drew first blood with a campaign to portray themselves as protectors of Social Security. One obvious purpose was to prevent the Democrats from repeating their 1996 success in identifying the Republicans as the enemies of American seniors. A contemporary Gallup poll showed the public trusted the Democrats more than the Republicans (by a margin of 50 to 38 percent) to preserve Social Security benefits.

An added aim of the GOP ads was to get conservative Democrats to back the GOP budget proposals while they were still being considered in Congress. Both parties were still struggling to complete the next year's budget without having to use Social Security funds as they had done many times in the past. The fact that both parties had already tapped into the funds did not prevent Republicans from claiming in the ads that they had not.

But this effort boomeranged in an unusual way in the mass media. One of those targeted was Rep. Earl Pomeroy, D-N.D., a long-time champion of Social Security. The program had enabled him to go to college after his father died and left few assets. *The New York Times* said Pomeroy found it "particularly galling" that he was one of the Democrats in swing districts singled out for attack by the Republican ads. Pomeroy told the paper: "Washington has gotten to the point where the sessions between the elections are kind of like the setup period for the next election."[7] Within two weeks, Democrats retaliated with an ad blitz of their own, blaming Republicans for failing to pass the legislation to allow patients to sue HMOs and authorize government subsidies to Medicare patients for prescription drugs. So much for polite debates among the gentlemen and "gentleladies" of the chamber.

Such advertising would not be so prevalent or effective if there were more complete news reporting from Washington. As described in Chapter II, serious news about the nation's capital is steadily going out of style. Yet there are more services than ever available to news outlets if they want to use them. Among them are Richard Thomas's Roll Call Report Syndicate and States News Service. Although both provide detailed weekly summaries of congressional voting records geared to local areas, only about one-third of daily papers regularly run such services. Local TV stations show little interest in such services, preferring to "ask incumbents puff questions," as Thomas puts it. The result, he said, is "often a free campaign commercial" rather than objective reporting.[8]

Nowhere has political advertising been as dominant as it was in California in 1998 where a gubernatorial election coincided with congressional elections. It was a battle of millionaires for the Democratic nomination for governor. Al Checchi, one of the losing candidates, spent more than $25 million. With news of the campaign at a low point and one poll showing only 6 percent of the public following the political shenanigans, ads clearly became the main event. In fact, it was one of the few ways for a candidate to get attention on television news programs in many areas. Reporter Todd S. Purdum found that when a poll first showed the eventual winner, Lt. Gov. Gray Davis, ahead in the heated race for the first time, CBS station KCBS in Los Angeles reported the news "but only after accounts about a rash of freeway shootings, a case of suspected child abuse, a veterinarian accused of torturing cats, pirated Titanic videos, a new kind of lie detector, a new car alarm that shocks would-be thieves, the Lakers, the weather, Monica Lewinsky and a wave of rattlesnake sightings induced by El Nino."[9] News of the race accounted for less than 1 percent of news programs, according to a survey by the Annenberg School at the University of Southern California.

Political ads were so pervasive and negative that they apparently generated a public backlash. As a result, said the Annenberg group, ads simply contrasting the records of opposing candidates began to exceed attack ads. Dean Kathleen Hall Jamieson cited evidence that the more negative attack approach had boomeranged. In an effort to combat unfair tactics, the Annenberg School aired its own public service announcements suggesting that voters concentrate on candidate records, so far as they become known.

MORE ADS THAN NEWS ON TV

Political advertisements also dominate political news elsewhere in the country. During one week in October 1998, a voluntary citizens group known as the Rocky Mountain Media Watch surveyed 128 TV news broadcasts in 25 states. It found that political ads, including issue and candidate ones, outnumbered political news stories by a margin of 4 to 1. It also found 47 broadcasts with no political news at all and a total of only 10 news stories relating to U.S. Senate races. The group's executive director Paul Klite said, "People are getting their election information from paid political advertising, and that's such a distorted, narrow view of the candidates."

Klite added: "Paid political advertising is at the core of what is wrong with the election process and the media's coverage of it. Massive amounts of money funneled into propagandistic advertising messages overwhelm journalism, even good journalism. A downward cycle of cynicism results among both journalists and citizens....With few exceptions, TV journalists have abandoned their responsibility to inform us about the candidates in a fair, balanced and substantive way."[10]

What happens when false or misleading claims are made in political advertising? The Federal Election Commission is known for its inability to adequately police campaign financing laws. The even split of Democratic and Republican commissioners, as required by law, assures ineffective policing. Besides, the agency has its hands full keeping up with the flood of campaign funds and reporting the details in a timely manner. News organizations have advertising standards, but they vary from one company to another. It is difficult and expensive for a particular firm to check the validity of technical claims. The Better Business Bureau's National Advertising Division (NAD) tries to monitor the truthfulness of advertising, but it rarely indicts a whole industry as it did the nuclear industry in December 1998. The ads, which were aimed at Washington policy makers mainly, ran in newspapers and magazines, including *The Washington Post* and *The New York Times*. The NAD said industry ads claiming that nuclear reactors make power without polluting the air or water were not supported by facts. Five months later, with the same ads still running in various weekly and monthly publications, NAD decided to refer the matter to the Federal Trade Commission. The FTC eventually decided not to get involved because of First Amendment issues.

How does a responsible newspaper such as *The Washington Post* deal with questionable ads? The paper's ombudsman E.R. Shipp tried to explain: "The person or organization responsible for the ad must be clear to readers; the ad must be distinguishable from news content; and if illustrations are used, they cannot be of a type that *The Post* would deem too graphic for publication with news stories." That was not too high a bar for a graphic ad about "partial-birth" abortions, nor did it prevent the paper from publishing an ad appearing like a news story and denigrating all Russians as "the source of evil." That ad led to an apology from the paper.[11] (But the hungry paper has never apologized for its multimillion dollar revenue from personal sex ads and local whorehouses.)

Questions of truth and taste are only the first level of problems arising from the influx of political attack ads. It was inevitable for such weapons to be sharpened for more personal combat in the congressional arena. One example was the battle over legislation backed by asbestos producers, insurance companies and others to limit their liability for injuries to workers. The bill was part of a much larger contest over so-called tort reform, a two-decade effort by business interests to limit compensation for victims of dangerous products.

The maneuvering turned nasty in January 2000 when a group representing asbestos victims under the name Montanans for Common Sense Mining Laws started running TV spots critical of Sen. Conrad Burns, R-Mont., because he favored the bill. With a cemetery in the background, a worker in the ad accused Burns of supporting "people who made me sick and killed my father." Two months later, an industry group used a similar cemetery backdrop for an ad blaming trial lawyers for flooding the courts with claims and thus delaying compensation to deserving victims. Some 200,000 cases are pending.

The Montanans' ad drew blood two months later when Burns decided to drop his support for the measure. His legislative aide called it "bare knuckles" politics. Then the bill's critics turned on Sen. Rod Grams, R-Minn., who called a press conference to claim they were trying to blackmail him into opposing the bill. He cited a telephoned message to one of his office aides warning that a future ad would target Grams unless he followed Burns and switched sides. The lobbyist who made the call claimed he was merely trying to be helpful, but Grams forwarded the message to the Justice Department.

It was a clear sign that attack advertising was entering a more ominous phase beyond the traditional give-and-take of political debate. What would Harry and Louise think about the sharper, personal edge to the ads they pioneered so successfully? They and their many clones were too busy shilling industry health care proposals in 2000.

Meanwhile, candidate ads were setting new record highs, while political news in the 2000 primary campaigns was disappearing. A study of 16 TV stations around the country by the Washington-based Alliance for Better Campaigns found that they averaged only 39 seconds of political news per night for candidate coverage. In the New Jersey U.S. Senate primary race, the figure for local stations was only 13 seconds. On the other hand, political advertising during the first four months of 2000 reached $114 million in 75 markets.

Such wholesale swapping of news for ad messages is an ominous sign for the future of public discourse. What chance does democracy have when news organizations are so willing to sell their souls?

CHAPTER VIII

Censoring the News to Please Business

There can be no press freedom to falsify the authorship of speech.

The Hutchins Commission

Steve Wilson and Jane Akre, a husband-wife investigative news team at WTVT-TV in Tampa Bay, Fla., thought they had a dynamite story in early 1997. They had discovered that despite promises to consumers, supermarkets in Florida were selling milk containing rBGH, a synthetic growth hormone developed by Monsanto to boost milk production. Some scientists believe that milk treated with the hormone may increase the risk of cancer. Wilson and Akre believed Florida milk consumers should have such information.

But they ran into a series of problems getting the story on the air. There were proposed revisions and cuts, then more revisions and cuts. Then conferences with lawyers in touch with Fox headquarters. The backing and filling were prompted by a letter from Monsanto to Roger Ailes, head of Fox News and former producer of the Rush Limbaugh TV show. The chemical company raised questions about Wilson and Akre's "objectivity and capacity for reporting on this highly complex scientific subject." It also charged that the reporters had "prejudged the safety [of rBGH] and the corporate behavior of Monsanto." The letter hinted at a lawsuit if the station didn't "get the facts straight."

In response, Wilson and Akre agreed to work with lawyers to produce a story that would be legally unassailable, but they insisted that they could not take part in airing a program that was false and misleading. After more discussion, the story was finally killed, and they were fired. They sued for breach of contract and violation of the Florida whistleblower protection law. They said station manager David Boylan told them: "We paid $3 billion for these television stations. We will decide what the news is. The news is what we tell you it is." The case was still awaiting trial three and a half years later.

Although such public confrontations are rare, they serve as sharp warnings to all journalists of the consequences lurking for anyone who defies the powers that be, especially large companies such as Monsanto that have the resources to advertise in many news outlets and to swing their considerable corporate weight in other ways. Stores selling milk were also a worry because of their potential advertising. Wilson and Akre became unemployable in their chosen line of work through no fault of their own. And milk drinkers in the area lost their right to know about ingredients that might be harmful.

It was not the first time that Americans had lost their right to be fully informed about vital health matters that might be embarrassing to a news organization because of its need to be friendly to advertisers. In fact, the problem is growing more serious as the news business becomes absorbed by other businesses. This chapter describes how the fear of displeasing advertisers and business in general robs the public of information that can deeply affect its health and welfare.

TV reporter Roberta Baskin ran into a similar problem at CBS with a hard-hitting report aired in 1996 on *48 Hours*. Her report, "Foul Ball," was about Vietnamese children making Reebok shoes and soccer balls for $6 a week while undergoing physical and sexual abuse. The programs set off an international uproar and some industry reform efforts. But when an article in *The Wall Street Journal* op-ed page attacked her reporting and she wanted to respond, her superiors said she couldn't. And when she sought to air some updates of her original report, a chill set in.

Two years later, she suddenly thought she saw why she was running into problems as she watched CBS coverage of the Olympics. There on the screen were network correspondents sporting the Nike "swoosh" across their shoulders. She fired off a memo to her superiors, citing the obvious violation of journalism ethics and the rules of CBS. The chill deepened to a mass shunning of her by colleagues. After finding out that there was indeed a deal between CBS and Nike that also included truckloads of free goodies from Nike for hundreds of CBS employees, she eventually quit to become a senior producer of ABC's *20/20*.

But her problems may not be any better there. Lowell Bergman, the former CBS producer who once worked at ABC, says he "discovered at ABC News that you could not do an enterprise story about a supplier or a major advertiser. You could try to do it, but you were taking a lot of risks getting close to the limit." The problem with television news, he says, "is that any obligation to report stories about unaccountable power...has been lost." He confirmed that censorship is rarely the result of external pressure but is usually subtle and unspoken. "It is no surprise," he adds, "that the commitment of media organizations to reporting without fear or favor has waned."[1]

Self-censorship is much more common than journalists will admit. Thus, when a substantial portion of them are willing to agree that it is common, it is likely that the actual amount is much more. A survey of 287 journalists by the Pew Research Center got two out of five to admit they had softened the tone of a news story because of company interests. When only investigative reporters were included, the figure rose to more than three out of five. But the proportion in actuality may be even higher, for only 10 percent denied that such manipulation ever happens.[2]

The problem of commercial pressure on the news began more than a century ago with the advent of mass retail advertising in newspapers. By the turn of the century, advertisements filled nearly half of the average paper. Thirty-five years later, reporter and press critic George Seldes wrote in his book *Freedom of the Press* that advertisers, not government, were the principal news censors in the United States. Since then, advertising has grown to about 60 percent of newspaper space and 100 percent of broadcast revenue. That kind of clout gives advertisers more than just the power to move goods and services. It makes them a major influence on what journalists say and how they say it.

In 1998, the ten leading national advertisers alone spent more than $18 billion in media outlets, according to *Advertising Age*. Robert J. Coen, senior vice president at Universal McCann in New York, predicted that marketers altogether would spend a record $233 billion in 2000. As revenue grows, so does the fear of losing advertising. Robert Hodierne, former Washington national editor for Newhouse News

Service, explains: "While the Tampa TV station killed its milk story because it feared that Monsanto would sue, that's not what scares most news outlets. They have learned to tell stories in ways that protect themselves from libel. What scares news organizations most is loss of advertising."[3]

A recurrent nightmare for media executives is an advertiser—no matter how small—who takes offense at something in the news or commentary and decides to withdraw its advertising. Although examples of such retaliations are few, they happen enough to sustain a high level of anxiety at the heart of journalistic operations. The fear is rarely mentioned in newsrooms, largely because journalists are too ashamed to talk about it. But it's a pervasive cloud that leads to self-censorship. Almost every issue of the leading journalism reviews carries examples of news executives altering news or commentary to please an advertiser, potential advertiser or close friend or relative of the owners or top officials.

Examples from the "Darts & Laurels" column of the *Columbia Journalism Review* in 1999 include:

- A fax to local businesses from Fox News's WDSI-TV in Chattanooga promising three positive mentions about "your company" on news programs plus promos for only "$15,000— that's 4.5 cents per household."

- A notice to local businesses from the Fall River (Mass.) *Herald News* offering one inch of news for every inch of advertising in the annual "Progress" edition, an idea encouraged for all papers by the Newspaper Association of America.

- Refusal of *The Atlanta Journal-Constitution* to mention a 40-page report of the Southern Regional Council in Atlanta documenting widespread employment discrimination in the state, a story other papers displayed prominently.

Such pampering of business interests, particularly advertisers, has had a depressing effect on journalists. When they begin to realize what they are up against, many either quit or decide to compromise their principles rather than risk becoming jobless. Few are willing to tough it out for years like Roberta Baskin. Although she still survives, she says, she has an uneasy feeling knowing that the next story may be her last. She adds, "The most serious threat to journalism is self-censorship." In her view, there is little prospect of improvement as long as the business is dominated by so many aggressive conglomerates. "It's enough," she adds, "to make many journalists wonder if they are long for this kind of world."[4]

Over the years, journalistic fears have led to serious restrictions on what can be covered as news. Perhaps the biggest casualty has been the hard-hitting, hour-long documentary on a single subject, the best way for TV to cover a complex matter. It was effectively killed on commercial television by corporate sponsors of Edward R. Murrow's pioneering documentaries after they saw the potential that his documentaries had for disturbing the status quo. Today's bastard child of Murrow's *See It Now* series, the proliferating TV "newsmagazine," would make Murrow roll over in his grave if he saw how hard such shows try to steer clear of major national problems that might upset powerful business interests. For example, evidence of tobacco health hazards was not fully told for nearly two decades, least of all by TV. Only after Congress banned tobacco advertising in 1971 did the issue finally begin to get full treatment on the air. PBS's *Frontline* comes closest today to the standards set by Murrow with its hard-hitting, well researched documentaries on topics that commercial networks won't tackle.

The success of ad censorship is reflected in the topics that win journalism awards. On the print side, only a handful of Pulitzer Prizes for investigative reporting have covered topics sensitive to large commercial interests. The same reluctance is apparent in editorial writing, with only three winners from 1917 to 1994 tackling such topics (two against land developers and one against a brothel). Typically, winners have focused on government and nonprofit organizations, adding further to public distrust of government while leaving large areas of interest relatively unexamined. The same pattern is evident in other awards. Conversely, half of the 10 "most censored" news stories of 1997, 1998 and 1999 selected by journalists for Project Censored involved issues sensitive to large businesses.

Even the best news organizations tend to shy away from serious reporting of topics with commercial conflicts. One of the industries most sensitive to unfavorable news is the country's network of nuclear power and processing plants, which have had their share of safety problems over the years. When *The Washington Post* decided in 1999 to do a series of reports on the topic, it chose to focus on a plant in Paducah, Ky., that recycles used nuclear reactor fuel. Three workers had sued earlier that year alleging that they had suffered from radiation by inhaling dust containing plutonium particles. In a four-week period in August, the paper ran eight stories, including five on page one, charging that the plant failed to properly screen metals for radioactivity, let radioactive waste seep from the plant and committed numerous other safety violations that led to devastating health problems for workers and some fatalities. The series was a good candidate for a major prize.

Two days after the first front-page story appeared, the Critical Mass Energy Project of Ralph Nader's Public Citizen group issued a detailed report claiming that for three years, 90 percent of the nation's nuclear reactors had been operating in violation of government safety rules and that the federal Nuclear Regulatory Commission, instead of policing these conditions, had set up an amnesty program to last through March 2001. Here was major news from a respected citizen group potentially affecting far more people. Yet the *Post* not only did not put this on page one, it could not find room for it anywhere, according to a data search. But it regularly found space for full-page ads from the Nuclear Energy Institute saying nuclear energy is good for the country. The Public Citizen story found its way into a few other news outlets, including *The New York Times*, NBC, National Public Radio and a few regional newspapers where the allegedly unsafe plants were located. But the news did not get far beyond these points.

Why would there be such reverse disparity in coverage between these stories, one very localized and one with national implications? One possible reason was the fact that the Paducah story had some strong personal angles, and the other didn't. Another was the fact that Paducah was a government-owned plant, while most of the others were privately owned and potential advertisers. Although news organizations have no stated policy of going easy on private industry, the record shows they prefer to target non-advertisers such as Uncle Sam. It's easier and safer. Jim Riccio, a publicist for Public Citizen, said he had noted the same pattern with other news releases about nuclear safety, noting that the *Post* occasionally covered the subject in a column of short items called "The Regulators."

The number of major news stories ignored or treated cavalierly because of such editorial timidity has become a national spectacle that is chronicled each year by the hardy band of volunteers called "Project Censored" at Sonoma State University in California. For 23 years, this group of students and professors has been issuing lists and copies of such stories, recently in the form of a book.

With each publication of "censored" news stories in book form, the news gets a little further into the public conscience. But the "censored" stories are effectively censored again by being largely dismissed by the major media. Also not welcome on high are the names of the journalistic organizations that are honored for exposing the embarrassing truths. Among the frequent sources of tough, independent journalism are *Covert Action Quarterly*, *The Progressive*, *The Nation*, *Multinational Monitor*, *San Francisco Bay Guardian*, *In These Times*, *Chicago Life*, *Slingshot*, *News From Indian Country*, *Earth Island Journal* and *Counterpunch*.

In 1998, these were the publications that one had to follow in order to know about an international trade agreement that undermined U.S. sovereignty, chemical companies that profited from breast cancer, genetically modified seeds from Monsanto that tainted world production, recycled radioactive metals that may be in your home, a U.S. nuclear program that subverted the comprehensive test ban treaty, gene transfers linked to dangerous diseases, Catholic hospital mergers that threatened reproductive rights of women, U.S. tax dollars that supported death squads in Mexico and environmental student activists gunned down at Chevron's oil plant in Nigeria. These were the ten "most censored stories" of 1998. They were typical of topics censored in other years.[5] There is an implication that such stories get no attention from major news organizations, but that is not necessarily true. Selections by the journalist judges merely mean the winning stories did not get the attention their newsworthiness deserved.

There once was hope that non-commercial broadcasting would fill in such major gaps in the news. But that hope vanished as the system became increasingly dependent on business sponsors in exchange for on-air credits that are growing closer and closer to full-fledged commercials. Financial problems for the Public Broadcasting Service flared up with the arrival of the Reagan administration and the rise of right-wing think tanks such as the Heritage Foundation, which have proposed drastic cutbacks in federal subsidies to public broadcasting. The biggest crunch came in 1995 as Republicans took over Congress and threatened to eliminate all of the approximately $300 million in federal funds. Their main complaint was that news broadcasts were unfair to conservatives, although most studies on the subject didn't back the claim. Pleas from viewers and listeners forced the Republicans to back down, but the continuing political pressure has only increased PBS's shift toward more commercial funding.

According to author James Ledbetter, virtually no phase of commercialism is alien to so-called noncommercial broadcasting today.[6] The Internet appears headed in the same direction despite a refreshingly open editorial approach at many Web sites. The reason: nearly all the major news sites use mainline sources or are branches of the same conglomerates that determine and distribute news and commentary.

TROUBLED TIMES IN LOS ANGELES

The take-over of journalism by industrial conglomerates and the accompanying corporate atmosphere have heightened the involvement of business interests in news and commentary. The most widely publicized example in recent years was the attempt of *The Los Angeles Times* to push aggressively for higher profits in order to appease investors. The hiring of Mark H. Willes, described elsewhere in this book, led to many firings and resignations as he sought to break down the traditional wall between news and business departments. It also led to an incident in 1999 that aroused widespread astonishment and considerable resentment by staffers as well as former publisher Otis Chandler.

The catalyst was a special edition of the paper's magazine devoted to promotion of the Staples Center, a new sports arena in downtown Los Angeles. Not mentioned in the magazine was the paper's secret agreement to split the profits evenly with the Center, thus severely compromising the paper's journalistic independence in covering events related to the Center and taking ads from it. Once these terms were disclosed—in another publication—300 editorial staff members signed a petition seeking an apology from publisher Kathryn M. Downing, a non-journalist before joining the company. She eventually issued an apology, attributing her misjudgment to a "fundamental misunderstanding." Willes also conceded that the deal was "a mistake." Editor Michael Parks claimed he did not know about it, adding that it was wrong to be "reporting on an institution with which we were going to share revenues." But months after all the smoke had blown away, nothing had changed. The top executives who set up the deal were still in place until eventually replaced by the new owners from Chicago.

In fact, the Staples deal was not much different from the common practice of setting up deceptive newspaper sections specializing on food, health, automobiles, travel, real estate and computers. Despite the occasional presence of real news, the main idea is not to provide news to readers but to attract advertisers. Space between ads is often taken up by promotional material interspersed with soft news not worthy of the main news section. The TV counterpart is the infomercial, so named because it looks like useful information but is actually a commercial.

Local merchants are the main source of tension for news staffs. A survey of news editors by *Advertising Age* in 1993 found that automobile dealers constituted the biggest problem for news executives because they are among the largest advertisers and are especially sensitive to news or commentary that casts them in an unfavorable light.[7] To complicate the matter, most auto ads are paid for by the manufacturers, which have even more editorial clout than local dealers. Now that about 80 percent of all daily papers are controlled by regional and national firms, the power of a General Motors, Daimler Chrysler or Ford has been enhanced still more. The three firms were ranked first, fourth and sixth among the nation's largest advertisers listed by *Advertising Age* for 1998.

Most efforts of large advertisers to censor the news are subtle. Not much needs to be said to a savvy news executive for him or her to understand the need to be extremely circumspect about any news that might offend such important sources of paychecks. So it was unusual in 1997 to see Chrysler's ad agency demand that magazines receiving ads submit articles in advance for review by company executives to determine whether the content was acceptable. The threat was clear. But it was even more unusual to see the co-founder of *New York* magazine, the graphic designer Milton Glaser, so shocked by Chrysler's action that he withdrew from consideration for a Chrysler Award for Innovation in Design. Comparing the company's policy to the earlier practice of submitting TV scripts to ad agencies in advance of airing a show, he said: "Censorship of this kind that acts to curtail the exchange of unpopular ideas is unacceptable for all those who care about human freedom and a healthy democratic society."[8]

GM is also not averse to using similar pressure. Fresh from getting NBC's apology for its unethical program about the safety of its pickup trucks, the automaker mounted an aggressive campaign against the syndicated show *Inside Edition*. While the program was preparing a segment criticizing GM's legal tactics in defending other trucks criticized by federal authorities, GM sent the program boxes of supporting documentation and a toughly worded letter. "If you broadcast the sort of story you described," it said, "we intend to use these GM responses as evidence of malice by *Inside Edition* in publishing a false, defamatory and grossly unfair story about General Motors." The company reportedly sent the same materials to more than 100 stations carrying the NBC program, asking each one whether the broadcast "conforms to your station's standards of journalistic fairness and balance." The experience illustrated why news organizations don't do more to probe big advertisers.[9] In 1996, consumer reporter David Horowitz learned how car dealers view fairness and balance when station KCBS in Los Angeles fired him after getting repeated complaints about his investigative reporting.[10]

BLURRING NEWS AND ADS

In contrast to the aggressive attitude of some large advertisers is the media's own submissive attempts to curry favor—and ads—from the same large firms. *USA Today* has built a record of blurring news with advertising. Sometimes the two are hard to distinguish from each other. The paper's page one spread for Nov. 2–4, 1990, featured a picture of Honda's new Acura NSX sports car, saying it was "so hot that the roll of early owners reads like the 'A' list for a celebrity bash." The free ad seemed to work. A few days later, the inside pages carried a large paid ad for the same car.

The paper also offers to redo its entire front page for an advertiser, complete with stories promoting whatever firm is willing to pay the price. The revised front page with its familiar logo and design—but not the rest of the paper—is then circulated as a promotional piece. One firm that used this device was Columbia/HCA, the giant health care firm that ran into financial trouble. Another was Glaxo Wellcome, which surprised some 7,000 delegates one morning at a 1998 AIDS conference in Geneva with what they assumed was an authentic edition of the paper but was not. Interestingly, Gannett got more criticism from outside the media than inside. The nonprofit Health Research Group, for example, called the practice "a craven violation of journalistic ethics." Gannett was not the only news organization selling its front-page format. A *New York Daily News* deal with supermarket chains allows them to "wrap" the entire front page of several thousand copies for an ad promoting in-store specials. By selling their journalistic trademark to all comers, these publications were displaying what the public could plainly see: their lost integrity.

However, these shenanigans must compete with Time Warner's efforts to woo advertisers before its purchase by AOL. One of its practices was to send top business leaders, key government officials and its star journalists on 10-day jet junkets around the world. Another was to turn over large chunks of *Time*, its flagship magazine, to business groups willing to pay the privilege. In September 1998, TW announced a deal with Ford Motor Co. to become the sole sponsor of a *Time* series of four extensive advertising sections on the environment entitled "Heroes for the Planet." According to press accounts, TW agreed to have its own staff produce the 40 pages of editorial material for each of the four issues, with Ford having the right to veto what it didn't like.

Nevertheless, *Time's* sister publication *Fortune* issued a blast in 1996 at fellow publisher and perennial GOP presidential aspirant Malcolm (Steve) Forbes for having "an unusually cozy relationship between those who edit the stories and those who sell the ads." John Huey, editor of *Fortune*, a competitor of *Forbes* magazine, defended the story by claiming: "Those of us who practice mainstream, ethical journalism don't believe in having advertising executives at your publication have influence over your stories or the slant that you take....If we did it, our staffs would be horrified."[11]

Beth Zacharias, editor of the *Washington Business Journal*, describes the type of pressure that journalists face from advertisers. She says that when one large advertiser—whom she did not name— got angry at the paper's news policy, "We met with him...to explain why our news pages weren't for sale. What he said in the middle of the meeting amazed me. 'I understand your philosophy completely,' he said. 'That's not what this meeting is about. I want you to change your philosophy.' He told us that because his company was a large advertiser, it deserved preferential treatment." When she and her publisher refused, he pulled his ads. "He couldn't buy the news," she said, "so he wouldn't buy the ads. It was a shame."[12] So was her failure to name the advertiser.

Rare is the case when all the names and details become public, such as when *The Boston Herald* decided to suspend its consumer reporter in April 2000 after BankBoston, a large advertiser, objected to articles about raising its fees. Robin Washington said he was already barred from negative reporting about supermarkets and auto dealers when he was ordered to stop writing about the bank. A bank spokesman admitted having complained to an editor. Washington was eventually reinstated by the paper.

None of this came as news to Lawrence Soley, a professor of communications at Marquette University. Sixty years after Seldes' book about advertising censorship, Soley said, "Advertisers are still muscling newspapers." He cited a survey of 55 members of the Society of American Business Writers at the group's 1992 conference revealing that advertiser pressure was common on business pages. "Business journalists have always struggled against advertiser pressures, but our members are telling us it's getting worse," said Sandra Deurr, business editor of Gannett's Louisville *Courier-Journal* and former society president.

In his own survey of members of Investigative Reporters and Editors, Soley reported that nearly three-quarters of those responding agreed with the statement that advertisers had "tried to influence the content" of news, and most also said advertisers had tried to kill stories. He added that more than two-thirds of the journalists reported that advertisers had threatened to withdraw advertising because of dissatisfaction with news stories and that more than half followed through on their threats. One respondent, who said he had been fired for offending advertisers, sent Soley a memo he had received from the news director. It said: "If you're involved in a story which you know might reflect badly on an advertiser, please let me know, so I can give sales a 'heads up.'"[13]

Under the circumstances, it is not surprising to see some journalists go over the line in the prevailing marketing milieu. All journalism suffered a black eye in 1998 from David Brinkley's indiscretion in allowing himself to become an ad spokesman for Archer Daniels Midland Co., the long-time sponsor of the Sunday ABC talk show featuring him. This is the same company whose top officials—including some known well by Brinkley—had been charged with criminal price conspiracy (and later fined and sentenced to prison). Neither ABC nor Cokie Roberts, co-host of *This Week,* covered themselves with glory in response to Brinkley's decision. The network allowed the ADM ad with the former newscaster to run for weeks on the same show he had moderated until his retirement. And Roberts offered her public congratulations to him. The headline on Maureen Dowd's column on the subject said it all with its reference to the pioneering *Huntley Brinkley Report:* "Good Night, David."[14]

FAREWELL TO THE WALL

In order to explore the status of advertising influence on the press, *Editor & Publisher* magazine polled editors and publishers around the country about their practices and policies and reported the results in its Dec. 4, 1999, issue. It reported that "the age-old image of a high, forbidding concrete barrier separating the newsroom from the business side has already been blasted into history—replaced (for better or for worse) by a low, approachable wall, made of glass." Flagrant breaches like the *Los Angeles Times*/Staples controversy are rare, *E&P* said, but "threats to, or breaks in, the Wall are common, perhaps even daily, occurrences at many newspapers." The survey showed:

- Three of four editors and publishers reported that advertising/editorial guidelines are breached "sometimes" or "frequently."

- Two out of five respondents disclosed that their papers had published special sections to obtain advertising even though they knew the focus of the sections had "little reader interest."

- One of three said they believed that "promotional ties or revenue-sharing arrangements" with institutions newspapers cover was a "common industry practice."

- More than half of the publishers labeled the *Times*/Staples arena deal an "acceptable" practice, compared to just one-fifth of the editors.

- Eight of 10 editors and nearly all publishers acknowledged that advertisers had pulled ads from their papers because of stories they opposed.

- A substantial number of publishers (19 percent) and editors (11 percent) said they found it acceptable for newspapers to consider "killing or holding a story that might negatively portray an advertiser." About one in 10 said their newspaper had killed or altered such a story.

- One in four publishers believe there is nothing wrong with asking reporters "to include advertisers in a story." Editors disagreed, but half felt it was acceptable for reporters to "be informed of certain advertisers who may be relevant to a story."

Only a decade ago, the wall was much more widely respected, especially by publishers and editors. The figures show that it is crumbling rapidly, with little chance that journalism or the public welfare will benefit. The state of the wall may be even worse than the figures indicate because of the likelihood that many editors don't want to admit what others consider irresponsible journalism.

The reaction of Leonard Downie Jr., executive editor of *The Washington Post*, was particularly noteworthy for his candor and lack of concern about the proverbial wall. He told the magazine: "This notion that there needs to be a wall is kind of a red herring." He said editorial and advertising people should communicate more, not less. "There needs to be discussion, ongoing dialogue, and joint planning," he said. It was the kind of remark that never would have been uttered by previous editors of his paper.

In contrast, *Wall Street Journal* publisher Peter R. Kann said the wall will remain firm at his paper. He put his finger on a key point: "Sophisticated advertisers," he wrote, "understand the importance of editorial independence and integrity to their long-term ability to deliver their message in a believable context." Max Frankel, former executive editor of *The New York Times*, explained more fully: "A wall is needed to insulate the gathering of news, which should be a selfless public service, from the pursuit of profit, which is needed to guarantee the independence of the business. Journalism, in other words, is a costly and paradoxical enterprise: it can flourish only when profitable, but it is most suspect when it seeks a profit at all costs."[15]

With almost every American city now served by a monopoly paper, one might expect all editors would report that they are free to pursue journalistic objectives without having to worry about offending advertisers. But the *E&P* survey clearly shows that is not the case. The prevailing corporate direction of newsrooms and the heavy emphasis on profits create an atmosphere of cooperation rather than confrontation with advertisers, especially among top officials.

Media corporations themselves are no strangers to pressure tactics when advertising revenue is involved. Their practices rarely become public because of their own tight self-censorship. But David McCord, an erstwhile competitor to Gannett Company, the nation's largest newspaper chain, managed to part the curtain a bit when he got to see sealed court records detailing numerous illegalities committed by Gannett in a fierce competitive struggle in Salem, Ore., in the 1970s. "When Gannett decides to kill something," wrote McCord, " it turns readily to a number of weapons that clean competition abhors: greed, lies, deceit, fraud, intimidation, bribery, fear, pressure, illegality."[16]

After exposing the details in his own weekly paper, the *Santa Fe Reporter*, McCord sought to interest major news organizations in exposing them. So he sent his documented account—covering six entire newspaper pages—to the commercial networks, major papers and chains as well as PBS's *Inside Story*. None would touch the story. He said *Editor & Publisher*, the industry "bible," carried only one small item. "This lack of interest mystified me," he said, "until someone pointed out that Gannett was *E&P's* biggest advertiser."[17]

Gannett is also a big advertiser in critical journalism reviews. The possibility that one of its purposes is to keep them from looking too closely at big media firms didn't seem to occur to one of those journals, the *American Journalism Review*. In a December 1998 article on budget cuts, Geneva Overholser, a former Gannett editor at *The Des Moines Register*, wrote about 1995 reductions that had "removed heart, soul and giblets" from the newsroom, then another $63,000 in cuts while corporate earnings soared another 22 percent. In retaliation, Gannett discontinued advertising in the magazine.

With that single act, the big chain brought an extra dose of reality to the worst fears of the magazine's executives. It showed that news organizations are not above using the very tactics they deplore most in the business world. And it made clear why there is little room in today's news charade for journalists like Steve Wilson and Jane Akre. In June 2000, Fox rewarded David Boylan, the TV manager who fired the couple, by making him manager of KTTV, Fox 11, in Los Angeles, the network's second largest station.

CHAPTER IX

Using Publicists to Cut News Costs

[The press] has lost the common and ancient human liberty...to offer half-truth for the whole.

The Hutchins Commission

"I saw the Iraqi solders come into the hospital with guns. They took the babies out of the incubator...and left the children to die on the cold floor."

So said "Nayirah," a 15-year-old Kuwaiti girl who shocked a public hearing of the Congressional Human Rights Caucus on Oct. 10, 1990. Her testimony rippled around the world, over and over, with no attempt by reporters to learn more about the witness and who was behind the hearing. Her tearful story became embellished with almost every repetition until Amnesty International cited a death toll of 315 babies. Her and other claims of atrocities were recited at another congressional hearing and later by "Citizens for a Free Kuwait" at a special meeting of the United Nations Security Council two days before that body set a deadline for Iraqi withdrawal from Kuwait. The allegations were restated frequently in the media and in the Congressional debate over granting war authority.

This remarkable propaganda coup was part of an $11.5 million public relations campaign conducted largely behind the scenes by Hill and Knowlton on behalf of the Kuwaiti royal family. Any PR campaign that could help get the United States to go to war over an oil patch halfway around the world should be considered one of the most successful of all time. Much of the credit was due to H&K's friends in the Bush White House and State Department. Especially effective were video news releases (VNRs), a type of audio-visual publicity that has become a common device in swaying public minds with rarely a mention of its source. The firm's video on Nayirah's testimony won fourth place on the top ten list of VNR successes in 1990, reaching a total of 35 million viewers, according to Medialink, a firm that distributes VNRs to TV stations for corporate clients. But the real coup by H&K was its success in staging hearings in Congress and the United Nations, then getting them reported as straight news despite the firm's unmistakable fingerprints all over the scenes. It helped convince Congress—by only five votes in the Senate—to approve war.

Not until five months later was John Martin, a correspondent from ABC news, able to go to Kuwait and find that Nayirah's claims were false. And it was not until January 1992 that another journalist found through a simple phone call to the Kuwaiti Embassy in Washington that Nayirah actually was the daughter of that royal fiefdom's ambassador to the United States. After the war, the Kuwaiti royal family hired Kroll Associates, an international investigative firm based in New York City, to look into the wildly varying claims of incubator deaths in hopes of confirming Nayirah's testimony.

Kroll eventually found the possibility of seven unexplained incubator deaths but concluded that her story "was based on a single incident…the sight of one infant on the floor and the presumption that other infants, not seen, had also been removed from incubators."[1]

This chapter describes how the increasing pressure on the news media to save money plays into the hands of professional propagandists grinding axes for powerful interests, leading to hidden conflicts of interest. It also tells how this melding of press and publicist can influence public policy often against the public interest and push legitimate news and commentary out of their proper place.

DEBATE REDUCED TO FLACKERY

Spin doctors are riding higher than ever in the nation's newsrooms, as the battle for public opinion and political power becomes increasingly partisan and bitter. Government officials have adopted the most sophisticated methods to promote programs and keep themselves in power. Members of Congress increasingly employ PR techniques to win debates with other members as well as to influence the general public. And, of course, private interests of all types use PR to get what they want from government. To today's cynical press corps, the spin is in. Reality is out.

By fall 1999, it looked as if winning the public relations battle was even more important to politicians than passing a budget. Mindful of how President Clinton and congressional Democrats had gotten the better of Republicans in the 1995 Christmas shootout over shutting down government, Republicans decided to conduct an intensive PR campaign. They didn't call it such, nor did much of the press. But they got what they wanted: a group photo on page one of *The Washington Post* and prominent play elsewhere for passing a tax cut bill that they knew the president would veto. A glimpse of the truth peeked out from the *Post* headline: "WITH EYES ON 2000, CONGRESS CRE-ATES ISSUES BUT NOT LAWS." They did better on TV with video clips of their own "bill-signing" ceremony and T-shirts announcing "Tax Cuts: A Home Run for America" and signs claiming "Real Tax Relief for Taxpaying Americans."

The aim was to convince the public that they, not the president nor Democratic legislators, were for tax cuts. It was pure public relations. The same type of show was presented as Congress adjourned a few weeks later, proclaiming with great hoopla that the Republicans had "saved Social Security" and "preserved Medicare" even though nobody had threatened those sacred programs. The semblance of legislating was replacing legislating itself.

The semblance even took the appearance of a gaudy pink "bus" labeled the "Pork Buster Patrol," a PR creation of the Seniors Coalition, a small right-wing version of the American Association of Retired Persons. Its ostensible purpose was to oppose wasteful spending that might threaten Social Security. The bus—actually an old motor home—was a gimmick created for hometown headlines around the country. But *The Wall Street Journal* gave the ploy a big front-of-section spread, saying it was part of a campaign of Republican congressional leaders to win the media battle of the budget in the fall of 1999.

Reporter Greg Hitt found that the scheme had a somewhat split mission since the vehicle was being used also to oppose a pending bill in Congress to extend drug patents for the popular allergy medicine

Claritin and others. Hitt reported that a lobbyist named McClain Haddow had hijacked the "Pork Buster" campaign for a client who made a generic version of Claritin. Haddow, described as a former Reagan administration official who had served prison time for a federal felony, called it "grassroots politics at its best."[2]

Candidates for president also seek success at the polls on the wheels of public relations. A year before the ballots would be counted in November 2000, frontrunners were blowing their own horns like never before. Eschewing the traditional news release to promote an important speech on foreign policy, Texas Gov. George W. Bush called key journalists with an offer to answer questions ahead of time. One call went to William Safire, *The New York Times* columnist who coyly granted the favor in his Nov. 12 column: "PRE-SELLING A SPEECH." Six days earlier, a page-one headline in *The Wall Street Journal* said: "GORE, THE EXECUTIVE, SHAKES UP MARKET-ING OF GORE, THE CANDIDATE." It used to be that journalists would discount, if not ignore, such sales pitches. Now, they have it both ways by playing along with the gag while sometimes revealing the inherent deception.

All politicians must play the game. Those who don't rarely win. Every special interest has its paid representative in Washington to score points as well as favors from government. The only interest not well represented in all the maneuvering is the general public's. Elected officials are supposed to do that job, of course, but it is becoming more and more difficult for them to do it because of the increasing pressure on them to raise campaign money from the same special interests they are elected to oppose.

LAWMAKERS BECOME ACTORS

So politicians turn to PR in part to cover up what they don't do for the public, particularly on Capitol Hill. Richard Sammon, a veteran newsman there for Kiplinger Washington Editors and earlier for *Congressional Quarterly*, explains: "So crucial is media coverage that some members appear more like hungry actors desperate for any TV face time than thoughtful legislators elected to serve the public." He said a joke among reporters is that the fastest way to get a black eye is to get between a television camera and Sen. Charles Schumer, D-N.Y. He added that Schumer holds more meetings with the press some days than with his staff and constituents. But his behavior is more a trend than an exception to it. Among the common ways used by legislators to get attention are:

- Responding rapidly to news events. Just moments after the shooting of two Capitol police officers in 1998, Sen. Bob Torricelli, D-N.J., issued a news release claiming the tragedy proved that stronger handgun laws were needed.

- Having press aides fashion releases with key quotes from legislators to make it easy for reporters to use them without requiring an interview.

- Using props such as poster boards on the floor of the chambers, with graphic details (of abortions, for example), then holding news conferences to increase mileage.

- Timing releases and press meetings on Mondays and Fridays to take advantage of slow news days and timing floor speeches for evening hours if member districts are in Western states.

There's also negative PR, the type Sen. Phil Gramm, R-Texas, employed in 1999 by scheduling a hearing for opponents of his industry-oriented banking bill for 5 p.m., a time he knew was too late for key reporters and TV cameras.

New members of Congress are even given coaching lessons in order to be at ease before television cameras. They are instructed on what to wear, such as a red tie to catch attention and help exude power and confidence. Political PR even has its own language, according to Republican pollster Frank Luntz, who helped create the GOP "Contract With America." To sell the Contract, he issued a 100-page manual for legislators, the main theme of which was to concentrate on the pitch, not the policy. By that he meant, for example, to accompany every statement about the federal budget with "cutting the government bureaucracy" and to speak of people, ideas and visions rather than actual numbers. And, of course, there was the paperback book to explain the Contract to voters.

It's a constant struggle for attention and one that is becoming more intense each year. It's also becoming more complex. Public relations is not only the practice of issuing press releases, holding news conferences and soft-soaping key people in the media. It's lining up lawyers and lobbyists, who are often part of the same firm. It's creating fake grassroots organizations to lobby. And it's advertising. It's often all these things in one package.

The inventors of the promotion business would not recognize today's version of what they pioneered. One of them, Ivy Lee, carved out a thriving business building images for corporations to help counteract the negative effect of journalistic muckrakers of the early 1900s. Sometimes called "Poison Ivy" by reporters, he was credited with having invented what is now called "crisis management," developing ways to reverse negative public images that may suddenly arise. He and others gained fame for the work they did in the government's Committee on Public Information to win public backing for America's entry into World War I. They set up civic committees, organized marches and delivered messages to churches, theaters and social groups with spectacular results. It was what Edward L. Bernays, another PR pioneer, called the "engineering of consent." Bernays himself became known for his use of "independent" third parties, often with secret deals, to push a common theme.

SWAPPING ACCESS WITH EXCESS

Public relations today involves an unwritten contract in which journalists give publicists free attention in exchange for free and reliable information. One result is a journalistic tendency to rely too heavily on promoters in an effort to save time and energy by news organizations. Another is the reluctance to fully identify information sources, a practice that can be misleading. The increasing pressure on news organizations to cut expenses and boost profits has added many opportunities for PR interests to get their way. Meanwhile, publicists have gained the skills and stature to win key roles inside business and government.

Thus, in 1991, when Sen. J. Bennett Johnston, D-La., wanted to overcome stiff opposition to an energy bill dear to his heart, he called in The Wexler Group, now a "government relations" subsidiary of Hill & Knowlton Public Affairs in Washington, to win support. The first thing Anne Wexler, the group's head, did was to arrange a meeting with some executives and lobbyists for numerous industrial firms. According to a newspaper report of the affair later confirmed by her, she gave each person at the meeting, including a representative of the

U.S. Energy Department, a packet of materials to help them lobby for Johnston's bill. But the public was not the prime target this time. Each executive was asked to lobby "those senators with whom you can be most effective in achieving the coalition's objective."

One reason why the campaign was not directed at the general public was that the legislation might not have been popular once its aim became widely known. Among its purposes was to open part of the Arctic National Wildlife Refuge to oil companies. Another was to speed up the licensing of nuclear generating plants. Still another was to deregulate the electric utility industry. The bill had Bush administration support as well as support in Johnston's energy and natural resources committee. Among those opposing the bill were consumer and environmental groups.[3]

The planetary alignment in this struggle tells a lot about the public relations business. Days before Wexler took charge, she had been lobbying *against* the bill on behalf of some electric utilities that were not satisfied with it. It showed how closely legislators work with publicists and lobbyists, particularly those representing business interests. It is not uncommon for members of Congress to join coalitions that support common interests. Two years earlier, Rep. John D. Dingell, D-Mich., an opponent of clean air laws that affect the auto industry, helped create the Clean Air Working Group, an industry-oriented group lobbying against strengthening the Clean Air Act. It was another example of the clout business interests have obtained due to their ability to pay the bills.

By 1999, the growing amount of political manipulation in Washington was attracting some of the largest PR firms in the world. Hill & Knowlton has become part of the large New York advertising conglomerate known as the WPP Group. And the largest lobbying firm in Washington, Cassidy & Associates, has been swallowed by Shandwick North America, the nation's eighth largest PR firm and itself a subsidiary of Interpublic, a large advertising agency in New York. In four years, its Washington office grew from 12 to 100 people while its annual revenue went from $1.5 million to $16.5 million. Cassidy already owned Washington's seventh largest PR firm, Powell Tate, which represents a political marriage between Jody Powell, former spokesman for the Carter administration, and Sheila Tate, formerly with the Reagan regime. Most PR firms now combine representatives of both major parties.

By combining public relations, lobbying, advertising, polling and direct mail campaigns, global firms can offer one-stop shopping to private interests who want to influence policy most efficiently. The rush to merge so many operations under one roof in recent years demonstrates how much the influence business has grown—and changed—especially in Washington. Advances in communication technology have also helped facilitate a type of grassroots lobbying called "Astroturf" that allows for top-down direction of multiple telephone, fax and e-mail operations. Such techniques were omitted from regulation by the 1995 lobby reform act.

Gerald S.J. Cassidy, founder of Cassidy & Associates, once explained to a reporter how conglomerated operations can accomplish what old-fashioned lobbying could not. He said that after the Bush administration had canceled the Seawolf nuclear submarines in 1992, his firm was hired by General Dynamics, owner of Electric Boat Division, to turn the decision around. He identified every supplier of materials for the sub from around the country, then brought them to Washington for some one-on-one lobbying with their members of Congress. Cassidy also launched a letter-writing campaign, induced retired admirals to give speeches in local districts, and arranged meetings with numerous editorial boards. As a result, he said, candidate Bill Clinton endorsed the cause, and so did Congress. It was typical of the manipulation that keeps so many people busy today in Washington.[4]

LET THE PUBLIC BE DECEIVED

But it also raises a point that is rarely discussed: that the high-priced maneuvering can drown out the public interest. To be sure, all elements of society have the right to be heard by the people's representatives in government, but the general public is losing out to private groups with the money and means to change almost any policy for the right price. The main problem is lack of disclosure: the large number of newsworthy activities not reported in the media because they are difficult to detect without time-consuming investigation. It is not often that an operator like Cassidy tells a reporter how he changed White House policy for the benefit of a paid client. Mark Dowie, former publisher of *Mother Jones* magazine, addressed the point in a book on deceptive public relations: "It is critical that consumers of media in democratic societies understand the origin of information and the process by which it is mediated, particularly when they are being deceived."[5]

An example of public and press deception occurred in connection with efforts of the tobacco industry in 1996 to combat increasing demands for details about their manufacturing process. A Washington PR firm called State Affairs, with ties to the law firm of Covington and Burling, set up a nonprofit organization entitled "Contributions Watch" ostensibly to monitor "the amount of special interest money that flows to candidates." But after it released an "independent" study on how much trial lawyers had contributed to candidates, internal company documents were passed to John Stauber, co-author of a book on PR, and Ken Silverstein, coeditor of a Washington newsletter Counterpunch. The papers showed that Philip Morris Co. was the biggest client of State Affairs and had the most to gain from any unfavorable publicity for trial lawyers, the industry's biggest enemies. The company was an ardent supporter of so-called tort reform legislation designed to limit court awards for victims of defective products. Among the papers that published the tainted State Affairs documents was *The Wall Street Journal*.

Microsoft was caught in a similar deception in an effort to influence the government's antitrust investigation of the firm. One of the groups running advertisements supporting Microsoft was the Independent Institute of Oakland, Calif. A full-page ad by it in *The New York Times* and *The Washington Post* in June 1999 contained a letter signed by 240 academic experts saying that the prosecution of Microsoft would be harmful to consumers, a point made frequently by the company. But three months later, reporter Joel Brinkley quoted Greg Shaw, public relations manager for Microsoft, acknowledging that the company had paid for the ads, a fact not known to the signers.[6] The disclosure gave the public a glimpse of a common ploy by PR agents, the exploitation of independent authorities for a cause they may not understand.

But it was just a blip on the screen of a larger effort by Microsoft to bolster its image, especially during its antitrust trial. A few years earlier, the company had little presence in Washington. Only after the telecommunications reform measure was wending its way through Congress did the firm belatedly started building a network of big-name supporters, including several former congressmen and Haley Barbour, former chairman of the Republican National Committee. It also jacked up its political contributions, particularly to Republican leaders of Congress. The effort to politicize the antitrust battle brought handsome dividends within minutes of the decision by the trial judge in November 1999 that said the firm had broken antitrust laws by hampering innovation and competition. Among those strongly criticizing the decision were House Majority Leader Dick Armey, R-Texas, and House Majority Whip Tom DeLay, R-Texas. Although the firm had lost a round in its long legal battle, it appeared to be aiming to trump any final negative decree with offsetting political action. It was putting its money and bets mostly on Republicans in the hope that a future administration in Washington would be friendlier than the Clinton crew.

In Washington, it is common for a legislative issue to become a public relations campaign. One of the biggest was the war over the Clinton health care plan in 1993. It started with an orchestrated White House offensive designed to sell the mongrel plan, a compromise between an all-inclusive, single-payer program such as in Canada or Great Britain and the existing system that left out 38 million Americans. It ended with the help of those celebrated masterpieces of spin, the already mentioned Harry and Louise ads against a perceived new government bureaucracy. In between was a steady flow of claims and counterclaims, largely from insurance industry sources, the most powerful opponents of the proposal.

EXPOSING FRONT GROUPS

In a complex contest like this one, many arguments are introduced to the news media via front groups set up by various interests to fight or back legislative changes. One group was the Council for Affordable Health Insurance, a name implying concerned consumers but actually consisting of insurance companies. Its vice president was Mark Litow, an actuary at Milliman & Robertson, who released a study contending that health care reform did not work in New York and suggesting that it would also not work nationally. Although the findings were later proved faulty, they nevertheless wound up in testimony before Congress that was repeated by leading news organizations as well as talk shows. The affair illustrated how easy it is to get devious propaganda circulated by the major media in an effort to block major legislative initiatives.[7]

One of the more sophisticated methods of influencing national policy is called "green PR" or "greenwashing." It was developed by E. Bruce Harrison, who started in PR work by devising ways of attacking Rachel Carson's historic book *Silent Spring* on behalf of business interests. The aim of going green is to help polluting firms publicize their environmental concerns through front groups, community advisory panels, "education" campaigns and other devices. Among the front groups created by Harrison were the Global Climate Coalition, which discounted the signs of global warming, and the Coalition for Vehicle Choice, which opposed government rules requiring emission controls. Harrison struck it rich with his efforts to neutralize several large environmental groups by getting them to accept large corporate contributions and add business representatives, including PR types, to their boards.

Harrison can also take much of the credit for co-opting Earth Day, an annual affair started in 1970 when young Denis Hayes called for Americans to resist business efforts to reshape the environmental movement into a mere anti-litter campaign that blamed the public. Hayes said: "Industry has turned the environmental problem over to its public relations men....If we want them to do what is right, we must make them do what is right." Two decades later, Gaylord Nelson, one of the founders of Earth Day, helped make it into a corporate commodity as a lobbyist for the Wilderness Society, one of the environmental groups depending in part on funds from corporate polluters. Nelson, a former senator with a liberal record, later defended the decision of Earth Day USA to hire Shandwick PR, one of the biggest greenwashers.[8]

Government is not only on the receiving end but is also the producing end of "engineering consent." The stated aim of government publicity offices, of course, is to dispense information to the public, but the ultimate impression depends on what is presented and how it is handled. With press secretaries and public information officers in every department or agency, the combination represents the largest PR operation in the world. Every member of Congress and all the committees have press assistants; some members even have "communication departments" responsible for everything from media coverage to issuing newsletters for constituents back home. Congress itself houses elaborate facilities for disseminating information via fax machines and e-mail plus specially designed radio and TV studios to beam messages to home states. Even the Supreme Court has a press office, although it is held in strict bounds by the justices who traditionally shun direct contact with reporters.

SPIN CYCLE POLITICS

Information central, of course, is the White House, which constantly faces a news corps suspicious of being manipulated for political reasons. Tensions have built in recent years largely because of the increasing skill of propagandists for the incumbent presidents. The first to take full advantage of television was John F. Kennedy, whose personal charm helped fashion a comparatively friendly press reception. It wasn't until Ronald Reagan, however, that the skills to dominate the news in the television age were brought to a peak. His communication staff headed by Michael Deaver succeeded so well that author Mark Hertsgaard summed up the media's stance in the title of his book on the subject, *On Bended Knee*. He contended that journalists became so subservient to the Reagan pitch that they "allowed loyalty to their executive superiors and official sources to take precedence over their obligations to the public and the country."[9]

With the arrival of Bill Clinton, the situation pretty much reversed course. Author Howard Kurtz reported that spinners for Clinton were highly competent but were constantly knocked off their guard by hostile questioning about various scandals, which inevitably drowned out official releases.[10] The tension can become unfair not only to incumbents but also to the public, a factor often submerged by the infighting between the press and the president's office. Author Michael Lewis says a reporter's desire to find the news without being co-opted often leaves "a huge void" in public discussion. "Whatever you think about Clinton and whatever his attempts to manipulate and mislead the press," he wrote, "there should have been someone with a sharp pen, an eye for detail and a high sensibility able to convey [Clinton's] point of view. A journalist the president could trust. Yet that person does not exist. And the problem is not confined to the Clintons."[11]

Manipulating perceptions is probably the best description of what public relations practitioners do, although they don't like to phrase it that way. A clue is sometimes revealed in advertisements for professional help. When the International Mass Retail Association sought a PR firm, it said it wanted the following results within 12 months: editorial board meetings with *The New York Times*, *USA Today*, *The Wall Street Journal* and *The Washington Post*; three to five articles, references or quotes in each of those publications; two or three quotes or references in national magazines such as *Time* and *Newsweek*; and national coverage of its annual trade show, including a spot on CNN and other business networks and an article in *USA Today*. Even for a skilled PR person, that's a tall order but in line with what business firms now expect—and get—for their money.

Meanwhile, publicists are swamping the Internet. This new medium can make the job of a PR agent or lobbyist infinitely easier and faster, especially for issues that demand quick action. It can also save money for business firms. To monitor customer satisfaction, one needs only to tap into various chat rooms on the Web. Some companies even hire flacks to keep tabs on customer complaints in such places, then sound off where needed. Chat rooms are becoming more and more like letters to the editors, whose columns are increasingly used deliberately by pressure groups and lobbyists to debate political issues.

COUNTERATTACK CONSULTANTS

The Internet is also becoming a battleground for competing interests in ways that were never contemplated only a few years ago. Companies aggrieved by what they deem to be overly aggressive journalism have discovered how to fight back through the World Wide Web. That's where Metabolife International went with a preemptive strike to counter ABC's plan to run a critical piece on *20/20* about the firm's controversial weight-loss pill in October 1999. After Michael Ellis, the company's president, was interviewed for over an hour but before the program ran, he posted his own video version of the interview on the Web. He then took out full-page ads urging people to visit the site. A company consultant said Ellis feared that the program would concentrate too much on adverse side effects of the pill. If he was trying to scare off the network, ABC did not buckle. In the three minutes it used from the interview, it managed not only to cite serious side effects of the pill but the fact that Ellis had no medical or scientific background and had a conviction for drug trafficking.

This was an example of crisis management in action. The expert for Ellis in the case was Mike Sitrick, a Los Angeles member of a new breed of hired guns helping firms fight adverse news reports mostly by TV newsmagazines. Another is Eric Dezenhall of Washington, D.C., who advised the Food Lion supermarket chain to make its own videotape from network outtakes and then distribute it to other news organizations in the company's battle with an ABC *Primetime Live* program in 1992. Writer Patrick J. Kiger calls them "attack flacks." As he explains, "It's an age where—as the Richard Jewells of the world have discovered—you can be put on trial and convicted on television and the Internet before you have time to punch the speed-dial to call your lawyer for advice." That's where crisis management comes in.[12]

Technology has even put a spin on spinning. Two days after the Columbine school shootings in Colorado in 1999, Robin Franzen, a staff writer at *The Oregonian*, needed sources for a story on teen-agers and the Gothic subculture that the shooters had reportedly embraced. But she faced a deadline. So she fired off an e-mail query to ProfNet, an online clearinghouse that caters to journalists. She wrote: "Looking for experts in cults, social sciences, and teens to discuss this timely subject. Need leads by 1 p.m. today." ProfNet staffers bundled her request with 22 others in one of three daily e-mail dispatches it sends to paying subscribers, which included more than 4,000 corporations, agencies, universities, nonprofits and other organizations. Franzen said she got leads on four "very useful" sources.[13]

One of the best known publicity services, PR Newswire, got into trouble for being too secretive about its practice of reporting to clients which journalists opened which release on its Web site. After *The New York Times* exposed the practice, PR Newswire agreed to stop it. Crossing an ethical line is not uncommon in the PR business, according to a survey of 1,700 professionals by *PRWeek*. One-fourth of the respondents admitted they had outright lied on the job, two out of five said they had stretched the truth and three out of five said they were not always able to check the validity of the information they imparted.[14]

The PR process is more institutionalized for smaller organizations. Publicists can score big by hiring a publicity service such as the North American Precis Syndicate Inc. (NAPS). For a fee, NAPS will distribute news releases to hundreds of news outlets. It says an average production will be used in some way by 100 to 400 newspapers, 100 to 150 TV talk shows, and 400 to 500 radio broadcasts. NAPS and companies like it use the latest technology to deliver stories, even art work, directly into newsroom computers.

Electronic delivery of press releases and other materials makes it especially easy for journalists to use them. Sometimes too easy. The *CBS Evening News*, for example, appeared to have put a lot of work into its June 13, 1991, segment on the hazards of automatic safety belts. Correspondent Mark Phillips' report included a videotape of a car being tipped on its side, the door opening and a strap allowing a dummy to fall out and be crushed beneath the car. But the videotape wasn't made by CBS, although the network's famous eye logo ran throughout the entire piece and there was no indication to viewers as to who performed the demonstration. In fact, the tape was part of a video news release created by the Institute for Injury Reduction, a lobbying group largely supported by lawyers whose clients sue auto companies for crash-related injuries. IIR lawyers, in turn, often show reports like the CBS segment in court to win cases and lucrative fees.[15]

The government's anti-drug office struck pay dirt in a big way with its publicity drive in 1997, a program that wound up making big money for broadcasters in a devious way. The scheme was unearthed by *Salon* magazine, which said it all started as part of a five-year $1 billion advertising campaign ordered by Congress. When the networks became reluctant to run some pitches, the White House Office of National Drug Control Policy (ONDCP) offered to give up some of the commercial time it had purchased if the networks would incorporate the anti-drug themes in their prime-time shows such as *Chicago Hope* and *7th Heaven*. The networks agreed, even changing some scripts to suit ONDCP though not revealing it to viewers. By January 2000, the drug office estimated that the networks had gained a $25 million bonus in ad revenue from selling the time. But they also gained a pot of bad vibes for their secret manipulation of programs.

SELF-PROMOTION EXPERTS

When it comes to self-promotion, however, nothing can beat the news business, despite its basic disdain for public relations sources. It holds the unique advantage of not having to pay cash for the time and space needed to reach an audience. The purpose often goes beyond merely attracting eyeballs for advertisers. TV networks are beginning to use their selling advantage by going retail with products such as audio and visual cassettes to promote their Web sites and pitch programs.

A contract to cover the Olympics can cause all sorts of cuts and disfigurements in news operations in order to make room for a steady blizzard of promos. During the 1994 winter Olympics coverage by CBS, its *Evening News* was snowed under with them, some featuring actual news of the Tonya Harding/Nancy Kerrigan controversy, a publicity bonanza. Did top executives put any pressure on CBS news flunkies to turn such cartwheels? "None. None. Zero. Not a phone call. Not a conversation." That was the response of Howard Stringer, president of CBS Broadcast Group, when asked by Tom Shales, *Washington Post* TV critic.[16] Shales neglected to ask the next question: "But was it all news?"

Networks are especially good at promoting their news magazines and entertainment shows on their news programs, thus taking away valuable news time. And the nets rarely skimp when it comes to building fancy sets and studios. ABC and NBC together spent a total of $85 million constructing street-front studios for their morning news programs in New York, the main purpose of which was to promote their corporate images in a dramatic fashion. *The New York Times* described the ABC version as "one part huge billboard for ABC and its parent company, Walt Disney, and one part Disney theme park." One of the most unusual billboards was created electronically by CBS so it appeared on camera to be on a nearby building. Adverse publicity made it disappear.

In the arena of self-promotion, nobody is more attuned than Al Neuharth, the man who built the Gannett media empire. His quest for fame once boomeranged when news stories described his unique way of becoming a bestselling author. For his autobiography, *Confessions of an S.O.B.*, he discovered which bookstores were tracked by the best-seller lists, then bought all available copies.

Neuharth also found a simple way to fix the credibility problems between the press and the public: build a $50 million "Newseum" for the tourist trade in Washington, D.C., and put the essence into two trailer trucks labeled NewsCapade for a continuing tour of the country. Since the exhibit opened in 1997, he has spent much of his time traveling with the trucks carrying the interactive Newseum—and his interactive self. The NewsCapade looks like a traveling circus as it rolls into one city after another, preceded by a full-page ad proclaiming "A 98-TON NEWS STORY IS HITTING TOWN." It says: "Step right up and watch the Newseum's award-winning film, 'What's News?'…Try your hand at being a news editor. Vote on the story of the century…" The ad explains that the effort is "designed to help the public and the news media understand one another better." Journalists are of mixed minds as to whether such tactics help or hurt the cause.

PR has become a big factor in efforts by news organizations to turn falling audience figures around. Instead of calling on successful publishers and broadcasters for free advice, they prefer to pay dearly for experts from other industries with little or no knowledge of this unique business. In 1997, the National Association of Newspapers, the main trade organization for daily papers, launched a $5.7 million, three-year public relations program to reverse declining circulation figures. It featured an advertising campaign starring actress Meryl Streep, quarterback John Elway, Barbara Bush and others to encourage children to read newspapers. Two years later, with circulation still falling and one more year to go on the contract, the NAA decided to double the ante to $11.5 million and switch to Coke. It hired Sergio Zyman, head of the Z Group noted for its success in marketing the soft drink. Zyman was hired to develop a five-year strategy for marketing newspapers, including a new readership survey.

News organizations have become obsessed with promoting star journalists and their work. But they rarely focus on what would appear to be their most valuable asset: credibility. When NBC bought newspaper ads to boost Brian Williams, its CNBC news anchor, it called him "the most interesting man in television." And when the network advertised its list of pundits the night before the Fourth of July 1997, Geraldo Rivera, Chris Matthews and crew were portrayed as "Freedom

Fighters." The same unrealistic puffery goes into the claim that NBC's *Nightly News* provides "all you need to know."

A year before the millennium arrived, both NBC and ABC decided that their viewers also needed a large book by their news anchors to keep abreast of events. At NBC, the title became *The Greatest Generation*, a large volume about people who experienced World War II and would be seeing the end of the 20th century. Thanks largely to a series of televised segments, the book became an immediate best seller at $24.95. What wasn't revealed was that author and anchor Tom Brokaw would be personally benefiting from the royalties, some of which he planned to donate to charity. ABC's book version, *The Century*, was a 600-page review of history often excerpted on the network's *World News Tonight*. It, too, did well in bookstores despite its $60 price tag, but co-authors Peter Jennings and Todd Brewster were reportedly not getting any royalties. A more thoughtful review, *The American Century*, by Harold Evans sold far fewer copies despite a price $10 less. For months, the network books crowded out legitimate news on evening news programs.

FRONT-PAGE PLUGS FOR BOB

The prize for star promotions, however, must go to *The Washington Post*'s quarter century of front-page promotions for itself and reporter/author Bob Woodward. The man who won a Pulitzer Prize for his Watergate reporting with Carl Bernstein produced ten books from 1974 to 1999, including *All the President's Men*, with Bernstein as co-author. When that one was published, the *Post* let loose a torrent of front-page publicity, starting with a pre-publication onslaught of recycled information that wire services helped spread to all points near and far. Two weeks before its June 18, 1974, publication, the paper's "Book World" section led with it. Two days before publication, the paper devoted most of the front page of its Sunday "Outlook" section to the book.

All of his other books also have been featured on the front page, usually for days at a time, often under the byline of reporter Haynes Johnson. All have depended greatly on unnamed sources in recreating scenes and conversations, a style that has been severely criticized by many other journalists. People described and quoted by Woodward have claimed that he did not present an accurate picture of events or conversations, though the percentage of public complaints to the total facts presented has been remarkably low. More remarkable is the degree to which the *Post* has gone to help Woodward and the corporation profit from the arrangements. Few of the page-one stories based on the books have been as newsworthy as their display would indicate. Editors left it up to Woodward to decide whether to release his findings as news before the book is published or to hold them for the book. Editor Leonard Downie insists each front-page story was news, but the paper's former ombudsman, Joann Byrd, said "the paper loses its head—and risks losing its credibility" by giving so much attention to Woodward's books.

The *Post* also lost its head over a seven-part series about Vice President Dan Quayle in January 1992 that turned into the book *The Man Who Would Be President* just as the presidential election was heating up. Many journalists called the effort a puff job, pointing out for one thing the failure to reveal how Quayle used the President's Council on Competitiveness, which he headed, as a cover to help raise millions in campaign contributions in return for relaxing regulations on automobiles, pharmaceuticals, airlines, utilities, insurance, air pollution, oil and gas, food and land developers.[17] Critics said Woodward and co-author David S. Broder got too close to their subject to allow for an objective and fair analysis. Much the same reaction followed a similar series by the *Post* on Texas Gov. George W. Bush in 1999. After it, too, was widely criticized, the paper decided to dig more deeply, resulting in a more probative series a few months later. Both series were typical of efforts designed more to win prizes than to disseminate news.

Post editors especially lose their heads when they encounter books critical of their work, often ignoring them even when they contain genuine news. Gene Lyons and the editors of *Harper's Magazine* alleged major errors in the paper's Whitewater coverage in their book, *Fools for Scandal*.[18] The paper not only refused to review the book, it declined to report the allegations. When *New Yorker* writer Jeffrey Toobin published his book on the Lewinsky scandal highly critical of then *Post* reporter Michael Isikoff,[19] the paper waited three months before having it reviewed jointly with one by Joe Conason and Gene Lyons.[20] And for a reviewer of the book, it chose a writer for *The American Spectator*, which they severely criticized for its use of paid informants in its campaign against Clinton. Both books contained major news and allegations about *Post* reporting that the paper ignored. But when a book friendly to Kenneth Starr and co-authored by *Post* reporter Susan Schmidt was published in April 2000,[21] the paper gave it a plug in its *Style* section and a page-one key to a big news story about it on page 2. For its review of the Conason/Lyons book, *The New York Times* chose one of its own Washington reporters, who chose to ignore the serious charges against the paper's performance in the Lewinsky affair.

Publicity has also been an occasional problem for CNN. Eight years after the cable network, like other news organizations, fell for the Kuwait publicity from Hill & Knowlton, the cable network fell into another Iraqi trap. This time it was due to CNN's efforts to capitalize on a "town meeting" planned by the White House to sell renewed military action against Iraq because of alleged truce violations. According to Frank Sesno, Washington bureau chief for the network, Clinton officials had asked if his organization would host an affair as a public service. He agreed on the condition that CNN would control the questioning. While other networks seethed over being excluded, the choice of CNN was said to be primarily due to its unique worldwide audience. The affair quickly turned into a shouting match between administration representatives and members of the audience who questioned the U.S. role, thus accidentally creating a serious debate over administration policy and turning a PR disaster into a positive force for public enlightenment.

Afterward, news stories focused on the failure of the administration's effort to get public backing for its planned military action. It was left to individual journalists to total up the damage inflicted on the news media by CNN in sharing the billing for such an obvious government promotion. Bruce Drake, managing editor for news at National Public Radio, summed it up by saying: "Given the degree of magnitude here—preparing the nation for military action and the possibility of lives lost—you don't play these kinds of games."

Clearly, the White House sought to use CNN as a vehicle for its own PR purposes. Then again, why not? Plenty of others did, too.

CHAPTER X

Chasing Ratings with Gotcha Journalism

The press must know that its faults and errors have ceased to be private vagaries and have become public dangers.

The Hutchins Commission

"This week," said ABC's Sam Donaldson, "we can talk about: Is this presidency over?" That same day, the *Los Angeles Times'* front page warned: "The president must tighten his grip or risk disaster." They echoed many others in the news business.

Perhaps after Travelgate, Filegate, Troopergate, Paulagate, Fostergate, Willeygate, Monicagate and the other Clinton administration media feeding frenzies such doomsday assessments might have been warranted. But Donaldson's comments came on Jan. 31, 1993—just eleven days after Clinton had taken office. By that time, the media were focused on two perceived disasters, both rendered pale by later ones. First, Clinton had softened the military ban on gays. And second, Zoe Baird withdrew as attorney-general designate because of the media firestorm over illegal aliens hired for child care and improper tax payments, a delinquency shared by millions of otherwise law-abiding Americans.

The media attitude was part of a growing syndrome known as "gotcha journalism," a new level of aggressive reporting that involves badgering vulnerable personalities for embarrassing stories designed to boost audiences without involving a lot of work in many cases. The driving force appears to be a combination of personal pique, arrogance and an urge to kill for a story, qualities that don't fit the traditional definition of political reporting. This chapter describes how the pace-makers of American journalism increasingly allow the bottom feeders to determine what qualifies as news.

Unlike previous presidents who traditionally enjoyed a press "hon-eymoon" for months after taking office, Clinton started taking heavy hits even before he was sworn in. From that vantage point, *Time* mag-azine, which had just featured him on its Jan. 4, 1993, cover as "MAN OF THE YEAR," offered a self-fulfilling prophecy: "As he takes office, Clinton's ponderous start and hedged pledges foreshadow a turbulent voyage." A week later, the newsmagazine's cover story heralded: "CLINTON'S FIRST BLUNDER" (Zoe Baird). By May, *The Washington Post* was headlining: "ANOTHER FAILED PRESIDEN-CY, ALREADY?" Its leading columnist, David Broder, pondered a "presidential meltdown." And Al Hunt, a columnist for *The Wall Street Journal*, was musing on "Meet the Press:" "I'm not sure he's going to recover from the problems of his presidency." It was becoming clear that the new regime was off to a rocky start in the nation's newsrooms if not on Main Street.

Helping to provoke the doomsayers was Clinton's reluctance to play up to the regulars of the Washington news corps during the cam-paign and later transition between administrations, particularly his occasional efforts to cut out the middle man by going on talk radio and TV. Adding insult was the decision by 32-year-old communications director George Stephanopoulos to close off part of the pressroom and clamp a partial gag on some mid-level officials. He came across to old hands as abrupt and arrogant, especially because of his lack of jour-nalism experience. Also unsettling was the decision to open press briefings to TV cameras.

An even bigger irritant was the widely publicized firing of travel office personnel. What apparently ticked off the press contingent most was the loss of old pals who treated correspondents like royalty with special favors in hotel accommodations, liquor and duty-free goods. However, this angle rarely crept into news reports. One exception was *Newsweek*'s: "DON'T MESS WITH THE MEDIA: THE WHITE HOUSE PRESS CORPS GETS ITS REVENGE." Thanks largely to the friendly testimony of Sam Donaldson of ABC, Jack Nelson of the *Los Angeles Times*, and others, travel office director Billy Dale was acquitted of embezzlement. Earlier, his offer to plead guilty and return $69,000 from his bank account had been rejected by prosecutors.

Yet comparatively little of the chumminess was reported. Nor was there much mention of Vincent Foster's suicide note saying: "The press is covering up the illegal benefits they received from the travel staff." Also not widely reported was an Associated Press dispatch saying major news companies owed lots of back taxes that the White House had failed to collect for air travel.[1] News stories and later congressional hearings focused instead on allegations that Hillary Clinton directed the firings in order to make way for friend Harry Thomason. In a review of the affair, editor Joe Conason of *The New York Observer* concluded: "If the Clintons handled Travelgate poorly, and they did, then the White House press hasn't done much better."[2]

No one disputes the need for aggressive probing if an independent press is going to adequately serve as a public watchdog over elected officials. The growing skill of federal administrations to put their own spin on everything adds to the need for doubt and suspicion. Ratcheting up the tension further is the journalistic competition for the fresh angle. The ingredients of verbal warfare are ready to burst forth whenever there is the slightest sign of weakness, ineptitude or embarrassment by those in power.

It's easy to see how an attitude of "us versus them" can turn barking dogs into pack attacks. Anyone whose work is not sufficiently hostile runs the risk of being shunned by colleagues and possibly reassigned. As it happened, ABC chose to replace a highly capable John Donvan with the more abrasive Donaldson just days before the Lewinsky story broke. Likewise, it looked to some that *Newsweek* had replaced Eleanor Clift at the White House because of her pro-Clinton stance as a regular on *The McLaughlin Group*. But she said she had asked to be shifted to columnist status after receiving a book contract. Later, however, she acknowledged: "It's awkward to be stating opinions on a talk show and be reporting the news the rest of the week. The balancing act can be difficult to handle."[3]

For most White House correspondents, pecking orders are more important than politics. Especially sensitive is any threat to established ways by newcomers from the boondocks like Arkansas and Georgia, the home states of Clinton and former President Jimmy Carter, who also took his share of cheap shots from the press. As

Donaldson had put it on the eleventh day of the Clinton presidency on his previous tour of duty at the White House: "What's happening here is people win the presidency and they come to town thinking, 'Well, I can do anything.' They're a little arrogant. They have a mandate, they think, and we have the power....Well, of course, it doesn't work that way." A lecture on arrogance by Donaldson helped set the stage.

The late *Newsweek* columnist Meg Greenfield brought the atmosphere into clearer focus shortly after Clinton's inauguration. In an unusually frank assessment of fellow Washington journalists, Greenfield wrote: "We are the dreadful children from a previous marriage. We are the insolent ones who live there, the brats who can't be sent away and absolutely refuse to be lovable. We roll our eyes to heaven and grimace every time the new man speaks. No one, it seems, has any real control over us. We are just there. And we never shut up."[4]

Pressroom attitudes soon deteriorated into a pervasive animus far from traditional reporting standards of objectivity and fairness. *The Washington Post's* Howard Kurtz described a "scandal crowd" that "never had anything nice to say about Clinton; their job was to dig up dirt. It was open warfare, and reputations were at stake. Each time these rock-throwing reporters nicked a White House official, they helped their own careers. And they were always nervous about being aced by the competition."[5] They were heading for an all-out power struggle to determine which would be left standing in the end, the Clinton presidency or the news corps. It appeared from his book title, *Spin Cycle*, that Kurtz set out to focus on White House propaganda efforts but wound up indicting fellow reporters, including some *Post* colleagues, for over-aggressive behavior.

Covering the nation's capital has not always been like this. Personal foibles, even of the adulterous kind, were traditionally considered beyond the scope of political reporting. Only in recent years has it become widely known that nearly every president in the latter half of this century carried on extramarital affairs, sometimes even in the White House, as Franklin D. Roosevelt and John F. Kennedy have been accused of doing. And it was not always because of reportorial ignorance of such shenanigans. Many of the facts were known to journalists and their bosses, but there was an unstated agreement in those days that political journalism did not extend to the private lives of presidents or other public figures.

Since then, media practices have changed with a vengeance, getting more personal and aggressive. In the department of presidential aspirants, one of the first victims of the new style was Sen. Thomas Eagleton, D-Mo., whose electric shock treatment was made into a *cause celebre* by columnist Jack Anderson. The resulting flood of news stories in 1972 effectively ruined his chances of becoming the vice presidential nominee on the Democratic ticket with George McGovern. Then there was former Sen. Gary Hart, D-Colo., who was trapped in his adulterous love nest by stalking reporters as he was preparing to run for the White House. His hopes sank with a flurry of headlines and an embarrassing photograph taken aboard the good ship "Monkey Business."

On the Republican side, media tempests included allegations of sexual harassment swirling around President Bush's selection of Clarence Thomas to the Supreme Court; accusations of drinking and womanizing that effectively killed Bush's appointment of John Tower as Secretary of Defense and political charges against his choice of Robert Bork for the Supreme Court. The latter case disturbed Republicans so much that they coined the verb "borked" to describe an unfair media attack. But the issue in his case, unlike the others, was not personal but his previous court rulings and partisanship. Other notable targets were President Gerald Ford for accidentally implying there was no Soviet domination of Eastern Europe; former Vice President Dan Quayle, who has constantly been depicted as a bubble-head unable even to spell the word "potato" because of a mental lapse as an observer at a spelling bee; and President Jimmy Carter, who was ridiculed for having detected a certain "malaise" in the populace and allegedly having been attacked in a small boat by a "killer rabbit."

Author Larry J. Sabato dramatically documented the early phases of "gotcha" journalism in a 1991 book titled, *Feeding Frenzy: How Attack Journalism Has Transformed American Politics*. He and his student helpers looked into 36 cases over four decades. Included were only one in the 1950s (Nixon's slush fund), three in the 1960s, seven in the 1970s and 25 in the 1980s. They made no attempt to separate cases where there might have been justifiable cause for extra attention, such as Nixon's fund and Ted Kennedy's accident at

Chappaquiddick, from others based on undocumented charges, such as rumors that Michael Dukakis was under the care of a psychiatrist, that Geraldine Ferraro's husband was somehow involved with the mafia and that Jack Kemp was a homosexual. The implication was that all matters were overplayed and to an unreasonable degree. Although that point could be argued in each case, there could be no disagreement that journalists were getting more of their kicks from personal attacks on public figures. Sabato concluded in 1991 that the phenomenon had reached "inquisitorial proportions."

But the proportions kept growing. Among targets of media overkill outside the Clinton White House in the last five years of the century were:

- **Richard Jewell**, who survived nearly three months of media stakeouts at his home after being named by an FBI agent as a suspect in the Olympic bombing in Atlanta in 1996 and essentially being proven guilty by, among others, NBC news, which paid for its excess in a private settlement.

- **Mike Espy**, former Secretary of Agriculture, who was acquitted of corruption charges in December 1998 after a spate of stories alleging that he traded minor favors with a large chicken processor under his department's jurisdiction.

- **Charles Robb**, U.S. Senator from Virginia who endured 19 months of adultery allegations in the news and an unsuccessful NBC attempt to get him and the woman in question on the same program. A grand jury decided not to indict him in 1995.

- **Henry Cisneros**, former Secretary of Housing and Urban Affairs, found guilty in 1999 of lying about an affair to prosecutors after the press had batted around intimate tape recordings furnished to the media by his mistress in a case going back to 1994.

- **Bruce Babbitt**, Secretary of the Interior, who was the subject of 47 stories in six months of 1998 by *The New York Times* and *The Washington Post* alleging bribery involving Indian casinos, triggering a special prosecutor despite what *The Washington Monthly* contended in a detailed analysis was a lack of proof. He was acquitted the next year.

- **Larry Lawrence**, a former ambassador to Switzerland, war veteran and political contributor to Clinton, whose burial at Arlington National Cemetery was propelled into a national feeding frenzy in 1997 by Rush Limbaugh alleging that burial plots were sold for political donations. No evidence ever turned up, according to Kelly Heyboer, who analyzed the case for *American Journalism Review* the following March.

- **Kelly Flinn**, a female Air Force pilot, the subject of many news stories in 1997 focusing almost entirely on allegations of adultery with an enlisted airman, even though the main charge against her was for lying about the relationship.

- **Rep. Henry Hyde**, the Illinois Republican chairman of the House Judiciary Committee and later the impeachment team, whose adulterous affair 33 years earlier was exposed by *Salon*, an Internet magazine.

Some would add former Sen. Bob Packwood, R-Ore., to the list because of the barrage of stories from nearly a dozen women charging him with various forms of sexual harassment in 1996. But his situation turned out to be quite different for three reasons: (1) the large number of accusers on record; (2) the timing of the first major news story (by *The Washington Post*) shortly *after* his narrow reelection; and (3) the failure to give as much coverage to a more important story: his dear-diary accounts of numerous conflicted dealings with lobbyists. The *Post* took pains to defend its delay in reporting the matter, claiming that the half-dozen documented cases it had well before the voting were not enough. Packwood eventually resigned to become a lobbyist.

Journalistic feeding frenzies go back to the days of Thomas Jefferson and Sally Hennings and earlier. But the intensity and frequency of them have increased, especially since 1991 when Sabato's book was published. Instead of sobering up, the news corps went on further binges, climaxing with the two long Simpson trials. When they were finally over, journalists became destitute for an encore. They grasped at relatively minor sensations such as the JonBenet Ramsey murder and the Marv Albert trial involving kinky sex. As authors Bill Kovach and Tom Rosenstiel put it, "The fascination with [these stories] might best be understood as this new hungry media culture trying to create another blockbuster. It didn't quite work."

Then came Monica, and the hound dogs were back in business with a vengeance.

EXPANDING PRESS FREEDOM

Helping to fuel the new aggressiveness was a 1964 Supreme Court ruling known as *New York Times v. Sullivan*. Up to that point, the press essentially had to prove that its statements were true in order to defend itself against libel claims. In the *Times* case, an Alabama sheriff said he had been falsely portrayed in an advertisement and sued for damages to his reputation. The court rejected his claim on the ground that he was a public official and did not need libel protection because elected and appointed officials face eventual approval or rejection by voters. According to the court, the press could even utter falsehoods as long as they were not done "knowingly or recklessly." Later court decisions expanded the press's near immunity from libel to all public figures such as movie stars and sports announcers. In Gen. William Westmoreland's libel case against CBS, Judge Pierre Laval went so far as to say a news organization "has no obligation under the libel law to treat the subject of (its) accusations fairly or evenhandedly."[6]

The increased freedom from libel suits has emboldened journalists to take action for the public good. Bob Woodward and Carl Bernstein of Watergate fame are often cited as models of gung-ho reporting, especially in the public sphere. The constant hunt for an exclusive story and competition among news organizations have inspired many reporters and news organizations to do exemplary work to keep the public informed of important events. But the results have often been public resentment as well as a noticeable decline in journalism standards as illustrated by the increase in unverified charges, anonymous sources and massive attention to relatively minor matters in the news.

An early example in the Clinton administration involved the famous $200 haircut that the new president reportedly got at Los Angeles International Airport on June 13 of his first year in office. News reports that were flashed repeatedly around the world—and still reverberate—said the tonsorial interlude had tied up air traffic, putting as many as three dozen planes into holding patterns. The simple truth—and White House denials—got trampled in the urge to spread an offbeat yarn. The facts did not arrive until three months later when *Newsday* reported that a search of official records under the Freedom of Information Act had found that no planes had been put on hold, and only one plane was delayed, a total of two minutes. Yet, according to David Shaw, the *Los Angles Times* media writer, *The New York Times* and the three major networks ran nothing to correct the record while *The Washington Post* ran only one paragraph. By that time, the *Post* had run 50 stories, including nine on page one, according to Joanne Byrd, its ombudsman.

The motivating force for many of the negative stories about the Clinton administration extended well beyond the Beltway, led by a band of bitter partisans seeking to ferret out and pass on any information that might lead to Clinton's political demise. Hillary Clinton finally put a public label on it during a January 1998 *Today* show when she cited a "vast right-wing conspiracy that has been conspiring against my husband since the day he announced for president." She was referring to a loose network of Clinton-hating news organs, ultra-conservative groups and assorted ideologues largely financed by Richard Mellon Scaife, an heir to the Mellon fortune.

Although Scaife denied he was leading a conspiracy, it was his millions that helped drive a large propaganda machine featuring his own *Pittsburgh Tribune Review* and the Scaife-financed *American Spectator*, the Western Journalism Center and Newt Gingrich's GOPAC fundraising organization. Media outlets most interested in distributing their allegations—often regardless of whether there was any evidence—ranged from cable news channels CNBC and MSNBC to Jay Leno and other late-night comedians; right-wing radio talkmeisters such as Rush Limbaugh, G. Gordon Liddy and Oliver North; politico-evangelists Pat Robertson and Jerry Falwell; book publishers such as Regnery; and filmmakers such as Jeremiah Films.

The scandal mania coincided with rapid changes in communications technology and news production that made it easier than ever for such forces to spread questionable allegations around the world without going through the traditional news processes. The emergence of talk radio and 24-hour cable news channels with their rapacious appetites for spicy material, plus the explosion of Internet sites, online magazines and chat rooms, assured the instantaneous transfer of information and opinions that don't fit the rules and standards of even a decade ago.

With all these outlets hungry for sensation, it became easy for Clinton haters to obtain generous time and space in the mainstream media, particularly the highly partisan editorial pages of *The Wall Street Journal*. Often it would take only a phone call from a young ideologue like David Bossie, Floyd Brown or David Brock (a self-described "right-wing attack dog" before his public apologia) promising hot tips. Brown, who helped create the infamous Willie Horton ads attacking Michael Dukakis in the 1988 presidential elections, ran an intensive anti-Clinton operation named Citizen United. Allegations were faxed around the clock to more than 1,000 reporters and talk show hosts. Working closely with Bossie, Brown found easy pickings with a mixture of unfounded rumors and documented allegations. In a fund-raising letter, Brown claimed: "Investigative television reporters from ABC and CBS have come to me and Citizens United so that we could present our evidence to them." He also named NBC, *The Wall Street Journal*, *The Boston Globe*, Gannett and the three main newsweeklies among his patsies.Although his claims were disputed by some of the named firms, he became wildly successful. Reporter Trudy Lieberman said a check of some 200 stories showed "an eerie similarity" to Brown's partisan reports in many reputable news outlets. Citing examples in the *New York Times*, *Washington Post*, *Los Angeles Times*, *Time*, *Newsweek*, *USA Today*, *Wall Street Journal*, ABC, CNN, and CBS, she concluded that the press had "shamelessly taken the handouts dished up by a highly partisan organization...without identifying the group as the source of their information."[7]

Another effective route to major news outlets involved the Internet and a transatlantic deviance, whereby rumors posted on the World Wide Web or in a fringe periodical such as the *Spectator*, were picked up by the London *Sunday Telegraph* via its American correspondent, Ambrose Evans-Pritchard. The unproven charges were then instantly blown back across the Atlantic to the persistently anti-Clinton *Washington Times*, *New York Post* and *The Wall Street Journal* editorial pages. Once an allegation reached this level in the media food chain, the rest of the press usually felt compelled to join the motley crew for fear of being accused of withholding legitimate news.

If an important news organization didn't fall in line, a blunter instrument was sometimes used: a full-page ad paid for by Scaife money to force recalcitrant papers to toe the line. According to author James D. Retter, that was how the Western Journalism Center helped spread the idea that Vincent Foster might have been murdered by someone in the White House. He found such ads in the *New York Times, Washington Post, Chicago Tribune, Los Angeles Times* and other papers.[8] Another Scaife-funded group using this ploy has been the oxymoronic Accuracy in Media.

Using advertisements for such purposes puts publishers and editors into a bind of being damned whether they accept or reject them. Newspapers have no legitimate reason for refusing such ads, but by doing so, they risk being seen as pressing their staffs to suspend the rules of good journalism for political purposes. The allegation that Foster was somehow murdered first reached critical mass when Rush Limbaugh blithely passed on an item from an obscure newsletter alleging that Foster was killed in a Virginia apartment maintained by Hillary Clinton and then dragged to the park where his body was found. Rather than be chastised by the rest of the press for such outlandish charges, Limbaugh was invited to participate in a Ted Koppel town meeting on press practices, where he was allowed to defend his performance without serious challenge. Although three formal investigations of the Foster affair concluded that it was a suicide, Scaife and many others continued to refuse to accept the rulings.

What made Hillary Clinton's departure from her long silence on the topic newsworthy was the failure of the mainstream press up to that point to let the public in on the extensive rumor factory from which many juicy leads were flowing. The White House had issued a 300-page packet more than two years earlier documenting the elaborate anti-Clinton media network, but it was greeted as a joke and ignored by reporters. According to a data search, *The New York Times* and *The Washington Post* did not address the matter until Mrs. Clinton's public remarks. Leading news organizations were not anxious to call attention to their own use of such dubious and partisan sources. Nor did they want to face the reality of how far they were drifting from traditional journalistic standards or how much public distrust they were engendering as shown by the polls, which seemed to indicate that the public was sated by scandal news.

The main thread running through the Clinton bashing was Whitewater, the first big target of the media and the impetus for several investigations. From the start, numerous nonpartisan observers considered the allegations surrounding the failed land deal substantially afflicted with hype, errors, unreliable sources and faulty interpretations of fact. Yet the two organizations most responsible for the poor journalism were not tabloids but the best of the lot: *The New York Times* and *The Washington Post*.

THE WHITEWATER WASHOUT

The *Times* broke the Whitewater story early in the 1992 presidential campaign and generally set the tone for all subsequent coverage. Based largely on tips from Clinton enemies in Arkansas, the original article on March 8, 1992, by Jeff Gerth laid out the now-familiar charges of unethical and illegal behavior by the Clintons in a speculative project in which they lost some $30,000. According to experts on the topic, however, his and other stories were replete with substantial errors from the start. One critic was Gene Lyons, a veteran journalist with the *Arkansas Democrat-Gazette*. After a detailed study of coverage, he concluded that America's two leading papers not only "bungled the Whitewater story" but made it their main goal "to protect themselves and their damaged credibility." With a few honorable exceptions, he added, "the rest of the media pack has obediently followed." In his book, *Fools for Scandal*, which the *Times* reviewed but not the *Post*, he called their work "possibly the most politically charged case of journalistic malpractice in recent American history."

Another authority who studied the record was Gilbert Cranberg, former editor of *The Des Moines Register's* editorial pages. He focused on what he saw as a basic error repeated countless times yet never corrected. In a magazine article, Cranberg demonstrated that the widely accepted "fact" that $50,000 of the felonious $300,000 loan from David Hale to Susan McDougal was used to prop up the Whitewater land development was false.[9] Apprised of this and other alleged errors, the *Times* and *Post* refused to respond. They also declined invitations from the editors of *Harper's* magazine to discuss the allegations in an open forum held at the National Press Club in October 1994. The *Post's* only response came when it printed an op-ed piece by Lyons.

The first independent prosecutor to investigate the Whitewater allegations was Jay Stephens, a former Republican U.S. attorney and adversary of the Clintons, who had tried to prevent his appointment. After spending nearly $4 million and two years looking into the matter, he concluded on Dec. 13, 1995, that "there is no basis to charge the Clintons with any kind of primary liability for fraud or intentional misconduct...nor...any claim of secondary or derivative liability for the possible misdeeds of others." *The New York Times* buried the news with a short story on page 12. The *Post* inserted it into the 11th paragraph of a front-page story devoted to a minor subpoena matter. The three major networks ignored the news.

Why were the acknowledged standard-setters of the news business so flippant with the facts, so one-sided in their presentations and so unwilling to discuss their performance? Mortimer Zuckerman, then editor-in-chief of *U.S. News & World Report*, offered a clue when he wrote in January 1996: "The press gives the impression that it has invested so much capital in the search for a scandal that it cannot drop it when the scandal evaporates." As for the Republicans, he said they "give the impression that if one slander does not work, they will try another." He added: "No wonder the nation holds Congress, the White House and the media in such contempt; the people know that the press seems to be acting like a baby—a huge appetite at one end and no sense of responsibility at the other."

As media interest in Whitewater began to subside, journalists turned to sex angles for kicks. One of the longest running subplots was Paula Jones's efforts to win an apology—and cash—from President Clinton because of an alleged encounter in a Little Rock hotel in 1991 while Clinton was still Arkansas governor. In a December 1993 article in the *American Spectator* entitled "Troopergate," David Brock quoted several state troopers who claimed they had set up numerous Clinton sexcapades. Some reporters were wary of the claims because the chief person pushing them was an ardent Clinton adversary, Cliff Jackson, the attorney for the troopers.

Based on Brock's casual mention of a woman named "Paula," news organizations apparently thought they had the sex angle that might end Clinton's political career. Within days, TV and cable channels were hot on the trail, along with many newspapers. But the dubious nature of her claims and the shifting allegations of the troopers who were looking to make big bucks on a book slowed coverage. By March 1997, her attorney had become thoroughly frustrated at the lack of progress in Jones' suit against the president. So he arranged an exclusive interview for Jones with *Post* reporter Mike Isikoff, who had become a key contact for the anti-Clinton crew. *Post* editors approved the interview but held up his story because of questions about her credibility.

Then CBS's *60 Minutes* gave Jones the platform she wanted. As weeks went by, Isikoff became increasingly frustrated. He finally blew up, was suspended for two weeks and eventually transferred to another *Post* property, *Newsweek*, where he became a lightning rod for other alleged and real Clinton misdeeds and later ran into some foot-dragging of a different kind. The *Post* published his edited interview on May 4 after a full-page ad was placed in *The Washington Post* by the right-wing Accuracy in Media asking "WHO IS PAULA JONES?" and "WHY IS THE POST SUPPRESSING HER CHARGE OF SEXUAL HARASSMENT?" Shortly afterward, Jones sued Clinton.

When the Lewinsky story broke, the three network anchors were in Cuba to cover the Pope's visit, a world-class event that was quickly relegated to also-ran status on the evening reports. CNN switched to live coverage of Mike McCurry's White House briefing in time to hear ABC's Sam Donaldson ask if Clinton would cooperate with an impeachment inquiry. What previously were occasional feeding frenzies turned into a non-stop binge. NBC led the way with around-the-clock Lewinsky on its two cable channels, CNBC and MSNBC.

The saturation coverage—and rush to judgment—became topics of a panel discussion later at the Columbia Journalism School. Attorney Floyd Abrams, an expert on the First Amendment, perceived "a tone, a mood, almost an exultation, as if to say: 'We've got him.'" Mara Liasson, White House correspondent for National Public Radio, called the matter "awful in every way you could imagine, for the presidency, for the American public, for journalism."[10]

CONSEQUENCES OF COMPETITION

The media didn't seem to be getting the message the polls were conveying to everyone else: The public wasn't as excited about Clinton's sex life as the media were. Instead, many journalists appeared to take offense at the poll data showing his popularity remaining high despite the embarrassing revelations. Journalists seemed determined to play up scandal morsels regardless of the possible adverse consequences to the public and the press itself. Competitive pressures to constantly find new angles made a difficult situation worse. A major embarrassment for the media was the erroneous report on Jan. 25, 1998, by ABC's Jackie Judd, NBC's Tom Brokaw and *The Dallas Morning News* that a Secret Service agent had caught Clinton and Lewinsky in an intimate moment. Other embarrassments included:

- **The Wall Street Journal's** false allegations that a White House steward had told Starr of seeing Clinton and Lewinsky alone next to the oval office.

- **National Journal** columnist Stuart Taylor's decision to talk secretly with Starr about a job offer while bashing Clinton regularly in his columns and on talk shows.

- **U.S. News & World Report's** "exclusive" about what was on selected Tripp tapes without revealing their source or being allowed to copy them in order to confirm accuracy.

- **NBC Tim Russert's** decision to have Drudge on *Meet the Press* and allow him to dish out falsehoods about other Lewinskys ready "to come out from behind the curtains this week."

- **Fox News'** speculation about an alleged second intern sexually involved with Clinton.

As errors and misjudgments proliferated, the public could plainly see. A poll by the Pew Research Center for The People & The Press in February 1998, only a month after the Lewinsky bomb had landed, reported that 63 percent felt the press was often inaccurate, a seven-point increase in one year. The public that the media so often dismissed as out of it was more observant than journalists assumed. After looking at 1,565 statements in the media, the Committee of Concerned Journalists found 41 percent not factual (being either analysis, opinion or speculation), 30 percent without a source and only 26 percent based on a named source. One problem was the long wait to confirm details from unnamed sources in the prosecutor's office. Although most of the undocumented points—the stained blue dress, for example—were eventually documented in Starr's report to Congress, others were left dangling, adding to the public's suspicions about the news business.

COMPROMISING ENTANGLEMENTS

As the Lewinsky saga unfolded, many journalists themselves expressed alarm at what they saw as declining standards. In the first edition of *Brill's Content*, publisher Stephen Brill quoted Starr as claiming that there was nothing improper about conversations between him and his staff and journalists despite the law prohibiting the release of grand jury investigations. Eventually, some 24 alleged leaks to journalists from Starr's office became the subject of a court investigation. Among news organizations defending Starr was *The Washington Post*, which called the complaints about his tactics "a coordinated smear campaign."[11] Not many people knew that the *Post* harbored a deep sense of gratitude to Starr for a favorable decision he made over a decade earlier as a judge in a libel suit filed by Mobil Oil.

Brill concluded that press performance was "a true scandal, a true instance of an institution being corrupted to its core." He added that competition "for scoops to toss out into a frenzied, high-tech news cycle seems to have so bewitched almost everyone that the press eagerly let the man in power (Starr) write the story—once Linda Tripp and Lucianne Goldberg put it together for him."[12] He lamented the way reporters and their organizations became involved in the investigation rather than retaining their independence.

With publication of the independent counsel's referral to Congress, news organizations expected to be redeemed. After five years of scandal headlines and breathless bulletins, here at last would be some serious charges. But few stories pointed out the failure of Starr to find any prosecutable offenses against the Clintons in the Whitewater affair. Nobody was ready for the next scandal. It came not at the White House but the House of Representatives as it prepared to vote for impeachment. The casualty was Rep. Bob Livingston, the Louisiana Republican chosen to succeed former Speaker Newt Gingrich, who himself had quit the speakership and his seat in Congress as the fall guy for the disappointing Republican results in the 1996 elections. Livingston's resignation on the House floor, with the nation poised to watch Clinton's public hanging, resulted from his fear of facing news stories about his own adulterous relationships, which *Hustler* publisher Larry Flynt was reportedly on the verge of exposing but did not do until months later. Suddenly, even a pornographer was playing gotcha, and many in the press felt embarrassed to have him on the team. Yet the rampant hypocrisy made it big news.

Those who expected to report Clinton's ouster from the White House wound up instead reporting Livingston's departure from Congress and Clinton's acquittal on perjury and obstruction of justice charges after a Senate trial in February. To the dismay of many Republicans and journalists, polls showed strong public disapproval of both institutions, particularly the GOP for its insistence on pushing impeachment rather than a possible censure, which had appeared likely to pass. The day after the House voted to impeach Clinton along party lines, *USA Today* reported the president's approval rating had hit 73 percent, the highest point in his presidency.

Gotcha journalism seemed to be boomeranging. While its editorial page continued to bash Clinton without letup, *The Wall Street Journal* led with: "ONE LIKELY CASUALTY OF THE CLINTON YEARS: THE SCANDAL GAMBIT." The subhead read: "ON THE RISE SINCE WATERGATE, MUDSLINGING FALLS SHORT OR BACKFIRES." The article quoted a number of political campaign consultants who felt that scandal mongering had lost its effectiveness.[13]

But the article did not signal the end of questionable media attacks against Clinton. While the Senate was preparing to begin its impeachment trial, Drudge set off another round by reporting that the *Star* tabloid of Gennifer Flowers fame was testing the DNA of a black Arkansas youth who his mother said had been fathered by Clinton in the 1980s. While the *Star* awaited results, the allegations quickly found their way into Rupert Murdoch's Fox News and his *New York Post*, the Hearst-owned *Boston Herald*, Mort Zuckerman's *New York Daily News*, the Moon-owned *Washington Times*, MSNBC, Jay Leno's monologue and numerous radio talk shows and Internet chat rooms. When the tests came back negative, the silence of the media was deafening. Here was a new phenomenon, a much-criticized supermarket tabloid behaving more responsibly than its uppity cousins. The media world was turning upside down.

Leading news organizations were even finding ways to make like tabloids without appearing like tabloids. They simply assumed the posture of an observer in order to report what awful things other news outlets were reporting while at the same time avoiding the ignominy of having to trumpet the sleaze in the same way. This form of journalistic "having your cake and eating it too" was perfected at *The Washington Post* by Howard Kurtz, its media reporter, and at *The New York Times* by Felicity Barringer and others. With this ploy, the *Post* had no problem, for example, spreading news nuggets from the *Globe* indicating that sportscaster Frank Gifford had cheated on his wife Kathy Lee without the stigma of big headlines. As Kurtz described it: "If [news organizations] eagerly report the allegations, they are accused of wallowing in sleaze. If they ignore the allegations, they are accused of covering up for one side or the other. If they try to check out the allegations, they are criticized for invading people's privacy."

When the Senate finally concluded its impeachment trial in February without mustering a majority for either perjury or obstruction of justice, many people assumed that it would end the political and journalistic marathon to target Bill Clinton. They were quickly proved wrong. Clinton's acquittal apparently merely raised some frustration and anger levels another notch. NBC soon joined other news organizations, including *The Washington Post*, in a determined search for more details about a 20-year-old rape allegation against Clinton by "Jane Doe No. 5" although the *Post* had already printed one story earlier. Kenneth Starr had checked out the accusations long before but found them not credible enough to highlight in his impeachment report to the House, although he had included them in the truckload of material sent there.

Nor did House leaders cite the matter in formal impeachment charges, although they sent delegates to interview the woman and sought to revive the issue in the Senate with a whispering campaign reported widely by the press. The *Post* obviously did not feel that the information it had dug up was substantial enough to print another story without further checking. Nor did NBC want to air its interview with Juanita Broaddrick by Lisa Myers on January 20. But the network's internal dilemma was publicized by Internet rumormonger Matt Drudge and echoed on other Web sites, radio and TV talk shows, including MSNBC, the *New York Post* and *Washington Times*.

POLITICS ABOVE PRINCIPLE

As days stretched into weeks, and with NBC showing no sign of airing what it had found, anti-Clinton operatives and their allies in the news media began to get desperate. *The Washington Times* led the way with a front-page banner: "THE CLINTON STORY THAT'S TOO HOT TO HANDLE."[14] Fox News, which broadcast the accusations without having interviewed the woman, showed anchor Brit Hume on the air wearing a "Free Lisa Myers" button in his lapel. On MSNBC, Rep. Chris Cannon, R-Utah, complained to a network representative: "Everybody knows in Washington, D.C., that your colleague Lisa Myers has Jane Doe No. 5 on videotape and you haven't broken the story." Frustrated partisans at *The Wall Street Journal* editors decided to force the issue. They dispatched right-wing media critic Dorothy Rabinowitz to Arkansas to interview Broaddrick. She returned with more detailed allegations, which the paper printed on its editorial page on Feb. 19 without further checking. The paper's news staff had possessed basically the same information since 1992 but had declined to publish it. One problem was the absence of any formal charges. Another was Broaddrick's earlier denials.

The *Journal* article set off still another round of below-the-belt journalism. Goaded by Fox's Hume and others, *Washington Post* editors suddenly saw no problem in printing the accusation on the front page after obtaining permission from Broaddrick to use an earlier off-the-record interview. Finally, three days later came NBC's extensive *Dateline* interview, followed by reports in countless other news outlets, including *The New York Times*, which said it and the *Los Angeles Times* had covered the story during the 1992 election campaign.

By this point, *The Wall Street Journal* dropped any remaining restraint. It ran a long article on its editorial page "In Defense of Tabloid Sleaze" written by Mark Steyn, a columnist for Britain's *Daily Telegraph*, who mocked the energy spent by respectable news organizations checking facts. "The responsible thing to do," he wrote, "would be to triple-check your sources a couple more times and sit on the story until, oh, sometime midway through Al Gore's second term." He added: "Enough with the dignity....America's mainstream media need more tabloid values, not less."[15]

Sabato had written about the overall damage to the democratic process from such journalism a decade earlier: "The abuses painfully visible during feeding frenzies damage the political fabric of America by cheapening public discourse, trivializing the campaign agenda, breeding cynicism and discouraging able people from seeking public office."[16] They also tend to drive moderate politicians out of office and lead to a steady increase in partisanship. Yet it is the moderates in politics who make democracy work with their ability to compromise and fashion legislation and regulations to meet public needs.

The more the press plays up personal scandal, the more likely there will be public furors followed by investigations and rounds of press attention to divert the public gaze from more significant matters. Kenneth Starr probably would not have engaged in some of his more questionable prosecutorial tactics had there not been plenty of news outlets and commentators anxious to play gotcha with him. The news media have the power to stop the cycle of sleaze, but the pressure to maximize profits by appealing to the lowest common denominator means that is not likely to happen soon.

During the 2000 presidential campaign, the gotcha crew went after George W. Bush early in the primaries. Reporters smelled blood because of rumors that he had sniffed cocaine and was a closet alcoholic well beyond his formative years. Queries were relevant because of his own push for tough drug legislation that might have landed him behind bars instead of in the governor's chair. Despite his denial of drug use after the age of 28 and lack of any evidence to the contrary, some reporters kept persisting. Their quest was ended by a CNN-Time Inc. poll indicating that 84 percent of Americans would not disqualify him from the presidency even if he had used cocaine in his 20s. Only then did reporters start a more relevant probe of his record as governor and the issues it raised for his presidential run.

His opponent, Vice President Gore, became a more classic victim of gotcha journalism. During the Clinton administration, pundits stenciled him as wooden even though all who knew him socially considered him anything but. Then in the primaries, reporters began relaying mischievous Republican jibes that he was a confused liar. His misworded claim that "during my service in the U.S. Congress, I took the initiative in creating the Internet" was turned into a boast that he had "invented" the Internet. The fact that he led congressional efforts to clean up toxic waste dumps was turned into a claim that "I was the one that started it all." And Gore's assertion that he was a model for the leading character in Erich Segal's *Love Story* was ridiculed even though Segal affirmed it. Like another vice president, Dan Quayle, Gore appeared to be marked forever by the media as a babbling dunce.

In the gotcha business, there was no more pitiful victim of journalistic excess than 6-year-old Elian Gonzalez, the Cuban boy found floating in an inner tube on Thanksgiving Day 1999 after his mother had drowned at sea trying to reach Florida. For four and a half months at his great uncle's home in Miami's "Little Havana," he was besieged and exploited by news crews as well as by his anti-Castro relatives. ABC, the Disney network, won a furious race to get an exclusive interview with the boy, in which he was questioned by Diane Sawyer about returning to Cuba, a clip that was repeatedly played on the air. ABC later joined many other broadcast outfits in airing a home videotape purporting to show the boy volunteering that he did not want to return to Cuba. The camera had been supplied by Univision, a Spanish language network. It was another example of how the mainstream media now outdo the supermarket tabloids in sleaze.

It showed that not even a child can escape the gotcha crews.

CHAPTER XI

Tilting News Toward the Powers That Be

[The press] will not without effort escape the natural bias of what it is. Yet this bias must be known and measurably overcome or counterbalanced if freedom is to remain.

The Hutchins Commission

In late 1999, a jury in Memphis ruled that a conspiracy between a businessman and the federal government led to the 1968 death of the Rev. Martin Luther King Jr. The December 8 verdict, following more than 30 years of debate, legal maneuvering and investigation, repudiated the official theory that James Earl Ray acted alone in assassinating King. The trial took a month and involved the testimony of more than 70 witnesses before the jury returned the first courtroom verdict on the mystery.

To some journalists, the trial and verdict were major stories. But leading news organizations played it as a minor event. Reviewing coverage afterward, *Washington Post* reporter Ruben Castaneda quoted the King family's attorney William F. Pepper as saying that "most people didn't even know this trial was going on." *The New York Times* and *Washington Post* ran a total of three stories during the trial and buried the verdict on inside pages, while the commercial networks ran brief items deep in their evening news programs. *Newsweek* and *Time* reported nothing. The verdict didn't put the festering mystery to rest, but it revealed some intriguing leads for further reporting if anyone were interested.[1]

The paltry coverage and its astonishing conclusion could also have reflected a lack of media interest in a matter appealing primarily to a minority audience that didn't fit the target population most wanted by editors and advertisers. Could news executives have become so much a part of the bored, elite class that they would downplay issues that don't resonate with their own set of values? Or could it have been another case—like the Kennedy assassination and the Iran hostage episode—where the news establishment strongly defends the official version against all challengers? Editors were skeptical of the conflicting stories and the fact that it was a civil, not a criminal, proceeding. Castenada quoted the *Times* managing editor as saying: "No offense to the jurors of Memphis, it was kind of like winning a verdict from Judge Judy and then proclaiming yourself vindicated." In any case, those who ran the larger news outlets again set the pace for smaller ones, which also largely dismissed the trial.

The fact is that American journalists, particularly those who set the news patterns for the nation, have become increasingly removed from the mainstream of American life. Their education and income levels, as discussed earlier in this book, have escalated well beyond what they were even a decade ago, setting them far above most of those for whom their work is intended. This chapter focuses on how these growing gaps affect the selection and treatment of news.

In their pursuit of maximum profits, corporations with news components have come to narrow their main focus on two especially desirable audiences: well-to-do people sought by advertisers and advertisers themselves. It means that journalism is more business driven than ever. Social welfare, the environment and consumer affairs tend to be covered for how they affect business rather than how they affect people as citizens, parents, workers or consumers. Consumer stories tend to focus on how to get rich, stay rich and use wealth wisely. People not participating in the economic boom often get painted out of the picture. News affecting minorities often gets stingy coverage or is portrayed in a stereotypical manner that does not necessarily reflect news values.

Leaders of media conglomerates and their top journalistic stars live like royalty. Top officials rank among the highest paid business leaders in the nation. In 1999, Steve Case of America Online pocketed $117 million in salary, bonuses and other compensation, making him the fifth highest paid chief executive officer in the country. He took home another $303 million over the previous three years despite the company's 119 percent negative return on equity. As of June 1999, he retained $1.26 billion in unexercised options. *Business Week* ranked him as the executive whose company "did the worst relative to [his] pay."

Other media chiefs were not far behind in pay levels. General Electric CEO Jack Welch received $93 million from his job in 1999, a one-third increase from 1998, placing him seventh among the highest paid executives. His compensation included $49 million from options and $31 million in long-term incentive payouts, making him one of the nation's top ten in executive compensation for five consecutive years. Disney's Michael Eisner got $50 million, landing him in the 19th spot, plus $636 million over the previous three years.[2] He signed an options contract in 1997 that could give him $771 million more depending on the price of company stock. Disney even managed to provide $97 million in a severance package in 1996 to Michael Ovitz, after his 14-month failure to fit in as company president. Stockholders could vote to reduce these immense sums, but they rarely do.

These executives could become richer should their companies do better in the stock market. Case stood to earn $1.3 billion from nonexercised options, while Welch could claim $436 million and Time Warner's Gerald Levin another $378 million. Bill Gates, often referred to as the richest man in the world as Microsoft's chief executive, had stock in his company worth $70 billion at one time.[3]

INCOME GAP WIDENING

Such phenomenal amounts are divisive enough for industrial firms because of the resentment that can cause with fellow employees and members of the public. But they are even more unsettling when they occur in organizations dealing with news and comment, for they create a fundamental conflict with the public service phase of journalism. They not only represent unprecedented greed but an unconscionable robbery from news operations whose budgets are constantly being tightened. They also don't make it any easier for journalists to claim they serve as watchdogs for the general public. According to the Center on Budget and Policy Priorities, the average pay disparity between top executives and average workers in American firms grew from a lopsided 42 to 1 ratio in 1980 to 419 to 1 in 1998. That story itself has received comparatively little attention by news organizations perhaps partly because of the invidious comparisons that might be made with their own compensation practices.

The diversity between the pay of ordinary journalists and super-stars has also been widening. Although the stars' pay scales don't measure up to those of top executives, they far exceed the bulk of working journalists at the other end of the line and often under the same corporate roof. Leading the constellation has been Barbara Walters, who teamed up with ABC to start the TV-news pay spiral in the 1970s with her million-dollar effort to become an evening news anchor. A generation later, she still led the pack, earning $10 million in 1999. In the same year, late-night TV show host Ted Koppel took home $8 million, while morning star Diane Sawyer got $7 million. Over at CNN, CBS and NBC, the highest paychecks in 1999 went to Tom Brokaw, Katie Couric and Dan Rather, each getting $7 million.[4] Around the same time King was negotiating a $7 million-a-year con-tract at CNN in the same year, the cable news firm was cutting 70 of the 300 jobs at its Headline News.

Newspaper barons are not in the same class, according to *Brill's Content*. The top lord in 1999 was John Curley of Gannett with $3 million in salary and bonuses plus $8 million in long-term compensa-tion. Next came J.W. Madigan of the Tribune Co. with $2.6 million plus $10.9 million in other compensation. Peter Kann, chairman and CEO of Dow Jones & Co., earned $1.4 million in 1999, while Arthur Ochs Sulzberger Jr. of *The New York Times*, got $1.1 million.[5]

As usual, TV correspondents lord it over their print counterparts. CBS Chief Washington Correspondent and *Face the Nation* Moderator Bob Schieffer earns $1.5 million, while CNN Anchor and *Newsstand* cohost Bernard Shaw makes $1.1 million. At *The Wall Street Journal*, top writers make $130,000 and editors $160,000. David Maraniss, national political correspondent for *The Washington Post*, earns $130,000 (plus book royalties) though most other leading Post reporters make closer to $100,000.[6]

But the level of pay still puts most journalists at leading firms far above the average American worker. In addition are numerous extra goodies that accrue to journalists, such as free use of public offices and parking facilities, free tickets to events and special consideration at police lines and social events. As *Washington Post* media writer Howard Kurtz has commented, "Reporters, editors, and pundits, particularly in Washington, have become card-carrying members of a socioeconomic elite that is comfortably insulated from many of the controversial issues they so glibly debate....Reporters may once have been champions of the little guy; now they are part of a smug insider culture that many Americans have come to resent."[7]

Many political pundits have become multimillionaires thanks mostly to regular stints on TV talk shows and the lecture circuit where fees can range from $5,000 to $35,000, the price of a Cokie Roberts or Sam Donaldson when they were hot properties. Robert Novak has become a mini-conglomerate with not only his column and lecture fees but a lucrative newsletter and conferences held regularly in Washington for business executives. Former priest and Nixon aide John McLaughlin has also hit the big bucks by pioneering the traveling panel show and the Sunday political food fight with his *McLaughlin Report*.

But the income level dips precipitously from there to the nation's newsrooms. Despite the riches made at the Tribune Company, for instance ($3.2 billion of sales in 1999), the pay scale at the flagship *Chicago Tribune* starts at $38,000 for reporters, editors and photographers and maxes out for reporters at $108,000.[8] That's only about half of the minimum $200,000 salary the company pays its employees who play losing baseball for the Chicago Cubs. Fifteen members of the team signed contracts for at least $1 million in 2000, led by Sammy Sosa's $11 million.[9]

Tribune scales for journalists are higher than for most big news firms. According to the Newspaper Guild, news assistants at *The Wall Street Journal* earn $27,560 while producers at CBS News start at $22,000. Time Warner pays its *Money Magazine* researchers $30,000, while Microsoft's editorial assistants in Redmond, Wash., earn $24,960. At *The Detroit News*, one of Gannett's largest papers, reporters had a top minimum salary of $39,000 in 1999, compared to $41,133 for newspapers covered by Guild contracts.

Yet the Guild tends to represent the larger papers, where staffers usually earn more than at smaller ones. The union could do no better than $28,480 after four years of experience for photographers at the Hazleton, Pa., *Standard Speaker* and $20,150 after five years at the

Utica, N.Y., *Observer-Dispatch*. With such mundane salary levels for such demanding work, it is not surprising that labor turnover at small print and broadcast news organizations is relatively high.

EDITORS LEARN TO TAILOR

While collecting modest salaries for the most part, journalists must routinely aim their work at people in higher economic levels in order to please advertisers. During the merger wave starting in the 1980s, the need to tailor the news to fit business needs grew apace. Newspapers have even been willing to give up large chunks of circulation if that will increase their usefulness to big advertisers. For years, the Newspaper Association of America, the largest publisher association, has endorsed "market effectiveness" by raising per-copy prices and trimming sales to areas where merchants see upscale customers. In the early 1990s, *The Rocky Mountain News* and *Des Moines Register* were among the first to cut off delivery of their papers to distant areas in order to make the papers more desirable to many advertisers, which want to focus on the upper-income areas of cities and close-in suburbs. Such moves also make it possible for newspapers to become more profitable by raising advertising rates.

But, as Gilbert Cranberg, former editor of the *Register*, has pointed out, such policies often work to the disadvantage of low-income people in the city and residents of rural areas. The papers themselves also lose in the long run by diluting their own ability to inform the total population and provide a public forum for ideas, two goals that editors constantly espouse. As the U.S. population grows increasingly diverse, newspapers thus run the risk of becoming even more irrelevant than they already are.

According to James Squires, former editor of *The Chicago Tribune*, that paper eliminated as many as 40,000 readers outside Chicago in 1980 because it was more profitable to strip the ads aimed at them from the paper and thus save newsprint than deliver the ads and charge advertisers for the additional circulation. He called this policy "the dirty little secret" of the industry. With few exceptions, he wrote, "the profitability of newspapers in monopoly markets has come to depend on an economic formula that is ethically bankrupt and embarrassing for a business that has always claimed to rest on a public trust."[10] One exception is *The Washington Post*, which has conducted an intensive drive for minority readers by frequently running soft news about them on page one.

At the same time, almost all news organizations have come to focus more and more on business news. The wave of new technology and the investor excitement created by it have helped inspire not only increased coverage of such developments but the growth of many new information channels and news services devoted to business topics. The trend has been especially noticeable in the international sphere, where interest in business and trade matters has led to an explosion in news coverage of such topics.

Rising to the challenge of satisfying growing investor interest have been organizations like Reuters and Bloomberg. The number of specialized computer screens installed by these firms and Bridge Information Services nearly tripled from 1993 to 2000, according to *The New York Times*.[11] The coincidental rise of cable television has brought financial news channels such as GE's CNBC, CNN's CNNfn and Bloomberg Television. As competition among them increases, so does viewership. There has also been a sudden growth of periodicals specializing in investment topics. The net effect has been to crowd out more general news with topics appealing to the most affluent segments of the population. News for other Americans is being shoe-horned into smaller and smaller pockets of media time and space. On the other hand, some observers say business news has been historically under-reported in newspapers and that only now is it coming into its own.

Ironically, much of the best reporting on poverty or working class issues gets done in places where it would be least likely to appear: *The New York Times*, *The Wall Street Journal* and *Business Week*. A case in point was the latter's May 1, 2000, report on government efforts to cope with poverty. Another was the *Journal's* April 27, 2000, front-page feature on blacks paying more for life insurance than whites. Former *Journal* labor reporter Alex Kotlowitz, who later made a name for himself writing books about urban poverty, said: "One of the wonderful things about the *Journal* is that they always appreciated a good story and will let reporters pursue them even if they take time and don't fit into the readership's normal field of vision. Sometimes it's better to do the great story, even if it is an internal political risk. If you're always trying to keep your bosses happy, in journalism, you'll probably never do anything worthwhile."[12]

Though the *Journal* doesn't extensively cover spot news outside the business world, it often does better than its more traditional competitors in reporting how the vast majority of Americans live. Michael Harrington, a long-time chronicler of U.S. poverty, once wrote: *"The Wall Street Journal*, whose editorial page is unimaginatively conservative, has, for instance, provided some of the most moving reportage about the human costs of the [early 1980s recession]. If there had been such articles and television spots two decades ago, *The Other America* [Harrington's seminal book on the neglect of America's poor] would not have been necessary, or, at least, would never have come to so many people as a revelation."[13]

But few enterprising stories, such as these *Journal* reports, get far beyond one airing. Reasons include intense editorial pride and strong "brand" competition, the fear that using such works would generate an unfavorable comparison with a competing news organization. The Associated Press was originated as a cooperative that would share such journalistic largesse, but in practice, most outstanding examples of journalism become like falling trees in the forest, neither seen nor heard beyond their point of origin.

ISN'T EVERYBODY WELL OFF?

Among journalistic topics, poor Americans remain largely off the media screen and therefore off the minds of most people. Princeton University's Julian Wolpert, an authority on charity and philanthropy, says journalists and others doing well economically "assume the prosperity is being shared by [the rest of] the population."[14] And since the media don't inform them otherwise, why shouldn't their audiences think so? When there is coverage, it tends to focus on one person or family in order to capture the human interest factor so vital to today's journalism. The result is often to distort the basic story and lead the public to blame the target of the story, according to a 1991 study done by Shanto Iyengar, a professor of communications at the University of California at Los Angeles.

In contrast to the *Journal's* occasional interest, American poverty earns a poverty of coverage at most news organizations. Of all the neglected issues, writes Michael Kirkhorn, "One of the most threatening and in a way most shameful…is the persistence of poverty in cities and the countryside and the growing gap between rich and poor that former U.S. Labor Secretary Robert Reich has said threatens the United States with a 'two-tiered society.'"[15] But such topics are not sexy enough for today's editors. Larry McGill, director of research for the Media Studies Center, summed up the feeling of newspaper editors, "You don't get promoted by covering the poor."

Coverage of the nation's lowest economic classes has generally followed a quote-the-expert-and-official-sources strategy rather than a serious effort by news outlets to get the facts. Or so charges Fairness & Accuracy in Reporting (FAIR), a liberal media watchdog group. It says the press has largely failed to ask why entry-level wages aren't keeping up with the rest of the economy, why the trend is toward temporary, part-time and contract employees, why many worksite health and safety problems involve chemical exposure and carpel tunnel syndrome and why work weeks are growing longer.

An example of the reporting problem occurred in 1996 when President Clinton signed a major welfare reform bill passed after years of debate by a Republican Congress. The law, known as the Personal Responsibility & Work Opportunity Act, ended a national entitlement to welfare that had existed in one form or another since the New Deal. In its place was created a program called Temporary Assistance for Needy Families, which requires parents to participate in education and training to receive benefits and which pays portions of child care and Medicaid costs while families move off the public dole and into self-sufficiency. The bill provides sanctions for those who fail to comply. The legislation created so much controversy that Clinton's own top political appointees responsible for welfare in the Dept. of Health & Human Services, Mary Jo Bane and Peter Edelman, resigned rather than implement it.

According to FAIR, the reporting left much to be desired. "What passed for debate," it said, "sounded more like a chorus exaggerating the burden of welfare programs on the federal budget and scapegoating the poor, the black, the foreign, the female and the young. Relatively powerless groups became the targets of politicians and most of the press, while their advocates were routinely excluded from or belittled in the discussion. Long-time critics of 'welfare' from the women's movement, trade unions and the left were sidelined."[16]

FAIR said the media attitude continued, noting in 1997 that "media critics could look back over the last two years and bemoan the overwhelming failure of reporters to challenge the assumptions that fueled talk of responsibility, dependency and shame." Left-wing periodicals such as *The Progressive*, *In These Times* and *The San Francisco Bay Guardian* have led attempts to find out what happened to welfare recipients. A notable exception was *The New York Times*, whose reporter Jason DeParle spent a year writing a 1999 series—which won a George Polk award—about what happened to families affected by welfare reform legislation.

Another topic of comparatively little interest to the news media is bankruptcy, what happens to victims of the credit economy. Because of the lack of coverage, credit companies can take advantage of the silence and work their will on Congress. That's what happened in 2000 when both legislative branches passed long-sought bills that would make it much more difficult for debtors to wipe the slate clean. Passage was greased by more than $23 million in payments to lawmakers and an array of industry allegations that were refuted by the U.S. General Accounting Office and others. The main reason why legislation like this gets anywhere is the failure of the media in general to expose the outright bribery and false claims of proponents. One big exception in this case was an article in *Time*[17] listing large payments to key legislators and profiling several victims of the current law.

The awkwardness of today's media in reporting what happens outside their traditional perspectives extends also to coverage of young people in general, particularly when violence is involved. A review of 3,174 California newspaper articles about youth in 1998 by a group known as Youth & Violence in California Newspapers showed that one-quarter involved violence and another quarter focused on education. "Giving nearly equal weight to violence and educational issues," said the study, "exaggerates the frequency of violence."[18]

As access to technology becomes increasingly necessary for personal success, those who are not up to date and can't afford the prices get left further behind. Perhaps more than in any other field, access to the media is becoming dependent on technology as the boom in cable has been followed by the emergence of the Internet. In a few years, the Internet may become the dominant source of news since it can handle an almost unlimited number of channels of information and requires less lag time before going to print or on the air. The percentage of households with Internet access jumped from 35 percent to 43 percent just between 1999 and 2000.[19]

DIGITAL GAP GROWING

But many people are being left by the wayside, according to the National Telecommunications & Information Administration (NTIA). In a 1999 study, it found that while more Americans are wired by telephones, computers and the Internet than ever, "there is still a significant 'digital divide' [that has] widened in the last year." NTIA found that urban homes with incomes of $75,000 and up were 20 times more likely to enjoy Internet access at home and were nine times more likely to have computers than those in the lowest income bracket. Blacks and Hispanics could access the Internet from home at about one-third the rate of Asian/Pacific Islander households and two-fifths the rate of whites. The gap between blacks and whites increased about five percentage points between 1997 and 1998.

The poor are left behind not only in coverage but in access to news. "Alternative papers sometimes take up the slack where mainstream papers drop the ball," says Laura Washington, publisher of the *Chicago Reporter*, which focuses on racial and social justice. She adds: "The mainstream press tends to do corporate and political corruption....There's been a lot more emphasis on the personality, public figure-type reporting. They'll bring down a big guy, but they won't bring down a system."

Media preoccupation with business news leaves labor as a small sideline. New Jersey Media Watch, a group affiliated with the Teamsters and Communications Workers of America, reported that Gannett papers in New Jersey all but ignored labor disputes at their own papers. Almost all newspapers include daily business sections but almost none have labor pages. And when the subject is addressed, it is usually related to its effect on business, not the general public. Yet nearly every paper devotes several full pages to daily fluctuations in price of stocks, mutual funds and bonds, space that could be used for general news.

Washington Post columnist David Broder readily admits the press's neglect of labor. Referring to a three-week strike by Los Angeles janitors who clean the buildings of the city's wealthiest moguls, he wrote "[t]his is part of the overlooked reality of this era of record prosperity—a story that receives far less attention in the press and on television than the gyrations of the Nasdaq. Understandably so, for the Nasdaq determines the value of the stock options held by the high-tech millionaires who are the 'masters of the universe' in the new economy..."[20] He could have added the new multimillionaires of the news business.

Liberal media critic Norman Solomon notes that "we rarely hear from American mass media...that downsides for corporate investors are apt to be important upsides for working people. In Germany, for example, the 'rigid labor laws' include a 35-hour workweek – a monumental victory for the German labor movement....Despite all the rosy economic reporting, many Americans are not counted as unemployed because they've stopped looking for work. Millions of others are working longer hours than ever while real wages remain stagnant."[21]

The emphasis on business begs a few questions: How influential have the media been in making the stock market the main measure of the U.S. economy rather than other economic indicators such as wage rates, housing starts, living costs and similar factors? And why do major newspapers place news relating to consumers and workers routinely in their business sections and discuss them mostly as they relate to business despite their general audiences?

Like many papers, *The Washington Post* regularly puts recall notices for consumer products ranging from cars to appliances in the business section, often buried in the roundup of executive milestones and earnings reports. For example, on April 13, 2000, the paper ran a story on a recall for swing sets in its Business section. When queried about it for this book, editor Jill Dutt explained, "There might be a better place for recall notices to run....But readers are accustomed to reading recalls in Business. My hope is that by offering useful information like recall notices, we can attract more readers."

Discrimination still lives in upper levels of the media world, although it rarely becomes as ugly and public as it did in April 2000 when David Weyrich, owner of the five weeklies in the Gazette chain in San Luis Obispo County, Calif., ordered his papers not to cover abortion or gays in any favorable way. He went so far as to pull a routine calendar listing for a gay support group. "This issue of traditional family values has more to do with integrity than journalistic ethics," he explained. In response, an editor and several staffers quit in protest, but Weyrich replaced them all. Some advertisers also left, but the papers found others to take their place, proving that individual ownership still has life.[22]

Native Americans also have trouble getting a fair shake in the news. When a federal judge found federal officials in contempt for mismanaging billions of dollars in Indian trust funds and destroying evidence, *The San Francisco Chronicle* gave the story only three inches while it placed a killing of a European billionaire on page one. It aroused a protest from News Watch, a project of the San Francisco State University Journalism Department. It asked: "Why is it only when the subject is Indians making money through casinos that they rate headlines in our news?"

INCREASING ROLE OF WOMEN

One group, however, has greatly increased its presence in the news business. Thanks to a concerted effort by news executives, women have accounted for the most new entries into television news in the past decade. They now comprise a majority of television news staffers, not counting sports, weather and photography. The news prompted *TV Guide* to trumpet "How Women Took Over the News," an article saying that stars like Katie Couric had "changed the face and focus of the stories we care about the most."[23] In response, *Extra!* woman's editor Jennifer L. Pozner agreed that women had made progress but said they still trail their male counterparts in large numbers and "are excluded from many of the most powerful aspects of the news business."[24]

But minorities are still lagging in newsroom hiring, according to Prof. Vernon Stone of the Missouri School of Journalism. He says that although Afro-Americans, Hispanics and others comprise about 26 percent of the population, their share of TV news staffs held steady at round 18 percent through the past decade, including about 8 percent of news director jobs. He said the 1990s brought losses for minorities in television news, especially as news directors, with only a few serving in such posts.

Since 1969, the Federal Communications Commission has required TV stations to diversify their staffs. In early 2000, it ordered broadcasters to step up their efforts but gave them flexibility to design their own methods to do so. But the agency can't breathe down the necks of print outlets. In 1978, the American Society of Newspaper Editors (ASNE) set a goal for news staffs to reflect the nation's ethnic and racial diversity by the year 2000. Despite some progress, newspapers failed to meet the goal. Whites still accounted for more than 90 percent of newsroom supervisors.

One trouble is that the goal line keeps changing. When ASNE set its goal in 1978, racial minorities accounted for 19 percent of the population but just 4 percent of news staffs. By 2000, the minority share of the population had risen to 26 percent and their share of newspaper journalists to 12 percent. There is no tablet on the mountain commanding news staffs to reflect the exact makeup of the total population, but the newspaper industry keeps trying. In spring 2000, the Freedom Forum announced a $5 million commitment to increase newsroom diversity, including providing $1 million to ASNE and the Associated Press Managing Editors to figure out ways to get more minorities into the newsroom—and keep them there. Freedom Forum's own study, "Newsroom Diversity," found that about 7 percent of minority journalists leave the field annually, compared with about 4 percent of white journalists.

It is ironic that after all the efforts and money spent so far, so little has really changed about newsroom character. There seems to be no evidence that the addition of blacks, Hispanics and women has improved relationships or the journalistic ability to report the news fully and fairly. In fact, political correctness in newsrooms sometimes gets out of hand, such as when race is omitted from the description of a crime suspect. *The Washington Post* ran into the problem on April 20, 2000, in reporting that an 8-year-old boy was stabbed to death in his grandparents' front yard. Neighbors were annoyed when they found that the paper had omitted the word "black" from the description given by police of a male, 20 to 30, wearing a brown sweater, dark blue T-shirt and dark pants.

LESSONS FROM THE RIOTS

The inability of the news corps to do better in covering all of society is a long-standing problem. The inner city riots of the 1960s opened many journalists' eyes to a world they never knew existed.

One of the main findings of various government studies of the bloody and destructive violence was a failure of journalists to recognize the depth of resentment in largely black communities before those feelings exploded into a degree of civil disturbance rarely seen in this country. As stated by the National Commission on the Causes and Prevention of Violence, "... the media have contributed to the widespread use of confrontation as an instrument of social change by their failure to report adequately the conditions underlying current protest..." Another finding was that reporters tended to focus almost exclusively on the most dramatic events to the exclusion of other factors.[25] Strong reactions to media behavior at the time forced many news organizations to take stock and begin efforts to connect better with such neglected topics.

But 30 years later, little had changed when street rioting broke out in Seattle where the World Trade Organization was meeting. Some journalists who were there reported later that leading news organizations seriously misrepresented not only the violent aspects of the affair but the reasons for the protests. In a review of the affair, media analyst Seth Ackerman said that "mainstream media treated protesters' concerns with indifference and often contempt."[26]

Television reporting was especially shallow, often reducing the complex issues involved to a mere battle between demonstrators and police. The main news theme, judging from print and broadcast reports from the scene, seemed to be that the demonstrators were against free trade even though that was an over-simplification of their views. Their main objection was the secret WTO procedure that allows the organization to repeal laws of any member country that protect public health and the environment. Some reporters were indiscriminant in their choice of witnesses to interview. For example, when police started using tear gas, CNN reporter Katherine Barrett turned for comment to Jerry Jasinowski, president of the National Association of Manufacturers.[27]

Network anchors and correspondents were almost unanimous in depicting WTO objectors as unreasonable youths who were there simply to cause trouble. Typical was Peter Jennings's comment that "it seems as though every group with every complaint from every corner of the world is represented in Seattle this week." As the demonstrators left, he added that they "will go home, or on to some other venue where they'll try to generate attention for whatever cause that moves them."

MAFIA-LIKE DISCIPLINE

Such a condescending attitude has become pervasive among journalists and readily discerned by the public, further distancing the news corps from the general population. When haughtiness is added to a legitimate concern for maintaining journalistic standards, the pressures may become too much for the news pacesetters to handle in stride. The problem becomes especially apparent when a journalist appears to depart from accepted policy toward certain sensitive topics. Such deviations are promptly and swiftly subjected to discipline not unlike that dished out by mafia bosses.

High on the list of sacred cows that are carefully tended by the media powers are centers of authority such as the military establishment, the Central Intelligence Agency, the Federal Bureau of Investigation and police at various levels. Under the usual working arrangement with such powers, journalists receive approved news tips in exchange for favorable treatment on sensitive matters, often resulting in no treatment at all. Over the years, there have been notable exceptions, but mutual advantages have kept the understanding in force at the expense of uncooperative journalists.

Among the more explosive disciplinary cases involving the military was the so-called Tailwind episode. It started with a joint production of CNN and *Time* magazine in June 1998 entitled "Valley of Death." The 18-minute telecast alleged that nerve gas had been used in "Operation Tailwind" against American defectors in Laos in 1970. The program quoted several veterans supporting the allegations and some who didn't. Immediately, CNN was besieged with complaints from a high-powered group ranging from Defense Secretary William Cohen, former Secretary of State Henry Kissinger and Gulf War hero Gen. Colin Powell to former CIA Director Richard Helms. They all insisted—without benefit of any review—that no such thing had happened.

Facing a flood of negative comments also from the media, top officials of CNN and Time Inc. contracted with media attorney Floyd Abrams to review the affair along with CNN senior vice president David Kohler. Meanwhile, *The Washington Post* published an article by producer April Oliver defending the show. She declared that she and producer Jack Smith had requested a full hour to tell the story but were denied, then were ordered to cut parts that would have made it more balanced. Another problem was that Admiral Thomas Moorer, retired chairman of the joint chiefs, who had voiced no objections during production of the program, did so afterward. Some others also recanted. Adding to the mix was Kohler's conflict in serving as a CNN official and fellow judge with Abrams. Abrams and Kohler severely criticized the program and recommended that CNN and Time issue an apology. The news organization did so, also firing Oliver and Smith. As a result, the public may never know the answer to the serious charges raised.

Another controversy over a long-past military event showed anew how controversial such issues can be. The dispute erupted in May 2000 a month after the Associated Press had won a Pulitzer Prize and a George Polk Award for a Sept. 29, 1999, story about an alleged massacre of civilians by GI's in the Korean War. The AP account was challenged by military affairs writers at three news organizations, *U.S. News & World Report*, *The Baltimore Sun* and *stripes.com*. They claimed that some of the GI witnesses cited in the AP story had not been at No Gun Ri in 1950 when American soldiers were said to have fired, under orders, into a crowd of unarmed Koreans, killing hundreds.

Reviews of the editing process at AP, as reported by *The Washington Post* and *New York Times*, revealed the extra caution that major news organizations use when facing an unfavorable story about the military establishment. After obtaining the basic facts, it took the wire service 18 months to agree on a final form for distribution, causing one editor's resignation and many strained relationships along the way. To settle the matter, the AP released enough details to convince the Pulitzer and Polk juries to confirm the awards. But the question of whether an order was given to shoot, which would have been a war crime, has been left unresolved.

THE MOST SACRED COW

The most sacred of all media cows is the CIA. The news business has never caught up to all the CIA's dirty tricks around the world and apparently doesn't really want to. The failure to report its devastating anti-communist sabotage in Italy for 45 years after World War II has already been cited. Another highly sensitive topic has been CIA involvement with drug traders, especially in connection with its recruitment and support of the Contras during the Reagan administration. Throughout its history, the CIA has enjoyed a charmed life with mainstream news organizations, avoiding serious attacks on its policies. One reason has been the close ties between "the company" and numerous highly placed journalists and media executives. A 1991 CIA memo cited by authors Alexander Cockburn and Jeffrey St. Clair admitted that the agency maintained "relationships with reporters from every major wire service, newspaper, newsweekly and TV network....In many instances, we have persuaded reporters to postpone, change, hold or even scrap stories that could have adversely affected national security interests or jeopardized sources or methods."[28]

Perhaps the friendliest news organization toward the CIA has been the one that should be the most skeptical, *The Washington Post*. Its long time chief, Katharine Graham, spoke with admiration to a group of CIA recruits in 1988: "We live in a dirty and dangerous world. There are some things the general public does not need to know, and shouldn't. I believe democracy flourishes when the government can take legitimate steps to keep its secrets and when the press can decide whether to print what it knows." Her paper's CIA expert for decades has been Walter Pincus, who once wrote about the subsidized travel he enjoyed around the world as an unpaid observer for the agency.[29] His stories about the CIA in the *Post* over the years have been so friendly to it that he has become known around Washington as "the CIA's house reporter."

So it was not surprising that when three stories alleging CIA involvement in drug trading in Los Angeles were published in August 1996 by the *San Jose Mercury News*, Pincus was among the first to defend the agency and lash out at its detractors. What set him off and many others in the media was the lead sentence in Gary Webb's series saying: "For the better part of a decade, a San Francisco Bay Area drug ring sold tons of cocaine to the Crips and Bloods street gangs of Los Angeles and funneled millions in drug profits to a Latin American guerrilla army run by the U.S. Central Intelligence Agency." It said it occurred mostly during a period when government funding of the Contras was banned by Congress.

Webb's articles and postings on the paper's Internet site along with a CIA logo and title of "The Dark Alliance" set off an uproar across the nation, especially on the radio. In African-American communities, the series was seen as proof positive of long-held suspicions of a government conspiracy to exploit disadvantaged people and encourage gang wars. U.S. Rep. Maxine Waters, a Democrat who represented south central Los Angeles, demanded congressional hearings, and CIA Director John Deutsch endured a hostile "town meeting" there to defend the agency. Deutsch ordered an extensive probe by the agency's inspector general Frederick Hitz, who was given no subpoena power to force testimony.

But Webb's series got almost no attention from the mainstream media until a month later, when Webb appeared on CNN along with Ronald Kessler, author of a friendly book on the CIA. Kessler took issue with Webb on the alleged CIA connection, the point that was to spark a fierce counter attack by the media powers that be. Chris Matthews, the CNBC talk show host, also attacked the validity of Webb's articles, claiming that the Contras didn't need the money in those years. Like many other detractors, Matthews went well beyond the stories, asserting what Webb had not claimed: a direct CIA connection. What bothered many journalists were the sweeping statements that implied a deeper involvement of the CIA and a larger role of local drug dealers in Contra funding than were supported by the stories.

The mainstream media offensive against the series began with six articles in two days (Oct. 2 and 4) in *The Washington Post*. It was part of what authors Alexander Cockburn and Jeffrey St. Clair called "one of the most venomous and factually inane assaults on a professional journalist's competence in living memory."[30] The main theme of the *Post* articles was that Webb had not produced sufficient evidence to prove that the CIA was behind the influx of crack cocaine into Los Angeles. In less than a month, *The Los Angeles Times* carried four lengthy accounts finding fault with the Webb articles. It was too much to expect that the *Times*, the paper that had been badly beaten before in reporting events in its own backyard, would simply pass on the *Mercury News* series without a whimper. *The New York Times* also launched a full-page defense of the CIA. Then the leading journalism reviews added their complaints.

Not only did the mainstream papers form a solid phalanx; they also didn't want to give the principal proponents of the articles a chance to speak for themselves. Webb's boss, Executive Editor Jerry Ceppos, responded to *The Washington Post* with a letter. When the *Post* refused to print it, Ceppos asked deputy editor Stephen Rosenfeld why. Ceppos was told to rewrite it, and he did, but still to no avail. When asked why by this author, Rosenfeld said Ceppos "had not addressed the issues."[31] *The New York Times* also chose not to print a letter from Webb complaining about its coverage.

It wasn't until May 11 that one chapter of the controversy ended with a column in the *Mercury News* by Executive Editor Jerry Ceppos. After having shepherded the whole series over many months and having defended Webb against his critics, Ceppos suddenly changed his mind completely. He accused Webb of having left out contradictory information and overreaching with his statements. Ceppos immediately was hailed by many other editors for his handling of the affair. And he won a National Ethics in Journalism Award from the Society of Professional Journalists. Two years later, he was named vice president for news for Knight Ridder, which owns the *Mercury News*, and the chain's headquarters was moved to San Jose. Six months after that, he was elected president of the Associated Press Managing Editors. Webb had resigned in December 1997 after being transferred.

One more opportunity for the mainstream press to set part of the CIA record straight came in March 1998 when Frederick Hitz, CIA's inspector general, testified before the House Permanent Select Committee on Intelligence about his 18-month investigation of the Webb affair. After complaining about getting little or no cooperation from some CIA personnel, Hitz made two highly newsworthy revelations. One was an admission that the CIA "did not in an expeditious or consistent fashion cut off relationships with individuals...engaged in drug trafficking activity or take action to resolve the allegations." The other was an admission that the agency had won a secret agreement in 1982 with then-Attorney General William French Smith removing a requirement that the agency report allegations of drug trafficking by its formal agents or contractual ones.

Here was the biggest confession the CIA had ever made about drug connections. It was an acknowledgement that its employees and "assets" not only had dealt extensively with drug traffickers in connection with the Contras but it had gotten approval to keep their crimes secret from prosecutors. Hitz confirmed what Associated Press reporters Robert Parry and Brian Barger had found in 1986 and what Sen. John Kerry, D-Mass., concluded after two years of hearings on the matter in 1989. Parry and Barger also reported that their story had been strongly resisted by AP officials and had gotten circulated only accidentally to Spanish language publications.

Despite the obvious newsworthiness of the testimony, however, the media were still not interested. A data search showed that of the big three newspapers so critical of the Webb stories, only the *Post* ran anything, and that was a small story deep inside the paper. Except for Knight Ridder's *Philadelphia Inquirer*, none of the 400 news other outlets on the database ran more than a brief line from wire dispatches.

Once again, the powerful media clique had managed to impose its will over other news outlets in regard to the nation's most secretive government agency. It resembled the news treatment of the King murder verdict on December 8, 1999, and its aftermath six months and a day later when the Justice Department announced that its own 18-month investigation had found "no credible information to support allegations of a conspiracy." True to form, the official theory got far more media attention than the trial verdict, according to Dow Jones Interactive data searches: 85 stories to 46. In fact, many first-day reports and nearly all follow-ups on the verdict led with official doubts.

Although the verdict did not settle the case, it at least warranted the lead sentence and headline in news reports. Instead of objectively reporting such highly controversial matters, the journalistic powers that be clearly prefer to try closing them with the official version, even if it is wrapped in impervious secrecy. Such behavior merely adds to the disconnect between the public and the press.

CHAPTER XII

Challenging the Press to Do Its Job

It is now the right of the people to have an adequate press.

The Hutchins Commission

For two days in April 2000, the U.S. Senate Committee on Aging listened to testimony highly critical of America's $18 billion funeral and burial industries. It was a rare occasion for the American people to learn some lessons from the experiences of others willing to tell how they were victimized by exorbitant prices, deceptive sales pitches and other factors causing great stress for buyers of such goods and services. Among the horror stories:

- An 81-year-old Florida woman who wound up paying $132,000 in advance for her funeral arrangements;

- A former seller of pre-need contracts who testified by videotape from a California prison about stealing thousands of dollars from so-called trust funds set up by buyers to pay funeral costs in advance;

- A solid copper casket oozing thick, malodorous liquid for most of a year from a mausoleum into a nearby flower garden in Uniontown, Pa.

- A large mound of dirt filled with casket fragments in a California cemetery that shut down without giving relatives of the deceased any information.

In his opening remarks, Committee Chairman Charles Grassley, R-Iowa, stated that, due to prices rising faster than inflation, the average bill for a traditional send-off, including a funeral, casket, burial and marker had reached $7,520. He said his staff had found that caskets are marked up an average of 500 percent above wholesale, some by as much as 2,000 percent. He said he was especially concerned about the confusion people have when confronted with the need to purchase a funeral, cremation or burial amid high-pressure sales tactics. And he said legislation might be needed to protect buyers of pre-need services.

One of the witnesses was the Rev. Henry Wasielewski, a priest for low-income Catholic parishes outside Phoenix, Ariz., who has been a vociferous critic of the industry in the face of death threats and tire slashings. He described one poor family that was making monthly payments for three funerals and was about to add a fourth before he offered to help. He said "the most lucrative fraud" was the sale of "protective seal" caskets. Such models, he claimed, "don't protect but bloat and destroy most bodies within a few months…spewing liquefied body parts out of the casket." He said many cemeteries and mausoleums prop open such caskets to avert explosions from anaerobic gases.

Wasielewski charged his own church with "nationwide ripoffs." In the Denver, Dallas and Los Angeles archdioceses, he said, Roman Catholic officials had contracted with large funeral chains that use deceptive practices and charge prices "two to five times more than needed for a fair profit." He even offered wholesale price lists to prove his point. His activities had previously been chronicled by *U.S. News & World Report*, *Dateline*, *Today* and other news organizations. Other witnesses at the hearings included representatives of the Funeral and Memorial Society Association, the American Association of Retired Persons, the Federal Trade Commission, the National Funeral Directors Association and the International Cemetery and Funeral Association.

Here was a rare peek into the mysterious world of last rites, a gold mine of newsworthy, even sensational, information of interest and relevance to all Americans. As a special dividend, the saga of the leaking casket caused the sobbing witness to produce some fresh tears, the mother's milk of gripping television. In addition, the lineup of witnesses created extra controversy when the top representative of the nation's funeral directors complained that the committee was being "unfair" to the industry for giving critics more time to testify. The affair also coincided with a formal review of the 16-year-old federal regulations imposed on the industry by the Commission, which must decide whether to drop them, strengthen them or leave them as they are. For skittish national news executives, the subject had the additional advantage of not involving big advertisers. Even at the local level, funeral and burial firms don't do much advertising.

THE BIG NEWS GETS BURIED

Despite this rare combination of sensation and relevance, little news got beyond the hearing room. A data search of 50 major dailies and some 400 other news outlets in all media, including the major newsweeklies and network newscasts, turned up stories in only six papers, a short TV segment on CBS and a snippet on CNN. NBC, the network that claims to present "all you need to know," ran nothing, and ABC News, which says it is the most watched, also ignored the news. No news report on the testimony mentioned Wasielewski's accusations against his church leaders, although C-SPAN aired the proceedings later.

CNN's snippet consisted of a one-sided question to a spokesman for the funeral directors who was asked: "Now it seems like the government is wanting to further regulate the funeral business. Do you think that's necessary?" The mortician was hitting that softball out of the park when he was interrupted by a voice announcing "our trivia question today: What's the average cost for an entire traditional funeral?" The answer was promised "when we return" from a commercial ending the "interview."

This little exchange plus the paucity of serious reporting about the hearings told a lot about today's news formula: entertain the masses with emotional trivia and skip relevant national news from government sources even when it has the required emotional clout. And in reporting unpleasant facts, be sure to favor the business side so there will be few or no repercussions, and certainly don't offend any large religious groups.

The scarcity of media interest was not due to lack of notice. Committee press aide Jill Gerber notified reporters well in advance, per custom in Congress. She spoonfed some with advance information, thereby inspiring detailed reports in two papers, *The Washington Post* and the *New Orleans Times-Picayune*, in the home state of Sen. John Breaux, the committee's ranking Democrat. Several other papers picked up Associated Press summaries of the hearings that were sent to nearly every news outlet in the country.

Committee members didn't show much interest either. Outside of Grassley and Breaux, only one of the other 18 members showed up. Sen. Richard Bryan, R-Nev., dropped in for a few minutes. The committee absenteeism was another function of the press. If more reporters had been there, more senators would have attended.

The big yawn given to this newsworthy event was not unusual for the nation's experts on newsworthiness. They preferred to concentrate at the time on safer emotional roller coasters such as the saga of Elian Gonzalez, pedophiles on the Internet and mass rapes in Sierra Leone. Other front-page topics of the day included radiation hazards, a scientific report on Vitamins C and E, and a new crop of Pulitzer Prizes. Then, of course, there was the attitude in many newsrooms that nobody is interested in government news.

This book has already described numerous major topics that have been grossly mishandled to the detriment of public knowledge and full political debate: from the fear of communism that dominated most of the 20th century to the overblown fear of crime during the last decade while violent crimes were dropping for eight straight years, and from the unrest of the inner cities that exploded in the late 1960s to the racial bitterness that seemed to be reaching a climax in the first part of the new millennium. Topics that get the full treatment—often to excess—tend to be highly personal ones with names like O.J., Tonya, Paula, Monica and Elian. The main aim is clearly to entertain, not inform.

Other major developments not often recognized for their newsworthiness include the growing international resistance to exported American culture and policies. The opposition—even contempt—for U.S. influence bodes ill for American trade, travel and hopes for security. And it comes at a pivotal time when isolationist voices are rising in the United States.

DEMOCRACY UNRAVELING

As the United States faces tensions abroad, it also faces a crisis of democracy at home. Most Americans do not read a daily newspaper or watch a network evening news program. Most potential voters don't vote, even for president. Those two trends test the future of democracy as never before. Some of the void in representation is being taken up by public referenda, a form of direct democracy used increasingly to circumvent glacial-like state legislatures. But the same deficiencies that weaken state and national lawmaking bodies also infect the referendum route: voter ignorance and apathy in the face of powerful private lobbies. The result is a declining degree of public representation, especially in Congress, and a declining willingness of the press to nourish the democratic system by doing its job well.

For most of the past century, elected officials were more responsive to their constituents than they are now. President Franklin D. Roosevelt and Congress reacted to the depression with a flurry of new laws setting up Social Security, workman's compensation, unemployment assistance, wage and hour standards and many other benefits taken for granted today. In the 1960s and early 1970s, another wave of federal lawmaking helped the nation answer the call for stronger civil rights, consumer rights, environmental protection and anti-poverty efforts. Since then, however, the responsiveness of self-government to urgent public demands—such as universal health care, meaningful campaign reforms, strong gun controls and a fairer tax system—has faded.

One reason has been an organized reaction by business and conservative interests to the wave of liberal legislation and efforts to push women's liberation, racial equality and gay rights. Understanding that the media were essential to changing public attitudes, business and conservative political groups began in the 1970s to set up media gadflies, think tanks and associations to generate news and commentary that supported their causes. Among the leaders of this New Right movement was Joseph A. Coors, heir to the family beer business based in Colorado. Coors helped found the Heritage Foundation and similar institutions to produce propaganda for reactionary causes, including the religious right. Over the years, Coors money has also helped finance right-wing periodicals such as *American Spectator* and numerous conservative newspapers on college campuses. Another prominent angel of reaction has been Richard Scaife, the Mellon heir, whose millions have helped push politics, the courts and the news media more to the right.

Along with the corporatization and consolidation of news organizations, these conservative forces have managed to narrow the scope of political debate by dominating the field of commentators. They also have helped slow new laws and rules in the federal arena. A high point for them was the takeover of both houses of Congress by Republicans in 1994 after a 48-year hiatus. The result has been a further slowing of the legislative process, as indicated by the drop in number of laws passed and the increase in vapid compromises that don't please either side. Typical was the skimpy 1997 minimum wage increase that was weighed down by large tax breaks for employers. Adding to the legislative inertia has been a form of political gridlock in which the same party has been able to control both the presidency and Congress in only two of the last 20 years.

Most observers blame the split-party control for the failure to respond better to major demands of the populace for campaign finance reform, better health care, stricter gun control and the like. But the political system was designed with such checks and balances, and this specific alignment had been approved by voters. Legislative gridlock in the 1990s was more likely related to the steady drop in news coverage of national and international affairs and increased public apathy, which have paralleled the growth of conservative political power and corporatization of the news process, especially in the past two decades. With less coverage of government activities, and with news audiences drifting away, it is no wonder that citizen interest in voting has been dropping. It is no wonder so many people don't know who represents them in Congress or how their representatives perform in office.

The quality of public representation in Washington is very much determined by the amount and quality of news reporting. Skimpy coverage of legislative proceedings not only robs citizens of the information they need to evaluate a legislator's performance, but discourages people from going to the polls. Poor coverage also gives elected officials more space to play *quid pro quo* with special interests without being exposed to voters. The persistent urge of journalists and politicians to discredit anything relating to Washington hasn't helped either.

WHAT BETTER REPORTING CAN DO

There is no doubt that government news can be dull. But it stands to reason that more serious news reporting could improve citizen knowledge of—and interest in—public affairs. Nothing is more critical to the proper functioning of democracy than the flow of information between voters and their elected leaders. Author James S. Fishkin has dispelled any doubts about that with his experiments in what he calls deliberative polling. In a televised National Issues Convention in 1996 at Austin, the University of Texas professor proved that organized efforts to expose a sample audience to politically balanced, in-depth information about specific issues would substantially raise the knowledge level of attendees and increase their interest in the subjects discussed. For example, the proportion of people approving the level of foreign aid in the federal budget rose from 26 percent to 41 percent after informative discussions on the subject.[1]

A more significant—but less recognized—effect was the political impact on people subjected to such polling. The more they learned about political issues, the more they tended to switch from conservative to liberal positions. For example, the proportion of people in favor of more education and training rose from 72 to 86 percent after discussion, while the proportion for a flat tax, like the one promoted by Steve Forbes, dropped from 44 to 30 percent. Such shifts were even more pronounced in a similar Fishkin experiment in England before the 1997 general election there. After listening to the key candidates at a weekend gathering, British participants moved from 11 percent Liberal Democrat to 33 percent and from 26 percent Conservative to 19 percent. The results presaged the sweeping Labour Party victory.

Here was what frightened conservative politicians: the clear evidence that more complete reporting and more balanced commentary could turn political control of government leftward as well as boost citizen interest in public affairs. Conversely, the results inferred that the decline of serious news reporting about government and the decline in voter participation in the past two decades had helped Republicans increase their electoral strength at state houses and legislatures as well as capture Congress. It also helped explain why conservative columnists such as George Will are not bothered by democracy for and by the elite.

Critics of Fishkin's U.S. experiment said the sample was not representative of the total population and that people don't behave normally before a live camera. Some charged that liberal forces were behind the exercise. Others questioned whether deliberative polling makes any more sense than a national town meeting, both concepts of which are impractical in such a large country, even with the Internet. But the shifts in attitudes were too large to be easily dismissed. It should not be surprising that exposing people to more information about a topic would change their views. What is surprising is that more has not been made about the implications for politics and the press.

The Fishkin experience may also help explain why the decline in serious news coverage has coincided with the increasing consolidation of media power with a strong conservative flavor. Rupert Murdoch, the head of News Corporation and the Fox network, is renowned for his contempt for liberals and the federal government. Other media chiefs with a strong conservative view of things include Jack Welch, chief executive of General Electric, NBC's corporate parent, and John Malone, head of AT&T's Liberty Media. A rare exception is Time Warner's Ted Turner. Clearly, the top rung of media combines is no place for progressive politicians or independent thinkers.

Despite glowing promises of better journalism after nearly every media merger, the news gap widens as stock values rise. Such a pattern cannot help democracy solve its most critical problems. At a time when the full attention of citizens and their elected representatives is needed, the nation's news business is losing the interest and ability to alert them.

A NEWS CORPS WITH BLINDERS

Numerous observers have warned of the dangers facing American democracy. As author and journalist Michael Janeway puts it, "Americans are in the eye of a storm—a democratic crisis in a republic of denial—that is the more threatening because of helplessness to date in coming to terms with it." Alluding to the media's role, he sees "a form of national blindness to avoid the paramount issues." Among the domestic issues he lists are political and government dysfunction, economic polarization, deepening racial division and cultural disintegration.[2] Beyond the borders lie other problems, such as the threats of military attack, terrorism and the previously mentioned resistance to U.S. policies and cultural exports at a time when the American desire for trade and travel is growing.

By failing to devote more attention to such matters, the media add to the disconnect between Americans and their government. And they make the problems more intractable. At the same time, press preferences for emotional topics help cause politicians of both parties to become obsessed with such distractions as abortion, flag waving, sexual deviance and school prayer. While these matters get the headlines, civic urgencies fester for lack of attention.

To make matters worse, the news media are spawning a crop of dangerous demagogues, mostly talk show hosts, whose main interest is to arouse the masses for personal profit. Radio is teeming with provocateurs who play on fears of a United Nations takeover of U.S. parkland and "jack-booted" federal agents invading private homes without reason. Largely due to the uproar they create, the U.S. House of Representatives has voted several times in recent years to reject a harmless U.N. program that designated certain nature preserves and cultural attractions such as Yellowstone National Park as "world class." Such a vote in July 1997 blocked Interior Department funds for environmental research in connection with a forthcoming world convention on the biosphere.

Another example of misleading the public occurred just months before the 1994 takeover of Congress by Republicans when House Whip Newt Gingrich was trying hard to obstruct Democrats in any way he could. He sent a fax to Rush Limbaugh stating falsely that a House-passed bill to tighten the rules governing lobbyists would require civic groups to disclose names of volunteers under penalty of a $200,000 fine. The Rev. Pat Robertson pounced on the same theme on his *700 Club* telecast. Capitol Hill was suddenly flooded with complaints that caused the Senate to hastily kill the measure, even though it mirrored one approved by a 95-to-2 vote one year earlier. Congress eventually approved lobby reform in calmer circumstances, but the episode showed the power of a few ideologues to distort majority rule.

A further example involved a GOP-sponsored bill to "reform" the Food and Drug Administration. The bill (S.830), fashioned almost completely by representatives of drug and medical device manufacturers, aimed to gut health and safety regulations. The measure was sent to the Senate floor in July 1997 without a public hearing or input from consumer groups. By railroading potentially embarrassing legislation, sponsors hoped to avoid probing reporters. Lack of coverage was a big reason why it passed by a vote of 98 to 2. The law allows device makers to form their own product-review committees and cuts in half the number of tests required for new drugs. Such undemocratic actions used to be rare; now they are common.

Some people might consider such episodes as messy examples of a healthy democracy. But with the great bulk of Americans out to lunch, the danger grows that mixed priorities of the media will help give unrepresentative interests an unfair advantage over a trusting, disinterested majority. When powerful media forces employ falsehoods or baseless fears to alter laws and policies for partisan or profit-making purposes, they effectively substitute a form of media tyranny for authentic democracy.

THE DANGERS WITHIN

Voting rates themselves illustrate the low degree of public representation in Congress. Only about one-third of eligible people cast ballots in congressional races, and only one fourth take the trouble to vote for governor of many states. Less than half of the eligible people vote for president. That means it takes only 17 percent of eligible citizens to elect a U.S. representative and only 13 percent to fill a gubernatorial office. Less than 25 percent of eligible adults voted for Bill Clinton's reelection.

Daniel Webster recognized the problem in 1837, when he warned that the greatest danger to democracy would come not from beyond the borders but from "inattention of the people to the concerns of their government, from carelessness and neglect." As civic awareness falls, it creates a growing void between the people and their representatives in government, a void that gets filled to the brim by special interests.

Against a total of 535 senators and representatives in Congress stands an army of 17,500 lobbyists, many of whom can create a flood of "grassroots" messages almost overnight, often in lockstep with narrow partisans in the media. Legislators spend increasing time meeting with lobbyists and begging for contributions rather than making laws. Most legislative business is done in secret, out of the range of reporters and TV cameras. Journalists occasionally lift the veil of secrecy, but the full story doesn't often reach a large audience.

Increasing political partisanship is another media byproduct. As journalists are drawn to the loudest and most divisive voices for news purposes, the news helps generate a more bitter political atmosphere. As a result, political moderates lose interest in active politics and quit rather than run for reelection. A study by the Brookings Institution on "The Disappearing Political Center" found that moderates in the House and Senate fell from about 30 percent of total membership in the 1960s and 1970s to only about 10 percent in 1996. Since then, the middle ground for compromise and cooperation has continued to shrivel.

TOTALING UP THE DAMAGE

These are but a few of the warts on the body politic, however, compared to the overall damage that the news business has inflicted on the American people and their creaky system of democratic government. This book's chapter titles describe some of the consequences of a press that has lost touch with its primary mission: to present the news that people need to know and provide an adequate forum for discussion of public matters.

Most inadequacies of today's news machine stem from the rise of corporate consolidations that became a tidal wave during the last 15 years of the 20th century. Mergers have evolved in large measure from pressures on family owners to sell out or go public in order to avoid oppressive inheritance taxes and to satisfy relatives demanding more of the financial action. The subsequent submersion of news operations into large industrial and entertainment conglomerates has encouraged the exploitation of press freedom for commercial profit and multiplied journalistic conflicts with business interests. To meet investor demands for maximum profits, media executives have been forced to reduce serious news coverage of national and international affairs and emphasize less costly stories appealing to human emotions. The pressure for profits and audience ratings lies behind "gotcha journalism," where journalists become executioners of fallible public figures.

At the same time, the news business has been transforming American politics to fit its own needs. The shift of the presidential selection process to state primaries and caucuses three decades ago helped the media to take over the process. In a similar vein, the introduction of TV cameras in the congressional chambers has transferred much of Congress's legislative power to the Fourth Estate. The political urge to ridicule anything relating to the federal government also has been encouraged by media interests partly because it resonates with the public and partly because it fits into the downsizing of news from Washington. As the amount of government news drops, political advertising fills the gap, adding to the deception, and conveniently filling media coffers with cash. As a result, the legislative process is turning increasingly into a battle of misleading images and messages that damage public discourse. Adding to the distortion is the tendency of media managers to tilt the news toward the privileged few and to self-censor news and views to please advertisers and publicists.

Along with the media responsibility to keep Americans fully informed about citizen affairs comes the obligation to provide a full and open discussion of public matters. That implies an equal opportunity for all shades of opinion. But the main avenues of commentary have become increasingly dominated by conservatives, leaving a declining portion of time and space for other points of view. And because of the declining amount of serious news coverage, topics for discussion tend to be frivolous. Hence the talk shows endlessly debating whether Elian Gonzalez should be allowed to go back to Cuba with his father and whether Hillary Clinton should have tipped a waiter.

Not all is bleak, however. Improvements in communications technology have been mind-boggling, helping to speed the development of many new channels of news, especially on the Internet. News itself moves infinitely faster and is more attractive than ever. And the quality of writing and the competence of journalists have also improved. National Public Radio, C-SPAN and CNN have filled in many of the news gaps while PBS becomes more commercialized. The Internet has added an infinite source of details for those who want them, plus a forum for the average person to sound off and be heard. In doing so, it turns upside down the complaint voiced so eloquently by noted press critic A.J. Leibling that freedom of the press is only for those who own one. Anyone can now become a publisher or broadcaster.

But these positive changes don't compare to the negative ones. The promise of the Internet is fading as it becomes dominated by media giants like AOL, Time Warner and the networks. According to

Media Metrix, general news sites with the most one-time visitors in March 2000 included MSNBC, CNN.com, TheGlobe.com and ABC. Media Metrix is to cyberspace as Nielsen is to broadcasting, generating the audience data that advertisers need. Although a few entrepreneurs and pioneering news organizations, such as *Salon*, have made a mark on the World Wide Web, they are bucking a reverse trend already underway: the growing presence of large advertisers and large media firms. The heralded promise of the Internet is proving to be no real threat to establishment powers.

WATCHDOG OR HOUND DOG?

Far more worrisome is the way media economic power is morphing into media political power. There are those who feel that unchallengeable media power is necessary to stand up to those who would threaten freedom, to be a watchdog for public interests and to fight the ever-present danger of government secrecy and propaganda. But today's media power has become a bigger threat to freedom than government. It's too busy making money and controlling politics to play traditional journalistic roles. It can't be a watchdog for the public and a hound dog for government favors at the same time. And it can't effectively fight government secrecy while keeping its own lobbying secret.

Nor can it cover politics objectively while shaping it to its own purposes. Issues that don't resonate in the press don't get attention, and candidates who don't excite the news corps seldom get elected. Party conventions must be geared first to interest members of the media, then to conduct party business. Members of Congress must think first of how to fight legislative battles in the papers and on TV then in the House or Senate chambers. Media images also guide the White House, even the Supreme Court.

But politics should be more than images, and political issues should extend beyond those that make money for media conglomerates. The workings of democracy cannot be limited by what TV producers or radio provocateurs think will draw the largest audience and the most profits. And the task of preserving individual freedom and representative government cannot be left primarily to a business that is more interested in maximizing profits than serving the public interest.

It's time to blow the whistle on the American news business. And it's time to challenge its commitment to freedom and democracy. The fundamental task is to find ways to reverse course by making national government more representative of the general public and less beholden to private interests. In order to do that, it is necessary to somehow convince the news business of the urgency of making a more serious effort. It requires that news operations be sufficiently freed from financial restraints to better inform the public about national and world affairs affecting their role as citizens. It means restoring a broader definition of news that puts more emphasis on the civic importance of events and less emphasis on what titillates the human animal. And it requires new efforts to make important news attractive enough to interest Americans in following the news as if their future depends on it, for it does. It also requires the media to offer a balance of political commentary more representative of public voting patterns and to open public debate to a wider array of views.

Many people in the media and elsewhere perceive what is wrong, but they are unable to make the necessary changes. They see no way of reversing the relentless economic pressures that continue to squeeze out efforts to inform rather than merely entertain the masses. The constant drive for higher profits steadily erodes the ability of journalists to provide the news necessary to maintain free society in a healthy state. Little effort is made to relate important news to a broad audience or to make it interesting. Yet NBC was able to win rave ratings for its primetime soap, *The West Wing,* in the 1999-2000 season, using many of the same themes that reporters consider too dull to report as news.

If the press were just another business, as Wall Street would like to have it, there would be no cause for concern. But journalism circulates the lifeblood of representative government. Without full and fair news and comment, there is no way for people to know what issues affect them, which candidates to vote for and whether to reelect the winners on the basis of their performance in office.

A free society requires more than the freedom to speak one's mind. As author Michael Parenti says, "A government is not a democracy when it leaves us free to *say* what we want but leaves others free to *do* what they want with our country, our resources, our taxes and our lives....Nor are elections and political party competitions a sure test of democracy. Some two-party or multiparty systems are so thoroughly controlled by like-minded elites that they discourage broad participation and offer policies that serve establishment interests no matter who is elected."[3]

Parenti, a noted university professor of political science, blithely suggests that a socialist movement could form a "truly democratic society." Robert W. McChesney, another distinguished professor, advocates a political renaissance of organized labor and leftwing politics.[4] Both Parenti and McChesney apparently see politics, not the media, as the basic problem and believe that political changes must come before journalistic ones.

RISKING THEIR OWN FREEDOM

But such sweeping changes in American politics are a pipe dream. There is more chance of changing media practices than political views. Besides, the news business has a proprietory stake in the outcome. It can lose its own press freedom, the basis of its existence, if it allows democracy to die and bring down all freedoms with it. Numerous polls show a high percentage of Americans who doubt the value of press freedom.

The big question is how to awaken those who run the business to what needs to be done before it is too late to discuss the matter freely. News organizations have a long history of failing to recognize major newsworthy developments, including warning signs about their own future. For years, they have dismissed falling audiences because profits kept rising. They also have ignored polls showing a steady drop in public trust, while claiming that they were giving the public what they wanted in saturation coverage of O.J. and Monica. And they obviously have not worried much about the likely connection between falling voting rates and shrinking news about national and international affairs.

One promising idea, borrowed from Scandinavia, has been to install an ombudsman in each news organization to ride herd on wayward journalists and smooth relationships with the public. But after several decades, only some three dozen news organizations have such an animal. Another positive move is to assign a reporter to cover media performance, but this idea also has had few takers.

There are a few critical media journals that do a creditable job in pointing out human errors and corporate miscalculations on a hit-or-miss basis, often dependent on voluntary contributions from concerned journalists working in their spare time. But their circulation is confined almost entirely to the industry. Stephen Brill broke the pattern in 1998 by creating *Brill's Content*, a critical review for the general public, but it has suffered from an uncertain identity and poor circulation compared to other consumer magazines.

The most concerted reform effort—and the most controversial—is an initiative called "civic" or "public" journalism. It is an attempt to combat public distrust by holding meetings and focus groups with private citizens to help formulate news policies that are more acceptable to the public. Its numerous experiments, however, have brought mixed results and strong opposition from traditional journalists who feel that the efforts distort the news process and fail to address basic problems such as budget cuts and profit demands.

One of the more persistent ideas for reforming the news business is the news council, a panel of journalists to answer complaints from the public about media performance. The first call for such a body came in 1947 from the Hutchins Commission, a committee of distinguished academics funded mostly by Henry Luce, head of Time Inc., and directed by Robert Maynard Hutchins, chancellor of the University of Chicago. The Commission recommended, among other things, an independent citizens organization "to appraise and report annually upon the performance of the press" and "promote the freedom, the public responsibility and the quality of mass communications." In addition, it would investigate allegations of "intentional falsifying," the "exclusion of minority groups from reasonable access to mass communication channels," and "give public recognition to excellent performance," among other things.

It wasn't until 1973 that media leaders succeeded in setting up a national news council, thanks to seed money from the 20th Century Fund, later called the Century Fund. But the effort failed to get the backing of key newspapers such as *The New York Times*, so its findings were not circulated far beyond journalism periodicals. Funds soon dried up, and the experiment died 11 years later. A state-wide council started in Minnesota two years before the national one continues to operate in much the same way: investigating complaints, seeking to settle disputes and issuing decisions in selected cases. Complainants must waive the right to sue, thereby showing they want fairness or vindication, not money.

One of the difficulties in getting media support for news councils is reflected by a major funder of the Minnesota council, The Ethics & Excellence in Journalism Foundation. It promotes the news council idea through national advertising with a telephone number that connects with the Minnesota organization. Callers are referred to a law firm in Oklahoma City that houses the foundation, a brainchild of Edith Gaylord Harper. She is the sister of the publisher of *The Daily Oklahoman*, which the *Columbia Journalism Review* calls "the worst newspaper in the country." While her Foundation promotes the idea of councils everywhere else, it has yet to form one even in its home state of Oklahoma.

A serious limitation of the council approach and others is that they merely react to complaints about what is printed or aired, thus restricting themselves from tackling more basic problems. Their effectiveness also depends on adequate funding and full cooperation by media firms, including publicizing their decisions. In 1998, CBS's Mike Wallace tried to regenerate interest in a national news council but ran into so many dissident voices that he backed off, saying that the best hope is at the state and local levels. But although several news councils have been formed, the long-term outlook for the idea is not sanguine.

Among other groups working to improve the craft are the Credibility Project of the American Society of Newspaper Editors, the Free Press/Fair Press project of the Media Studies Center in New York City, the Media Management Center of Northwestern University, the Pew Center for Civic Journalism, the Project for Excellence in Journalism, the Robert C. Maynard Institute for Journalism Education, the Journalism Ethics and Integrity Project of the Radio and Television News Directors Foundation and the Joan Shorenstein Center on the Press, Politics and Public Policy at the Kennedy School of Government at Harvard University.

Hardly a day goes by without a panel discussion, a critical survey or a new publication assessing its current state. There are even program guides to keep track of the programs. But when all these efforts are added up, the question remains whether they have made any difference. Although they may have kept a bad situation from getting worse faster, polls don't show any improvement in public trust. Nor have newspaper or network news audiences stopped drifting away.

RAISING JOURNALISTIC INTEGRITY

Meanwhile, Bill Kovach, a former newspaper editor and curator of the Nieman Foundation at Harvard University, has been pushing a revolutionary concept: better journalism. He insists that stronger efforts to attain excellence will restore public trust. He could point to some impressive evidence that quality journalism can attract large audiences. Examples include ABC's *Nightline*, which has survived for two decades against late night comics such as Jay Leno and David Letterman; Ross Perot's blackboard talks about the federal budget that outdrew entertainment programs at the time; and the persistent though modest financial success of *The New York Times*, everybody's "best" paper in the country.

Kovach could also point to new signs that the hoary formula for sex and scandal may be losing its punch. In a 1999 survey of 59 TV stations in 19 cities, the Project for Excellence in Journalism found that quality news programming was twice as likely to bring commercial success as tabloid formulas featuring crime, scandal and celebrity.[5]

But it will take more evidence than that to reverse a basic news formula imbedded in U.S. journalism for more than a century largely by tabloid pioneers Joseph Pulitzer and William Randolph Hearst. It's not simply a matter of choosing quality over sleaze or serious over silly. It means finding a way to reverse the relentless pressure from on high to cheapen the basic product in order to increase short-term profits. Conscientious, competent working stiffs can exert some pressure for change, but only higher authorities can actually produce it.

The only people who can stop the news budget slashing and downsizing of serious news have names like Gerald Eisner (Time Warner), Michael Eisner (Disney), Rupert Murdoch (News Corporation), Sumner Redstone (Viacom) and Jack Welch (General Electric). But even they don't have the final say. They have to please a still higher level, the key fund managers of Wall Street, who are not likely to give up their love affair with media profit margins without a struggle. Two years of efforts by some members of the National Press Club to use its good offices merely to host a meeting of such bigwigs failed. The ques-

tion remains: How to get the news business to recognize its basic fail-
ings and consider steps to correct them? It is a dilemma that has
plagued society as long as there has been a press.

The Hutchins report cited a laundry list of shortcomings that have
only worsened since then. They included dwindling competition,
increasing tabloidization, an aversion to serious news and a heavy corporate hand directing how news is treated. It said the "faults and errors
have ceased to be private vagaries and have become public dangers,"
adding that "the preservation of democracy and perhaps of civilization
may now depend on a free and responsible press." The last five words
formed the title of the voluminous Hutchins report.

In order to offset the tendency of the press to concentrate only on
the most profitable type of news, the Commission suggested that the
press accept the notion of being a common carrier of information and
opinions, offer material "of high literary, artistic, or intellectual quality" and present "vigorous mutual criticism." It said the press had "an
obligation to elevate rather than degrade" public discourse. It even
proposed an expanded government effort to inform the public about
its current activities.

But sponsor Luce was not pleased with the critical tone of the
report. Nor were leading newspaper publishers of the time. The headline greeting the findings in Robert McCormick's *Chicago Tribune*
read: "A FREE PRESS (HITLER STYLE) SOUGHT FOR U.S." The
story called the report "a major effort in a campaign of a determined
group of totalitarian thinkers…to discredit the free press of America."
The failure of Hutchins to include any representatives of the press
proved to be the kiss of death. It ruined any chance of getting cooperation from key publishers like McCormick.

Since the demise of the National News Council in 1984, there
have been scattered calls for a broader, Hutchins-style study to assess
the news media's role in democracy. But it wasn't until March 1999
that a formal proposal was offered by a media organization. It came
from the Committee on the Future of Journalism, a group comprised
mostly of working journalists put together by The Newspaper Guild, a
unit of the Communications Workers of America. Declaring that the
news business "cannot bring about the reforms needed to guarantee
that the press as we know it can continue to fulfill its mission," the
committee urged creation of a group of prominent citizens from out-

side the industry to accomplish the task. It said such a group should study all parts of the media, including newspapers, magazines, books, radio, television and the Internet.

But the announcement by the Guild group has fallen on deaf ears. One reason for that, just as with the Hutchins project, was its failure to include members of the media on the proposed commission. The Guild took pains to "invite all participants in this industry to join with us to develop the framework for a new independent examination." But it made clear that the group "would be independent of the industry and government."

In order for such an ambitious venture to succeed, it must include members of the media in all phases of the work for they have the knowledge and the experience to know what can and cannot be done. And they know how to investigate and report when they want to. One reason why so many thoughtful books on the news business have not had much impact has been the authors' lack of journalism experience and unfamiliarity with the factors that motivate journalists and their superiors. Members of the media should share equally with outsiders in controlling such a project but not have control because so many of them have a stake in changing nothing.

TOPICS FOR INVESTIGATION

A possible agenda for such a group overflows with urgent problems for study, including:

- **The declining degree of public representation.** This part of an overall study would concentrate on the media's role in the growing contrast between what polls show people want and what Congress and the White House deliver. Among topics to be considered are declining voting rates, the growth of campaign contributions, the role of political advertising and the growing power of private interests to defeat public interests in legislative arenas. One possible proposal would require some free TV time for candidates during their campaigns.

- **Shrinking news coverage of Washington and the world.** The focus here would be on causes of the decline and the effect on public knowledge and voting patterns. Proposals might include ways of increasing such reporting and involving the government more directly in informing citizens about how their tax dollars are being spent. There is nothing in the First Amendment preventing such government activity.

- **Investor influence on news operations.** Topics for study would include the impact of financial pressures on the reduction in serious news coverage, increasing tabloidization of mainstream news outlets and the rise of "gotcha" journalism. One possibility would be to seek broad agreement with Wall Street to allow media managers to remove news operations from the same profit goals imposed on other divisions and lower short-term profit goals in order to preserve long-term profitability and foster more responsible journalism.

- **The shrinking scope and balance of political discussion in the media.** This section needs to examine media accessibility for all shades of opinion and measure the degree of balance in views presented to the public. Consideration should be given to re-establishment of the Fairness Doctrine for broadcasters, the principle of which has been supported by the Supreme Court, and a voluntary pledge of more balanced political commentary by news organizations.

- **Concentration of media ownership.** A comprehensive study should be done on the effect of corporate mergers on news operations over a period of several decades. There should also be a review of antitrust standards to see if there is a need to break up combinations that have already been approved and a thorough examination of the increasing collaboration of the largest media firms to see if it violates antitrust law or circumvents the principles of a free press.

- **Commercial pressures on news and commentary.** The focus here would be on the effect on news and commentary due to pressures from advertisers, publicists and other commercial interests. The study should include public broadcasting and the Internet. One possibility would be a plan to substantially expand public broadcasting with a new scheme to provide the necessary funding—at last.

- **The failure to relay enterprising journalism.** Unless a reporter is working for a newspaper or wire service with its own broad distribution system, there is little chance that his or her most outstanding work will be circulated to competing outlets. A way needs to be found to repeal this unwritten law so that such works reach the widest possible audience. A cooperative system to do so is already in place. Its name: the Associated Press.

- **Media secrecy.** One way to regain public confidence in the press would be to investigate the practices that undermine it the most, including the journalistic failure to fully disclose conflicts of interest, both personal and corporate, and the widespread reluctance to report lobbying and business activities that may affect news and commentary. More openness is necessary.

As these words were being written in May 2000, the two largest media conglomerates, Time Warner and Disney, demonstrated their arbitrary power to control what Americans get—or don't get—in television news and entertainment. For nearly two days, some 7 million people in seven major metropolitan areas including New York, Philadelphia and Los Angeles lost all ABC programs because Time Warner had dropped them from its cable systems in a dispute with ABC parent Disney over how much Time Warner should pay Disney for the right to carry its ABC programs on Time Warner cable systems. Only after some members of Congress hinted at holding hearings and the FCC chastised Time Warner did the latter agree to reinstate ABC programs.

It was not the first time that TV viewers had lost their pictures because of disagreements between media conglomerates over cable access. This book has described other blackouts involving Cox, Fox and Time Warner. But the May blackout served as the sharpest reminder to date of how millions of innocent people can be robbed of news, commentary and entertainment by angry tycoons bent on controlling everything. It proved that nothing is sacred to the powers behind drive-by journalism, not even our rights and freedoms.

Is it already too late to save ourselves from such media tyranny? That's what former Boston Globe editor Michael Janeway glumly believes: "The powers of inertia at work today are too persistent to permit meaningful reform." He says things must get worse before they can get better.[6]

But Americans have risen to other challenges in time to prevent democracy's funeral. Many of the problems threatening this nation would ease if journalists would be freed to do what they claim to do and what the Founding Fathers expected them to do: exercise their obligations as well as their freedoms.

Confidential Mail Survey of Correspondents Covering Congress

1) Circle box describing your main outlet.
   [daily paper, 45%] [radio, 7%][TV,23%]
   [newservice, 23%] [web, 2%][dna, 0%]

2) Circle the box that fits your years covering Congress.
   [1-4, 41%] [5-9, 15%] [10-20, 20%]
   [over 20, 9%][dna, 15%]

3) Do you usually have adequate time to do the job assigned to you?
   [yes, 62%] [no, 38%]

4) Is your work often edited/cut enough to hurt your relationship
   with sources?   [yes, 6%] [no, 94%] [dna, 0%]

5) Has your employer Cut/Added personnel on the Hill in the past
   5 years?   [C, 26%] [A, 29%] [dna, 45%]

6) Are budget pressures on news operations seriously hurting
   coverage?   [yes, 35%] [no, 56%] [dna, 9%]

7) Do you feel your news outlet gives adequate attention to
   Congress?   [yes, 65%] [no, 35%] [dna, 0%]

8) Do the news media in general give adequate attention to
   Congress?   [yes, 56%] [no, 44%] [dna, 0%]

9) Do you get sufficient help from Congressional sources you deal
   with?   [yes, 70%] [no, 30%] [dna, 0%]

10) Do you often find lobbyists more helpful than Hill aides?
[yes, 32%] [no, 68%] [dna, 0%]

11) Do you find Members adequately accessible for your needs?
[yes, 73%] [no, 27%] [dna, 0%]

12) Has there been an increase in the presence of lobbyists on the Hill? [yes, 56%] [no, 21%] [dna, 23%]

13) Does the media's own lobby ever get in the way of objective reporting? [yes, 18%] [no, 66%] [dna, 26%]

14) Do you have enough time to fully report the influence of lobbyists? [yes, 18%] [no, 82%] [dna, 0%]

15) Are there other major stories not covered because of time restraints? [yes, 91%] [no, 9%] [dna, 0%]

16) Has there been a major increase in undemocratic procedures in Congress? [yes, 32%] [no, 53%] [dna, 15%]

17) Has the degree of partisanship in Congress increased on your watch? [yes, 85%] [no, 15%] [dna, 0%]

18) Do you feel that the public is adequately represented in Congress? [yes, 38%] [no, 56%] [dna, 6%]

19) Who ultimately has more political clout?
[Congress, 59%] [media, 15%] [neither, 26%]

(Based on one-time mailing to 260 members of Press and Radio and Television Press Galleries listed in the Official Congressional Directory, 106th Congress, U.S. Government Printing Office, then verified as active via telephone to major news organizations in November 1999. Total responses: 34, representing 13 percent.)

Confidential Mail Survey of Press Aides to Members of Congress

1) Circle the box describing your work situation.
   [House] [Senate] [Rep] [Dem] (not tallied)

2) Which box best fits your years in Congress?
   [1-4, 55%] [5-9, 31%] [10-20, 11%]
   [over 20, 3%] [dna, 0%]

3) Do you have adequate time to do the job assigned to you?
   [yes, 57%] [no, 43%][dna, 0%]

4) Do you have adequate resources to do the job assigned to you?
   [yes, 75%] [no, 25%][dna, 0%]

5) Do you feel that reporters covering your bailiwick do an
   adequate job?   [yes, 65%] [no, 33%][dna, 2%]

6) Do you feel that the news media overall do a good job covering
   Congress?   [yes, 47%] [no, 52%] [dna, 1%]

7) Do you feel that publicity concerns of Members are excessive?
   [yes, 29%] [no, 63%][dna, 8%]

8) Do you feel that lobbyists have too much influence over
   Congress?   [yes, 50%] [no, 48%][dna, 2%]

9) Have the media gained influence in Congress in recent years?
   [yes, 70%] [no, 28%][dna, 2%]

10) Before arranging a hearing, do you check the interest of key
    reporters?   [yes, 38%] [no, 62%][dna, 0%]

11) Does reporter bias seriously affect news coverage of Congress?
                                        [yes, 71%] [no, 26%][dna, 3%]

12) Does your Member adequately represent the people of his/her
    district?   [yes, 99%] [no, 1%][dna, 1%]

13) Does Congress overall adequately represent the American
    people?   [yes, 69%] [no, 30%][dna, 1%]

14) Has the level of public representation gotten better or worse?
              [better, 26%][worse, 25%][same, 46%] [dna, 3%]

15) Has the propensity for closed-door dealing increased in recent
    years?   [yes, 29%][no, 63%][dna, 8%]

16) Do you believe large contributors have too much clout over
    legislators?   [yes, 43%][no, 55%][dna, 2%]

17) Has the number of lobbyists on the Hill increased in recent
    years?   [yes, 62%] [no, 22%][dna, 16%]

18) How much Member time is spent raising money?
              [0-20%, 60%][21-40%, 24%][41-60%, 6%]
              [over, 60%, 1%][dna, 9%]

19) Which institution is ultimately more powerful?
        [Congress 29%] [media 30%] [neither 19%][dna 22%]

(Based on one-time mailing to 725 press aides to Members of Congress
in November 1999. Total responses: 96, representing 13 percent.)

APPENDIX C

DAILY NEWSPAPERS SURVEYED FOR COMMENTARY
(circulation as of Sept. 30, 1998, per *Editor & Publisher Yearbook*)

Newspaper	Circulation
* New York (N.Y.) *Wall Street Journal*	1,740,450
* Arlington (VA) *USA Today*	1,653,428
* Los Angeles (CA) *Times*	1,067,540
* New York (NY) *Times*	1,066,658
* Washington (DC) *Post*	759,122
New York (NY) *Daily News*	723,143
* Chicago (IL) *Tribune*	673,508
Houston (TX) *Chronicle*	550,763
* Dallas (TX) *Morning News*	479,863
San Francisco (CA) *Chronicle*	475,324
* Boston (MA) *Globe*	470,825
New York (NY) *Post*	437,467
Phoenix (AR) *Arizona Republic*	435,330
* Philadelphia (PA) *Inquirer*	428,895
Cleveland (OH) *Plain Dealer*	382,933
Detroit (MI) *Free Press*	378,256
San Diego (CA) *Union-Tribune*	378,112
* Orange County (CA) *Register*	356,953
* Miami (FL) *Herald*	349,114
* Portland (OR) *Oregonian*	346,593
* St. Petersburg (FL) *Times*	344,784
Denver (CO) *Post*	341,554
St. Louis (MO) *Post-Dispatch*	329,582
* Atlanta (GA) *Constitution*	303,698

(Asterisk marks one of "Best 21 Newspapers" chosen by editors, per *Columbia Journalism Review, November/December 1999*. Papers among top 30 in circulation not included in survey for technical reasons were: *Long Island Newsday*, 572,444; *Chicago Sun-Times*, 485,666; *Newark Star-Ledger*, 407,026; *Minneapolis Star Tribune*, 334,751; *Rocky Mountain News*, 331,978; and *Baltimore Sun*, 314,033.)

APPENDIX D

SIX WEEK SURVEY OF NATIONAL POLITICAL COMMENTARY IN 24 LARGE NEWSPAPERS OCTOBER–NOVEMBER 1999

Newspaper	No. of Editions	No. of Editorials	No. of Op-Ed Commentaries	Total Items
Arizona Republic	37	8	39	47
Atlanta Constitution	37	25	26	51
Boston Globe	37	25	49	74
Chicago Tribune	37	26	42	68
Cleveland Plain Dealer	37	8	34	42
Dallas Morning News	37	23	50	73
Denver Post	37	14	61	75
Detroit Free Press	37	19	33	52
Houston Chronicle	37	24	63	87
Los Angeles Times	37	29	37	66
Miami Herald	37	21	36	57
New York Daily News	37	9	36	45
New York Post	36	27	66	93
New York Times	37	53	77	130
Orange County Register	37	14	36	50
Oregonian	37	27	40	67
Philadelphia Inquirer	37	16	31	47
San Diego Union-Tribune	37	15	67	82
San Francisco Chronicle	37	17	53	70
St. Louis Post-Dispatch	37	23	49	72
St. Petersburg Times	37	27	65	92
USA Today	31	23	6	29
Wall Street Journal	31	32	47	79
Washington Post	37	50	89	139
Total	875	555	1132	1687

Conflicting Connections of Large Media

Among the outside connections represented by directors of the largest five media conglomerates are:

- **AOL** directors also were affiliated with Netlink Corporation, Nextel Communications, General Instrument Corp., Palm Computing Inc., Sun Microsystems Inc., Homegrocer.com, 3Com Corp., Harrah's Entertainment Inc., MCI Worldcom Inc., Metro-Goldwyn-Mayer Inc., Interneuron Pharmaceuticals, Organogensis Inc., BarnesandNoble.com., Cendant Corp., Six Flags Entertainment Corp. Gulfstream Aerospace Corp., Fannie Mae, Pfizer Inc., Pepsico Inc., Boeing Co. and Conagra Inc. **Time Warner** (before being purchased by AOL) had directors also representing Bank of New York, Hilton Hotels, Dow Chemical, American Express, United Airlines, Aetna Inc., Chevron Corp., Lucent Technologies, Citigroup, Colgate-Palmolive Co., Phillip Morris, Allstate Corp., Dell Computer, Morgan Stanley, Dean Witter, Sears Roebuck, Forstmann Little & Co., Dime Savings Bank, General Cigar, Oakwood Homes and Westfield America Corp.

- **General Electric** directors also sat on the boards of Avon Products, Fiat SpA, PepsiCo Inc., R.H. Macy, Kimberly-Clark Corp., State Street Bank & Trust, Chubb Corp., Knight-Ridder Inc., Tandy Corp., Quaker Oats Co., Baxter International,Tricon Global Restaurants, Home Depot Inc., Baby Superstore Inc., Telefonos de Mexico, Kellogg Company, Lockheed Martin Corp., Bellsouth

Corp., Dell Computer, Coca-Cola Co., Delphi Automotive Systems, Penske Truck Leasing Corp., Gulfstream Aerospace Corp., Honeywell International, Allied Signal, Bristol-Myers Squibb, Champion International, Chemical Banking Corp., J.P. Morgan, Anheuser-Busch Companies Inc., Sun Microsystems Inc., Liz Claiborne Inc. and Goodyear Tire & Rubber Co.

- **News Corporation** directors linked to Commonwealth Bank of Australia, Nike Inc., Apple Computer Inc., Mallinckrodt Group Inc., Phillip Morris Companies Inc., Compaq Computer Corp., Royal Philips Electronics, E*Trade Group Inc., Gateway Inc., MCI Worldcom Inc., Telefonica de Espana, Rit Capital Partners, Cato Institute, Bayou Steel Corp., Hudson General Corp. and the Markle Foundation.

- **Walt Disney** directors also represented Cisco Systems, Northwest Airline, Phillip Morris Co., Infoseek Corp., City National Bank, Jenny Craig Inc., Federal Express Corp., Sun Microsystems Inc., Rockwell International Corp., Columbia HCA Healthcare Corp., Doubleclick Inc., Texaco Inc., International Business Machines Corp., Riggs National Corp., Staples Inc., Xerox Corp., Koor Industries Ltd., Northwest Airlines Corp., Mitchell Energy & Development Corp., Tejon Ranch Co. and Bankamerica Corp.

- **Viacom** directors also represented Bell Atlantic, American Home Products, CVS Corp., Allied Signal, Hartford Finance, Avnet, Bear Stearns, Simon & Schuster and Credit Suisse First Boston. **CBS** (before its merger with Viacom) included directors who also served at Amazon.com, Atlantic Richfield, Prudential Insurance, Rockwell International, Chase Manhattan Bank, Warner-Lambert, Union Pacific, U.S. Airways, Banc One, Gillette, New York Life, Smithkline Beecham and American Express.

(Source: Bloomberg News Service, 1999, 2000.)

DAILY NEWSPAPER ENDORSEMENTS FOR PRESIDENT

Candidate, Party, Number and Percentage of Endorsing Papers.
Winners underlined

Year	Candidate and Party	Number of Endorsing Papers	Percentage of Endorsing Papers
1940	Wilkie (R)	813	64%
	Roosevelt (D)	289	25%
	No endorsement	171	13%
1944	Dewey (R)	796	60%
	Roosevelt (D)	291	22%
	No endorsement	237	18%
1948	Dewey (R)	771	65%
	Truman (D)	182	15%
	No endorsement	182	15%
1952	Eisenhower (R)	93	67%
	Stevenson (D)	202	15%
	No endorsement	250	18%
1956	Eisenhower (R)	740	62%
	Stevenson (D)	189	15%
	No endorsement	270	23%
1960	Nixon (R)	731	58%
	Kennedy (D)	208	16%
	No endorsement	328	25%
1964	Johnson (D)	440	42%
	Goldwater (R)	359	35%
	No endorsement	237	23%
1968	Nixon (R)	634	61%
	Humphrey (D)	146	14%
	No endorsement	250	24%

1972	Nixon (R)	753	71%
	McGovern (D)	56	5%
	No endorsement	246	23%
1976	Ford (R)	411	62%
	Carter (D)	80	12%
	No endorsement	168	28%
1980	Reagan (R)	443	42%
	Carter (D)	126	12%
	No endorsement	439	42%
1984	Reagan (R)	381	58%
	Mondale (D)	62	9%
	No endorsement	216	27%
1988	Bush (R)	195	29%
	Dukakis (D)	51	8%
	No endorsement	416	63%
1992	Clinton (D)	149	18%
	Bush (R)	125	15%
	No endorsement	542	(67%
1996	Clinton (D)	65	4%
	Dole (R)	111	27%
	No endorsement	415	70%

(Source: *Editor & Publisher*, Oct. 26, 1996 Third parties omitted)

Endnotes

The quotations marked by asterisks at the beginning of each chapter were taken from *Freedom of the Press: A Framework of Principle*, by William Ernest Hocking, and the report of the Commission on Freedom of the Press (the Hutchins Report) University of Chicago Press, 1947.

Chapter I: Corrupting the News with Business Mergers

1 Ben Bagdikian, *The Media Monopoly*, Beacon Press, 1983.
2 Interview with author, Dec. 3, 1999.
3 Ken Auletta, *The New Yorker*, July 26, 1999.
4 *Editor & Publisher*, Nov. 20, 1999.
5 Elizabeth Lesly Stevens, *Brill's Content*, December 1998/January 1999.
6 Lawrence K. Grossman, *The Electronic Republic*, Viking, 1995, p. 83-84.
7 Steve Weinberg, "Smoking Guns: ABC, Philip Morris and the Infamous Apology," *Columbia Journalism Review*, November/December 1995.
8 Lawrence K. Grossman, "Lessons of the 60 Minutes Cave-In," *Columbia Journalism Review*, January/February 1996.
9 James Fallows, *The Nation*, June 3, 1996.
10 *Columbia Journalism Review*, July/Aug. 1998.
11 Paul Farhi, *The Washington Post*, Sept. 12, 1999.
12 Robert McChesney, *Rich Media, Poor Democracy*, University of Chicago Press, 1999, p. 22.
13 Paul Farhi, "Does Big Media Mean Bad Media?" *American Journalism Review*, December 1999.
14 Lou Uraneck, "Newspapers Arrive at Economic Crossroads," *Nieman Reports, Special Issue*, summer 1999.
15 Douglas R. Cliggott, "Industry Index Performance," J.P. Morgan Securities Inc., Jan. 12, 1998.
16 *Broadcasting & Cable*, January 3, 2000.
17 John M. Higgins and Price Colman, "The Powers That Buy," *Broadcasting & Cable*, Aug. 17, 1998.

18 Marc Gunther, "Dumb & Dumber," *Fortune*, May 29, 2000, and confirmed by e-mail.

Chapter II: Downsizing News of the Nation and World

1   Marvin Kalb, *The New York Times*, Aug. 29, 1990.
2   Charles Layton, "Hocus Focus," *American Journalism Review Special Report*, 1999.
3   Ken Auletta, *Three Blind Mice*, Random House, 1991, p. 159.
4   Layton, *Op. cit.*
5   Howard Kurtz, *The Washington Post*, Sept. 19, 1999.
6   Tom Rosenstiel, Carl Gottlieb, and Lee Ann Brady, "Quality Brings Higher Ratings, But Enterprise is Disappearing," *Columbia Journalism Review*, November/December 1999.
7   *Censored 1999*, Seven Stories Press, New York, 1999.
8   Penn Kimball, *Downsizing the News*, Woodrow Wilson Center Press, 1994, p. 23.
9   Penn Kimball, *op. cit.* pg. 12.
10 *Ibid.*
11 Thomas Mann and Norman Ornstein, *Congress, the Press and the Public*, American Enterprise Institute and Brookings Institution, Washington, D.C., 1994, p. 4.
12 "Washington Journalism, Changing It Is Harder Than I Thought," by James Warren, *The Business of Journalism*, edited by William Serrin, The New Press, 2000, pp. 77-139.
13 Jill Geisler, "Blacked Out," *American Journalism Review*, May 2000.
14 David S. Broder, *The Washington Post*, June 18, 1997.
15 Martin Plisser, *The Control Room*, The Free Press, New York, 1999.
16 The total number of weekday editions—excluding Sundays—was 37 for all papers except those that didn't publish on Saturdays. One edition of one paper was unavailable. The papers included 14 of the 21 "best" papers, according to the *Columbia Journalism Review*. See Appendices C and D.
17 Carl Sessions Stepp, "Then and Now," *American Journalism Review*, September 1999.
18 Interview with author, June 14, 2000.
19 Richard Morin and Dan Balz, *The Washington Post*, Jan. 29, 1996.
20 See Arthur E. Rowse, "Gladio," *Covert Action Quarterly*, Summer 1994.

Chapter III: Exploiting the First Amendment for Profit

1   Howard Kurtz, "Post Taken to Pillory," *The Washington Post*, Oct. 7, 1994.
2   Mike Mills, *The Washington Post*, Nov. 11, 1994.

3   James H. Snider and Benjamin I. Page, "Does Media Ownership Affect Media Standards? The Case of the Telecommunications Act of 1996," Paper delivered at the 1997 annual meeting of the Midwest Political Science Association, April 10, 1997.

4   Citizen Publishing, 394 U.S. at 139, 89 S. Ct. At 932 quoting Associated Press v. United States, 326 U.S. 1, 20, 65 S. Ct. 1416, 1424 (1945).

5   *America Inc.*, Dial Press, 1971, p.88.

6   Bryan Gruley, *Paper Losses: A Modern Epic of Greed & Betrayal at America's Two Largest Newspaper Companies*, Grove Press, p.171.

7   Mintz & Cohen, *Op. cit.*, p. 84.

8   Jan. 31, 1970.

9   Ben Bagdikian, *Media Monopoly, First Edition*, Beacon Press, 1983, pp. 96-7.

10 Paul Farhi, *American Journalism Review*, September 1999, p. 50.

11 Bryan Gruley, *Op. cit.*, p 395.

12 Robert Schiff, *The Progressive*, December 1997, p. 23.

13 *Virginia State Board of Pharmacy v. Virginia Citizens Consumer Council*, 425 U.S. 748.

14 Cass Sunstein, Ronald K.L. Collins and David M. Skover, "Speech and Power," *The Nation*, July 21, 1997.

15 *National Journal*, Aug. 2, 1997, p. 154.

16 Bruce W. Sanford, *Don't Shoot the Messenger*, The Free Press, 1999, p. 184.

17 Ibid.

Chapter IV: Trashing Washington for Media Purposes

1   *The Washington Post*, July 6, 1997.

2   Cook, *Op. cit*, pg. 48.

3   Wills, *A Necessary Evil*, 1999, p. 236.

4   E.J. Dionne, *Why Americans Hate Politics*, Simon & Schuster, 1991.

5   Chris Matthews, "How Pols Play Hardball," *Chicago Sun-Times*, July 31, 1988.

6   Lou Cannon, "President Stumps in Parched South Carolina," *The Washington Post*, July 25, 1986.

7   Howard Kurtz and Dan Balz, "Clinton Assails Hate Through Media," *The Washington Post*, April 24, 1995.

8   Ibid.

9   "How Dangerous Are Our Airwaves," *The Atlanta Constitution*, May 5, 1995.

10 Robert L. Hilliard and Michael C. Keith, *Waves of Rancor: Tuning in the Radical Right*, Armonk, New York, 1999.

11 Sean Paige, "Talking the Talk," *Insight*, Feb. 9, 1998.

12 Hilliard and Keith, *Op. cit.* p. 228.

13 Kevin Berger, "Hate Radio," *San Francisco Examiner*, May 1, 1995.

14 Ibid.

15 Jason Vest, "The Spooky World of Linda Thompson; Her Videos Inflame the Militias," *The Washington Post*, May 11, 1995.

16 Thomas Halpern, David Rosenberg and Irwin Suall, "Militia Movement: Prescription for Disaster," *USA Today Magazine*, January 1996, p. 16.

17 Susan Tolchin, *The Angry American*, Westview Press, 1999, p. 90 and 135.

18 "The Road to Paranoia," *The New Yorker*, July 19, 1995.

19 Jack C. Doppelt and Ellen Shearer, *NONVOTERS*, Sage Publications, Thousand Oaks, Calif., 1999, p. 17 and pp. 222–232.

20 George Will, *Restoration: Congress, Term Limits and the Recovery of Democracy*, 1992.

21 David Broder, "Cure for Nation's Cynicism Escapes Its Leaders," *The Washington Post*, Feb. 4, 1996.

22 *Ibid.*

23 Editorial, April 27, 2000.

24 Garry Wills, *A Necessary Evil*, Simon & Schuster, 1999, p. 320.

Chapter V: Narrowing Political Debate for Profit

1 Peter Laufer, *Inside Talk Radio*, Carol Publishing Group, 1995, p. 208.

2 Norman Solomon, *The Habits of Highly Deceptive Media*, Common Courage Press, 1999, p. 277.

3 Arthur E. Rowse, *Slanted News*, Beacon Press, 1957, pp. 123–128.

4 January/February, 1993.

5 *Time*, July 8, 1974.

6 S. Robert Lichter and Stanley Rothman, "Media and Business Elites," *Public Opinion*, October/November 1981; and Linda Lichter, S. Robert Lichter and Stanley Rothman, "The Once and Future Journalists," *Washington Journalism Review*, December 1982.

7 Herbert J. Gans, "Are U.S. Journalists Dangerously Liberal?" *Columbia Journalism Review*, November/December, 1985.

8 *Forbes Media Critic*, Fall 1996.

9 David Croteau, "Challenging the 'Liberal Media' Claim," *Extra!*, July/August 1998, p. 4.

10 Richard M. Cohen, "Extra! The Press is Liberal (So What?)," *The Nation*, May 26, 1997.

11 Robert Parry, "In Search of the Liberal Media," *Extra!*, July/August 1998 p. 11.

12 Telephone interview with author, Oct.19, 1999.

13 *Ibid.*

14 Louis Wolf, "Accuracy in Media Rewrites the News," *CovertAction Information Bulletin,* Summer 1989.

15 Telephone interview with author Oct. 26, 1999.

16 *Media Monitor,* April 1991.

17 *Newswatch,* Sept. 9, 1999.

18 Bill Lueders, *An Enemy of the State,* Common Courage Press, 1994, p. 272-3.

19 *Extra!,* June 1987.

20 "In Search of the Liberal Media," *Extra!,* July/August 1998, p. 11.

21 *Rolling Stone,* Sept. 10, 1987.

22 *Extra!, Op. cit.* p.12.

23 Malcom Byrne and Peter Kornbluh, "Iran-Contra: The Press Indicts the Prosecutor," *Columbia Journalism Review,* March/April 1994.

24 L. Brent Bozell, *Wall Street Journal,* July 6, 1999.

25 March 6 and April 28.

26 Bill Messler, "The Spy Who Wasn't," *The Nation,* August 9/16 1999.

27 Michael Dolny, *Extra!,* November/December, 1997.

28 *Fortune,* July 23, 1984.

29 "All the Usual Suspects," *Extra!* Winter 1990.

30 Reese Cleghorn, "The Press Shifts to the Right But Slowly," *American Journalism Review,* December 1994.

31 Norman Solomon, "Politics: What is Disinformation?" *Bay Guardian,* Aug. 8, 1996.

Chapter VI: Tailoring National Politics to Media Needs

1 *The Wall Street Journal,* Dec. 15, 1999.

2 Thomas E. Patterson, *Out of Order,* Random House, 1993 p. 34.

3 Martin Plisser, *The Control Room,* The Free Press, New York, 1999.

4 Kevin Cash, author of *Who the Hell is William Loeb?,* makes a strong case that the letter was actually concocted by Republican operatives led by the late Pat Clauson from the White House.

5 Jeff Greenfield, *The Real Campaign,* Summit Books, 1982 p.13.

6 Howard Kurtz, "Forget the Final Tally: The Media Declare the Real Winner," *The Washington Post,* Feb. 13, 1996.

7 Eleanor Randolph, "GOP Convention '96: Frustrated Networks See an End to Hours of 'Live' TV Coverage," *Los Angeles Times,* Aug. 15, 1996.

8 Kathleen Hall Jamieson, *Spiral of Cynicism,* Oxford University Press, 1997, p. 33.

9   Interview with author, Nov. 26, 1999.

10 *USA Today,*June 7, 1995.

11 Interview with author, Dec. 10, 1999.

12 July/August 1998.

13 Richard Harwood, *The Washington Post,* Oct. 23, 1993.

14 Interview with author, Nov. 21, 1999.

15 Timothy Cook, *Governing With the News,* University of Chicago Press, 1998, p. 131.

16 Memo from Moyers to Robert Kintner, president of NBC, April 8, 1966, as quoted by Timothy Cook, p. 133.

17 As quoted by Cook, p. 159, from Kenneth S. DeVol, *Mass Media and the Supreme Court,* Hastings House, 1982, p. 139.

18 Edward Lazarus, *Closed Chambers*, Penguin, 1998, p. 428.

19 *Op. cit.*, p. 157.

20 Slavko Splichal, *Public Opinion*, Roman and Littlefield Publishers, 1999, p. 255.

21 Meg Greenfield, *The Washington Post,* May 12, 1997.

22 Sally Quinn, *The Washington Post,* Nov. 2, 1998.

23 *Ibid.*

Chapter VII: Trading News Negligence for Political Ads

1   David S. Broder, *The Washington Post,* May 12, 1999.

2   Melinda Henneberger, *The New York Times,* May 22, 1998.

3   *U.S. News & World Report,* June 29, 1998.

4   Remarks at the Annenberg Washington Program, Washington, D.C., Nov. 29, 1990.

5   Interview with author, Dec. 13, 1999.

6   Ira Teinowitz, "Paid Ads Loom Larger on the Political Landscape," *Advertising Age,* Oct. 5, 1998.

7   Alison Mitchell, *The New York Times,* Oct. 28, 1999.

8   Interview with author, Dec. 9, 1999.

9   Todd S. Purdum, "Race for California Governor Is Not Necessarily News," *The New York Times,* May 6, 1998.

10 Paul Klite, "No News Is Bad News," *Extra!*, January/February 1999.

11 E.R.Shipp, *The Washington Post*, Nov. 21, 1999.

Chapter VIII: Censoring the News to Please Business

1   "Network Television News: With Fear and Favor," *Columbia Journalism Review,* May/June 2000.

2   Andrew Kohut, "Self-Censorship: Counting the Ways," *Columbia Journalism Review,* May/June 2000.

3   Interview with author, Dec. 20, 1999.

4   Interview with author, Dec. 16, 1999.

5   Peter Philips, *Censored 1999,* Seven Stories Press, New York, 1999.

6   James Ledbetter, *Made Possible By ...: The Death of Public Broadcasting,* Verso, 1997, p. 208.

7   *Advertising Age,* Jan. 11, 1993.

8   Milton Glaser, "Censorious Advertising," *The Nation,* Sept. 22, 1997.

9   Howard Kurtz, *The Washington Post,* Apr. 17, 1993.

10 Lawrence Soley, "The Power of the Press Has a Price," *Extra!,* July/August 1997.

11 Howard Kurtz, "Forbes Feels the Wrath of Fortune," *The Washington Post,* Jan. 16, 1996.

12 Beth Zacharias, *Washington Business Journal,* Dec. 3, 1999.

13 Lawrence Soley, "The Power of the Press Has a Price," *Extra!,* July/August 1997.

14 *New York Times,* Jan. 7, 1998.

15 *The New York Times Magazine,* Jan. 9, 2000.

16 David McCord, *The Chain Gang,* University of Missouri Press, 1996, p. 85.

17 *Op cit.* p. 89.

Chapter IX: Using Publicists to Cut News Costs

1   H&K Vice Chairman Frank Mankiewicz continues to claim that Kroll supported Nayirah's story of deliberate murder, per letter to author, Dec. 22, 1998.

2   Greg Hitt, "How a Bus of Conservatives Joined Anti-Claritin March," *The Wall Street Journal,* Nov. 22, 1999.

3   Thomas W. Lippman, "Johnston Turns to PR Firm for Energy Bill Aid," *The Washington Post,* Sept. 29, 1991.

4   Neil A. Lewis, "Spheres of Influence Grow in Washington," *The New York Times,* Nov. 16, 1999.

5   Mark Dowie, "Torches of Liberty," pp. 1-4, *Toxic Sludge is Good for You,* by John Stauber and Sheldon Rampton, Common Courage Press, 1995.

6   Joel Brinkley, "'Unbiased' Ads for Microsoft Came at a Price," *The New York Times,* Sept. 18, 1999.

7   Trudy Lieberman, *Columbia Journalism Review,* January/February 1995.

8   John Stauber and Sheldon Rampton, Op. cit. p. 123-135.

9   Mark Hertsgaard, *On Bended Knee,* Farrar Straus Giroux, 1988, p. 348.

10 Howard Kurtz, *Spin Cycle,* Free Press, 1998, p. 302.

11 Michael Lewis, "I Like a Pol," *New York Times Magazine*, Nov. 21, 1999.

12 Patrick J. Kiger, "Attack Flacks," *Regardie's POWER*, March/April 2000.

13 Jeff Pooley, *Brill's Content*, October 1999.

14 *PRWeek*, May 1, 2000.

15 David Lieberman, *TV Guide*, Feb. 22, 1992.

16 Tom Shales, *The Washington Post*, Feb. 18, 1999.

17 Arthur E. Rowse, "Regulatory Creep: Dan Quayle Clears the Way for Industry," *The Progressive*, May, 1992.

18 Franklin Square Press, 1996.

19 *A Vast Conspiracy*, Random House, 1999.

20 *The Hunting of the President*, Thomas Dunne Books, 2000.

21 *Truth at Any Cost*, Harpercollins.

Chapter X: Chasing Ratings with Gotcha Journalism

1   "White House Press Corps Owes Back Taxes, IRS Says," *The Washington Post*, Oct. 19, 1994.

2   *Columbia Journalism Review*, March/April 1996.

3   Interview with author, Oct. 10, 1999.

4   Meg Greenfield, "Love and Marriage," *Newsweek*, Feb. 15, 1993.

5   Howard Kurtz, *Spin Cycle*, The Free Press, 1998, p. 177.

6   *Westmoreland v. CBS Inc.*, 601 F.Suppl. 66,68, S.D.N.Y., 1984.

7   *Columbia Journalism Review*, May/June 1994.

8   James D. Retter, *Anatomy of a Scandal*, General Publishing Group, 1998.

9   *Nieman Reports*, Winter 1997.

10 "The White House and the Media," *Columbia Journalism Review*, May/June 1998.

11 *The Washington Post*, Sept. 15, 1998.

12 Stephen Brill, "Pressgate," *Brill's Content*, August 1998, p. 151.

13 *The Wall Street Journal*, Dec. 11, 1998.

14 Feb. 4, 1999.

15 *The Wall Street Journal*, Mar. 2, 1999.

16 Sabato, *Op. cit.* p. 23.

Chapter XI: Tilting News Toward the Powers that Be

1   "A Conspiracy of Silence?" Ruben Castaneda, *American Journalism Review*, March 2000.

2   *Business Week*, April 17, 2000.

3   *The New York Times* Report on Executive Pay, April 2, 2000.

4   "1999 Salary Survey," *Brill's Content*, May 1999.

5   *Ibid.*

6   *Ibid.*

7   Howard Kurtz, "When the Press Outclasses the Public," *Columbia Journalism Review*, May/June 1994.

8   Ibid.

9   CBS SportsLine.com.

10 James D. Squires, *Read All About It*, Times Books, 1993, p. 91.

11 March 21, 1999.

12 *The Medillian*, Northwestern University, Spring 2000.

13 Michael Harrington, *The New American Poverty*, Holt, Rinehart & Winston, 1984.

14 *National Journal*, April 15, 2000.

15 Michael Kirkhorn, "Widening Gap Between Haves & Have-Nots," *Nieman Reports*, Fall 1998.

16 Laura Flanders and Janine Jackson, "Reforming Welfare Coverage: Five Issues Reporters Need to Address," *Extra!*, the magazine of FAIR, May/June 1997.

17 May 15, 2000.

18 "Study Suggests Media Coverage of Youth Violence is Misleading," *The San Francisco Chronicle*, April 24, 2000.

19 *Business Week*, May 8, 2000.

20 April 16, 2000.

21 "Media Beat: Mass Media: Hatred of American Labor," www.fair.org/media-beat.

22 "Quitting in Protest," *American Journalism Review*, April 2000.

23 October 9, 1999.

24 "Woman Have *Not* Taken Over the News," *Extra!* January/February 2000.

25 *Violence and the Media*, Vol. XI, p. 152.

26 "Prattle in Seattle," by Seth Ackerman, *Extra!*, January/February 2000.

27 "Prattle in Seattle," *Extra!*, January/February 2000.

28 Alexander Cockburn and Jeffrey St. Clair, *Whiteout: The CIA, Drugs and the Press*, Verso, 1998, p. 32.

29 The Washington Post, February 17, 1967.

30 Cockburn and St. Clair, *Op. cit.* p. 29.

31 Interview by phone with author, June 6, 2000.

Chapter XII: Challenging the Press to Do Its Job

1   James S. Fishkin, *The Voice of the People*, Yale University Press, 1997.

2   Michael Janeway, *Republic of Denial*, Yale University Press, 1999, p. 14 and 172.

3   Michael Parenti, *Democracy for the Few*, St. Martin's Press, 1980, p. 50.

4   Robert W. McChesney, *Rich Media, Poor Democracy*, University of Illinois Press, 1999.

5   Tom Rosenstiel, Carl Gotlieb and Lee Ann Brady, "Quality Brings Higher Ratings, But Enterprise is Disappearing," *Columbia Journalism Review*, November/December 1999.

6   Janeway, Op. cit. p. 176.

Acknowledgements

This book has been a joint product of some dedicated and competent people. First, I want to thank my wife, Ruth Fort, for helping immensely to perfect this mammoth project. She is an unexcelled editor with the rare ability to see detail as well as the large picture, a necessity for an up-and-coming writer. Next to her, I owe the most to the book's editor, Robert Hodierne, the Pulitzer embodiment of journalistic excellence who last directed the national staff of Newhouse Newspapers. I particularly want to thank Morton Mintz, the prize-winning former reporter and colleague of mine on *The Washington Post*, who helped in more ways than I can count. I also want to express deep appreciation to Greg Bates and Arthur Stamoulis of Common Courage Press for the wisdom and courage to see the potential of my proposal.

In addition, I am deeply grateful for superhuman assistance from Mary Rowse, her husband George Lang and the following journalist pros for superb assistance in researching and reporting important sections: Rita Colorito, George Clifford, Alan Dessoff, Fiona MacKintosh, David Martin and Charles Pekow. Among others who helped were Bill Eaton, Amy Fitch, Dick Kleeman, Howard Kurtz, Leonard Reed, Richard Sammon, Martin Schram and Richard Thomas.

I add my most sincere thanks to the library staff of the National Press Club, especially Ginny Blodgett, Heather Crocetto, Laura Falacienski, Sarah Gehring, Jackie Vick and director Tom Glad, without whose assistance this book would be a lot thinner. I would also like to thank *The Washington Monthly* for permission to lift portions of my article, "The Lobby the Media Won't Touch," in the May 1998 issue. Needless to say, however, none of these people or organizations share any responsibility for mistakes or omissions in the book. They are my responsibility alone.

Index